BUSINESS
COMMUNICATION
TODAY

Study Guide to Accompany

BUSINESS COMMUNICATION TODAY

Fourth Edition

Courtland L. Bovée

Professor of Business Communication
C. Allen Paul Distinguished Chair
Grossmont College

John V. Thill

Chief Executive Officer
Communication Specialists of America

McGraw-Hill, Inc.
New York   St. Louis   San Francisco   Auckland   Bogotá
Caracas   Lisbon   London   Madrid   Mexico City   Milan   Montreal
New Delhi   San Juan   Singapore   Sydney   Tokyo   Toronto

Study Guide to Accompany
BUSINESS COMMUNICATION TODAY

4 5 6 7 8 9 0 SEM SEM 9 0 9 8 7 6

ISBN 0-07-006910-7

Permissions Acknowledgment
page 15: Adapted from Patricia A. Thompson and Brian H. Kleiner, "How to Read
Nonverbal Communication," *The Bulletin of the Association for Business Communication*
LV, no. 3 (September 1992): 81-83. Used by permission of the Association for
Business Communication

The editor was Bonnie K. Binkert;
the production supervisor was Cindy Regan.
Semline, Inc., was printer and binder.

CONTENTS

EXPERIENCE IS THE BEST TEACHER ...

A college course in business communication can teach you quite a bit about how people in business write and speak, read and listen. The textbook, the teacher, and the interaction of students eager to learn all contribute to the educational process, but if you really want to learn how to communicate in business, you must practice and get feedback on your work. You must actually write letters, memos, and reports and speak in small meetings and before large groups. Although your first efforts may be amateurish, they are the necessary forerunners to more polished communication.

"Great," you say. "I know I need practice, but how am I going to get it? Many employers hire only people who already have on-the-job experience." We'd like to propose a solution to this dilemma. First, realize that communication skills are obvious to employers as you go through the application and interview process. Your writing skills show in your résumé and application letters; your speaking skills, in conversations with potential employers. Thus you get a chance to demonstrate your skills without having previous job experience, a privilege not available in many other fields. Our second point is this: If you take advantage of every opportunity to practice business communication while you're still a student, you will enter the job market with an advantage.

This *Study Guide* has been designed to guide your practice. Used in conjunction with its companion textbook, *Business Communication Today*, Fourth Edition, this guide can help you accomplish important goals.

- Understand the content of the textbook chapters
- Prepare for quizzes and tests
- Apply what you have learned to practical problems
- Understand related issues in business communication
- Improve your spelling and expand your vocabulary
- Improve your knowledge of grammar, punctuation, and mechanics

These goals are achieved through a wide variety of exercises. Simply by reading, you can gain a new perspective on the chapters in the textbook and new insights into peripheral issues. Fill-in and essay exercises test your understanding and recall of chapter content, and vocabulary activities test your ability to spell and use words correctly. (Because the answers to these exercises are provided at the end of each chapter, you can check your own work and get immediate feedback on your progress.) Crossword puzzles in the last three chapters further test your ability to spell and use words correctly. Application exercises allow you to take the role of a professional communicator—whether writer, editor, or speaker. A separate section at the end of this book offers a short course in the basics of English, with explanations and exercises interwoven.

We propose the following study program for making the best use of these aids:

1. Read the one-paragraph summary/statement of objectives at the beginning of each chapter in the *Study Guide*.
2. Read the corresponding chapter in *Business Communication Today*.
3. Immediately complete two sections of the *Study Guide*—Master Key Concepts and Quiz Yourself—checking your answers right away and rereading any portion of the textbook that seems to have given you trouble. (The answer section provides textbook page numbers to make this task easier.)
4. When you feel comfortable with the textbook's content, do the application exercise described in Build Your Skills; then read Expand Your Knowledge and respond to the questions. (Ask your instructor for feedback on your solutions.)

5. Work through Develop Your Word Power. (The answers are at the end of the chapter, but keep a dictionary at hand so that you can look up any spelling or vocabulary words you have trouble with.)

6. Do one of the English Essentials lessons at the back of this book. (Ask your instructor for feedback on your answers.)

If you work at this program consistently and diligently, we guarantee that it will give you practice in many of the skills that are important to business communicators. [1]

---

[1] The vocabulary and grammar sections of this *Study Guide* have used the University of Chicago *Manual of Style*, the *Harbrace College Handbook*, and *Webster's Collegiate Dictionary* as authorities.

STUDY GUIDE

to Accompany

BUSINESS COMMUNICATION TODAY

PART ONE

FOUNDATIONS OF BUSINESS COMMUNICATION

Chapter 1

Communicating Successfully in an Organization

The main point of Chapter 1 is that communication is the glue that holds organizations together. As you read the chapter, think of the many ways that people in business communicate; think, too, about the role that communication plays in the various activities of organizations. When you finish reading, analyze your own communication skills and preferences and plan how you can improve your weak areas.

MASTER KEY CONCEPTS

Use the following terms to fill in the blanks in the outline. All terms are used, but none is used more than once.

approach	effective	formal	intercultural
audience-centered	efficiently	grapevine	link
climate	ethical	horizontally	power
communication	external	information	technology
crises			

I. Organizations cannot function without effective _____ (p. 4).
   A. Every member of an organization is a _____ (p. 5) in the information chain.
   B. The flow of information is essential to a company's operations. Outsiders provide the fuel—information, people, raw materials, and capital—which the organization transforms into goods and services that can be sold to customers.
   C. Within the company, you and your co-workers use the information you obtain from outsiders and from one another to guide your activities.
   D. When making and implementing decisions, managers must gather and evaluate _____ (pp. 5–6) and must communicate their decisions to others in the organization.

II. The _____ (p. 6) to communication varies from organization to organization.
   A. Through _____ (p. 6) communication channels, information flows upward and downward following the official chain of command; official channels also permit messages to flow _____ (p. 6) from department to department.
   B. Informal communication channels, also called the _____ (p. 11), are an important source of information, both accurate and inaccurate.
   C. In many cases, the informal communication network is the real _____ (p. 11) structure of the company.

III. The marketing department and the public relations department plan an important role in managing the flow of _____ (p. 12) messages.
   A. One of the public relations department's most visible functions is to help management plan for and respond to _____ (p. 12).
   B. The way a company handles a crisis can have a profound impact on the organization's subsequent performance.

IV. _____ (p. 15) communication exhibits six important characteristics.
   A. An organization's communication _____ (p. 16) affects the quantity and quality of the information transmitted.
   B. _____ (p. 17) communication includes all relevant information, is true in every sense, and is not deceptive in any way.
   C. Both internationally and domestically, firms are working with an increasingly diverse work force and paying more attention to _____ (pp. 20–21) communication.
   D. The growing amount of information and increasing speed of communication are making it necessary for all businesspeople to understand and adapt to _____ (p. 21).
   E. When you use an _____ (p. 22) approach, you focus on the person or persons who will be receiving your message.
   F. Messages can be handled more _____ (p. 24) by reducing the number of messages, making instructions and assignments clearer, distributing communication responsibility more evenly, and training employees to be better writers and speakers.

Check your answers at the end of this chapter.

QUIZ YOURSELF

1. Give three examples of downward information flow in an organization.

2. Give three examples of upward information flow in an organization.

3. Give one example of horizontal communication flow.

4. What is the major advantage of informal communication channels? What is the major disadvantage?

5. List three main limitations of formal communication channels.

6. Which two functional units of an organization are particularly important in managing the flow of external messages? How do their functions differ?

7. Give two examples of recommended actions to take when a crisis occurs, and two examples of actions to be avoided.

8. What six organizational characteristics contribute to effective communication?

9. Give an example of a business area in which laws provide ethical guidelines.

10. Give three measures that a manager can take to more efficiently handle the flow of routine messages.

Check your answers at the end of this chapter.

BUILD YOUR SKILLS: WHAT ARE YOUR STRENGTHS AND WEAKNESSES AS A COMMUNICATOR?

Knowing your strengths and weaknesses as a communicator helps you set priorities for self-improvement. Ask yourself the following questions. Then put a *W* by the items that require the most work, a *P* by those that need polishing, and a *U* by those you can use to the fullest right away.

Reading

_____ Do you read fast enough for your work?

_____ Are you able to pick out and remember key points?

_____ Can you vary your approach to reading to match different types of reading situations?

Listening

_____ Are you able to focus your attention on what a speaker is saying?

_____ Can you identify and recall key points of a speech to your satisfaction?

_____ Are you able to put aside your preconceptions and judge the speaker's message on its merits, regardless of whether you agree or disagree with the ideas or like or dislike the speaker as an individual?

_____ Are you able to analyze a speaker's message and ask questions to test its logic and accuracy?

_____ Are you satisfied with your ability to take notes during a lecture?

Engaging in Casual Conversation

_____ Are you confident in conducting casual social conversations?

_____ Can you think of interesting things to say to keep up your end of a conversation?

_____ Do you ask good questions?

_____ Do you listen empathetically to the other person and draw her or him out?

_____ Are you comfortable talking with a wide range of people, including those who differ from you in background, age, and interests?

_____ Do you give the other person a chance to talk too?

_____ Are you sensitive to the other person's reactions?

Interviewing

_____ Do you prepare adequately for interviews by developing a list of questions to cover and by preparing answers to anticipated questions?

_____ Are you confident in interview situations?

_____ Are you able to remain objective in difficult interviews?

_____ Can you use different types of questions to obtain the information you want?

_____ Are you able to match your interview style to the situation?

_____ Can you draw out the other person?

_____ Are you able to give and receive criticism effectively?

_____ Are you relaxed in interviews with people who outrank you or have more power than you do?

_____ Are you considerate in interviews with people in a subordinate position?

Dealing with Small Groups

_____ If you are in charge, do you lay the proper groundwork for the meeting by preparing an agenda and making necessary arrangements well in advance?

_____ As the leader, are you able to keep the group focused on the business at hand?

_____ Are you familiar with the rules of parliamentary procedure?

_____ Can you facilitate interaction by balancing the contributions of group members?

_____ Are you able to build consensus among group members?

_____ Are you able to summarize results and assign responsibilities?

_____ As a group participant, do you make useful and constructive comments?

_____ Are you sensitive to the needs and concerns of other group members?

Delivering Speeches and Presentations

_____ Are you able to plan a speech or presentation that is suitable for various situations and times?

_____ Are you able to control your stage fright?

_____ Can you speak clearly and distinctly so that people understand you?

_____ Do you sound natural and engaging?

_____ Are you able to use visual aids effectively in a speech or presentation?

_____ Can you handle unexpected or hostile comments effectively?

_____ Can you deliver a speech from notes?

Writing Letters, Memos, and Reports

_____ Do you have an adequate command of basic grammar and punctuation?

_____ Are you able to vary the style and tone of your writing to suit different situations?

_____ Can you write clearly, accurately, and concisely?

_____ Are you able to organize messages logically and persuasively?

_____ Are you familiar with different formats and their uses?

_____ Can you construct tables, charts, and other illustrations to supplement your writing?

_____ Are you careful about editing and proofreading your work?

EXPAND YOUR KNOWLEDGE: WHERE THE JOBS ARE

It is hard to imagine a career that doesn't require some sort of writing. Thus, everyone should acquire the basic skills. Some people, however, develop a better-than-average ability to write. If you're one of them, you may want to consider one of these business-writing careers:

- _Business and industry._ Writers are employed in advertising, public relations, sales promotion, and training departments, and as publication editors and speechwriters.

- _Copywriting._ A flair for writing ads, commercials, booklets, and brochures may land you a job as a copywriter in an advertising agency or with the media. Jobs for copywriters may also be found with manufacturers, retailers, banks, hotels, and public utilities.

- _Public relations._ If writing news releases and articles interests you, consider a career in a public-relations or advertising agency, in the PR department of a large company, in a trade or professional association, or in a government agency.

- *Fundraising.* Staff writers develop grant proposals, ads, features, and promotional material for the media. They also write speeches that administrators deliver to business and civic groups.

- *Publishing.* Book publishers have jobs for manuscript readers, editors, copyeditors, staff writers, and advertising and promotion writers. Business magazines, newspapers, wire services, and syndicates employ editors, staff writers, rewriters, copyeditors, correspondents, and advertising copywriters.

- *Government.* Thousands of jobs exist in federal, state, and local government agencies for writers and editors, as well as for radio, TV, and film script writers. Their assignment: to write about government and agency activities for the media. They also create pamphlets that describe public benefits and services.

Other career opportunities for business writers include radio and TV writing and editing, science writing, and technical writing. Writers are needed by chambers of commerce to write and edit publications, handle publicity for special events, and create materials to promote business and tourism in the area. Some interesting free-lance opportunities also exist: writing articles for business magazines, ghostwriting material for leaders in business and industry, writing new-product releases for small manufacturers, creating audiovisual materials for business, operating a resume-writing service, or even writing manuscripts for business-book publishers. Professional secretaries, too, often are called on to write for their bosses. These and other challenging opportunities can be yours as a business writer.

1. Do any of these business-writing careers sound interesting to you? If so, do a little research to find out more about the job requirements. Talk to someone who holds such a position. What are some of the person's duties? How did she or he prepare for this career? If you don't know anyone who has a job like this, look in the Yellow Pages for advertising or public-relations agencies, newspapers or magazines, government agencies, and businesses that employ writers; if approached courteously, they may connect you with someone willing to share information.

2. Over the next few weeks, develop a collection of business-writing samples: direct-mail and other letters that you receive, ads from magazines and newspapers, product brochures, news stories about companies, government pamphlets. Keep your eyes open. You may be surprised at how many samples you accumulate. What can you conclude from your collection?

DEVELOP YOUR WORD POWER

Spelling Challenge   Identify the misspelled word in each of the following sentences, and spell it correctly in the space provided. If all the words in a sentence are spelled correctly, write *C* in the space.

_____   1. Congratulations on your many acheivements over the past year.

_____   2. Our building is adjascent to the hospital.

_____   3. They plan to aquire a small manufacturing company.

_____   4. In Mark's absense, you can assist me.

_____   5. Refinancing would be an acceptable alternative.

_____   6. How many new workers can that plant accomodate?

_____   7. His skills are not adaquate for the position.

_____ 8. You are absolutely right!

_____ 9. Jennifer accidently sent those memos to all staff members.

_____ 10. Speed and acuracy are the two qualities most valuable in a typist.

Vocabulary Challenge   Match the words in the first column with the definitions in the second column.

_____ 11. acumen   A. opponent

_____ 12. adversary   B. something not in its correct historical time

_____ 13. antecedent   C. something going before

_____ 14. affinity   D. keen insight

_____ 15. anachronism   E. natural likeness or agreement

Circle the best definition of the highlighted word in each of the following sentences.

16. We should make computers **accessible** to all office workers.

     A. easily modified   B. extra   C. available

17. Some modest people prefer to work in **anonymity**.

     A. without recognition B. loose-fitting clothing   C. solitude

18. George volunteered with **alacrity** to take on the new project.

     A. willingness   B. reluctance   C. ignorance

19. The customer was **adamant** about getting a refund.

     A. angry   B. unyielding   C. unsure

20. An **ambiguous** answer will only postpone resolution of the problem.

     A. two-sided   B. small-minded   C. indefinite

Select one of these words to complete each of the following sentences, and write the word in the space provided.

   acrimonious   **acute**   **adroit**   **aloof**   **amicable**

21. Contrary to her claims that she wants to get involved, Stacey has remained

    _____ from all the group's activities.

22. Thanks to Deborah Sweeney's _____ handling of the malfunctioning control mechanism, a disastrous accident has been avoided.

23. After an _____ exchange between Eric and his boss, Eric stormed out.

24. To maintain goodwill, we train all our customer-service representatives to seek

_____ settlement of complaints.

25. An _____ shortage of petroleum products would have severe effects on our ability to keep the plant open.

Follow-up Word Study   Check your answers at the end of this chapter. In the spaces below, write the words that you spelled or used incorrectly. (Use a separate piece of paper if you missed more than five words.) Then look up each word in your dictionary, and carefully study its spelling, pronunciation, definition, and history (etymology). Finally, to help fix the word in your memory, write it in a sentence.

Word   Sentence

_____   _____

_____   _____

_____   _____

_____   _____

_____   _____

CHECK YOUR ANSWERS

Master Key Concepts

I. communication
   A. link
   D. information

II. approach
   A. formal, horizontally
   B. grapevine
   C. power

III. external
   A. crises

IV. Effective
   A. climate
   B. ethical
   C. intercultural
   D. technology
   E. audience-centered
   F. efficiently

Quiz Yourself

1. Examples of downward information flow would include any communications from executives, managers, or supervisors to those below them in the organizational hierarchy, such as memos to employees, instructions on how to perform various jobs, policy directives to all employees, or motivational pep talks. (pp. 8–9)

2. Examples of upward information flow would include any communications from lower-level employees to supervisors, managers, or executives, such as written or oral reports, employee exit interviews, grievance filings, or group meetings. (pp. 9–10)

3. One example of horizontal communication is a memo sent from the director of marketing to the head of production. (p. 10)

4. The main advantage of informal communication channels is that they provide employees with their major sources of information. The main disadvantage of informal communication channels is that they are often sources of misinformation. (p. 11)

5. The limitations of formal communication channels are
   a. They may restrict lower-level employees' access to decision makers.
   b. They are subject to distortion and misunderstanding.
   c. Information may become fragmented because each person in the communication chain knows only about one specific area. (p. 6)

6. The two most important functional units for managing the flow of information to outsiders are the marketing department and the public relations department. The two differ in their central focus: Marketing is focused on selling goods and services, whereas public relations is more concerned with developing the organization's overall reputation. (p. 12)

7. When a crisis occurs, be prepared for trouble and get top management involved as soon as the crisis occurs. Avoid blaming anyone for anything and avoid speculating in public about unknown facts. (p. 14)

8. The factors that contribute to effective communication are as follows: management fosters an open communication climate, the organization is committed to ethical communication, employees understand the difficulties involved in intercultural communication, employees are proficient in communication technology, employees use an audience-centered approach, and messages are created and processed in a timely, efficient manner. (p. 15)

9. Human resource management is one area where the law provides guidance; another area is advertising. (p. 19)

10. Managers can facilitate the flow of routine messages by
    a. Reducing the number of messages being produced
    b. Speeding up the preparation of messages
    c. Making writers and speakers better at their jobs through training programs (p. 24)

Develop Your Word Power

1. achievements	6. accommodate	11. D	16. C	21. aloof
2. adjacent	7. adequate	12. A	17. A	22. adroit
3. acquire	8. C	13. C	18. A	23. acrimonious
4. absence	9. accidentally	14. E	19. B	24. amicable
5. C	10. accuracy	15. B	20. C	25. acute

Chapter 2

Understanding Business Communication

The main point of Chapter 2 is that the communication process consists of a series of steps and is effective only when each stop is successful. As you read the chapter, think about how misunderstandings can arise, especially in business communication. When you finish reading, mentally review some personal experiences with misunderstandings and try to figure out how they could have been overcome or avoided.

MASTER KEY CONCEPTS

Use the following terms to fill the blanks in the outline. All terms are used, but none is used more than once.

audience	credibility	formulating	perception
barriers	decoding	key points	repeating
channel	encoding	listening	sender
complexity	feedback	media richness	specific and accurate
control	filtering	nonverbal	time and space

I. Communication occurs in two basic forms: verbal and _____ (p. 30).
    A. Nonverbal communication, which conveys most of the emotional meaning of a message, can be grouped into six main categories: facial expressions and eye behavior, gestures and postures, vocal characteristics, personal appearance, touching behavior, and use of _____ (pp. 30–36).
    B. Verbal communication involves speaking and writing to send messages and _____ (pp. 35–36) and reading to receive messages.

II. Communication takes place in a _____ (p. 37) process of five phases.
    A. The _____ (p. 37) has an idea.
    B. The idea is put into a message the receiver will understand. This phase is called _____ (p. 37).
    C. In order to transmit the message, the sender selects a communication _____ and _____ (p. 37).
    D. Once the receiver gets the message, that person absorbs and understands the information by _____ (p. 37) the message.
    E. Finally, the receiver sends _____ (p. 37) to the sender.

III. Misunderstandings are common, and they may arise at any point in the communication process.
    A. Problems in _____ (pp. 37–38) a message may result when the sender can't decide what to include in a message, isn't sure about how the information will be used or who will use it, or finds it difficult to express ideas.
    B. If you communicate well, other people will understand you, whether they agree with you or not.

IV. Communication _____ (p. 39) can exist between people and within organizations.
    A. To overcome incorrect _____ (p. 40), establish more than one communication channel so that information can be verified through multiple sources. Also try to eliminate as many intermediaries as possible.

   B. To overcome language barriers, use the most _____ (p. 40) words possible.

   C. To overcome message _____ (p. 42–43), use strong organization and be sure to ask for feedback.

   D. _____ (p. 44) is determined by a medium's ability to use more than one informational cue, facilitate feedback, and establish personal focus.

V. Successful communicators have several traits in common.

   A. Because of their _____ (p. 45), they are able to predict how you'll receive their message.

   B. Because of their _____ (p. 45), you have faith in the substance of their message.

   C. Their _____ (p. 45) allows them to shape your responses.

VI. One of the ways effective communicators overcome communication barriers is by creating the message carefully.

   A. The first thing to do to create messages carefully is to learn about your _____ (p. 47).

   B. Another way to create careful messages is to call attention to your _____ (p. 48).

Check your answers at the end of this chapter.

QUIZ YOURSELF

1. List six types of nonverbal messages.

2. Identify the five phases involved in the communication process.

3. Which phase in the communication process allows you to evaluate the effectiveness of your message?

4. List three problems that may arise when a message is being developed.

5. What measures can you take to overcome poor listening?

6. Every message contains both a _____ meaning, which deals with the subject of

the message, and a _____ meaning, which suggest the nature of the interaction between the sender and the receiver.

7. Describe three ways business messages are particularly complex.

8. What can you do to overcome competition barriers?

9. Briefly summarize six steps you can take to create your message carefully.

10. List four ways that you can make feedback more useful.

Check your answers at the end of this chapter.

BUILD YOUR SKILLS: CAN YOU READ THE BODY LANGUAGE
IN THESE PHOTOS?

Take a close look at the photographs that follow. What can you infer from the pictures? What do you think is happening? Who are the people? What is their probable background? What are their relationships to one another? What are their feelings?

Even Ken the line space in your own office to indicate
bita ais and position, to simulate bullhorn so tech are

EXPAND YOUR KNOWLEDGE: READING THE NONVERBAL COMMUNICATION OF OFFICE SETTINGS

Your ability to read nonverbal communication in the business world is a valuable tool. Subtle, silent messages are constantly being communicated, and not just in body language or manner of dress. The placement and arrangement of offices can tell you a lot about a company and its employees. If you were responsible for arranging office space for your company, what points would you consider?

One of the first things you might consider about a U.S. office is the placement of walls and partitions. Offices built on the open plan with few walls and partitions can cause difficulties for employees, especially higher-level employees. Some people believe that this type of arrangement will encourage openness in employees, but in the United States, your insistence on this setting would probably give the impression that company executives don't trust their employees and want to keep an eye on them. On the other hand, if you provide plenty of walls and partitions, be careful not to isolate people from each other all day. At least a coffee room or a "watering hole" will provide employees with a place to interact with each other.

Office location on a particular floor communicates a lot about a person's power and position within a U.S. organization. Offices are usually based on a corner power system: the senior executives are located in the corner offices, which tend to be larger and more desirable. The closer an executive's office is to the center of an area, the less powerful he or she is. A related consideration is the proximity of an executive's office to the boss's office. This is especially important to new, young executives whose location may yield more opportunity to interact with the boss and perhaps receive special attention or a larger variety of new projects.

The proximity of certain people within an office is also important. Personal interaction drops off markedly beyond a distance of 25 or 30 yards, so pay close attention to the location of employees who are part of a special team within the organization. Core members should be close together, even if it means sacrificing status space for some members.

You can use the space in your own office to influence personal interactions. You can demonstrate authority and position by arranging furniture so that you talk across a desk to a person seated on the other side. In a second area, you can place chairs at right angles to each other or group them around a coffee table to encourage more informal, sociable communication. If you control the personal furnishings in your office, that fact enhances your power and authority.

You can use office decor to make a statement about a company's values. A good example of this is seen at Digital Equipment Corporation (DEC). The top managers' offices, in an old mill, are simple and almost Spartan, with plywood partitions and few "extras." The intended message is that hard work and functionality are important at DEC. Basically, physical space conveys the essential values of the company.

Color can help you establish the visual image of an area. You might consider hiring an "executive color consultant" to analyze a manager's or company's character and appearance to find the colors most conducive to the statement that is being projected. However, as a general rule, dark blue is regarded as a very powerful color, red is frightening, yellow is frivolous or weak, beige is too neutral and white gives people a sense of openness and freedom. Perhaps the most effective use of color in an office decor may be white and dark blue, with a touch of red to inspire fear or control.

The best way you can become skilled in reading the nonverbal communication of office settings is to keep a log listing what settings conveyed a particular message or feeling. With practice, you can improve your ability to read and send these messages. Your business effectiveness depends on successful interactions with people. These interactions are affected by what you learn about individuals through nonverbal language. Taken alone, an office setting is incomplete and unable to give you the whole message; however, when combined with nonverbal cues from other nonverbal cues such as dress and body language, the combination can enhance your understanding of communication and people.

1. How would understanding office settings help you do your job as a new employee?
2. How would understanding office settings help you do your job as a senior executive?

DEVELOP YOUR WORD POWER

Spelling Challenge   Identify the misspelled word in each of the following sentences, and spell it correctly in the space provided. If all the words in a sentence are spelled correctly, write *C* in the space.

_____   1. What would it cost to advertize in *Newsweek*?

_____   2. Bill is anxous because he has not heard from his associate yet.

_____   3. Ms. Hansen will analyse your income statement.

_____   4. Standish Corp.'s anual meeting will be held on August 17.

_____   5. That typewriter is ancient!

_____   6. We will issue stock when it is advantageous to do so.

_____   7. What kinds of returns are allowible?

_____   8. I must apologise, Mike, for being unable to attend your meeting.

_____   9. What did you think of her analisis?

_____   10. It is not adviseable to wear your Sport watch while swimming.

Vocabulary Challenge   Match the words in the first column with the definitions in the second column.

_____ 11. benign   A. gentle

_____ 12. apathetic   B. independent

_____ 13. bilateral   C. haughty

_____ 14. arrogant   D. two-sided

_____ 15. autonomous   E. uninterested

Circle the best definition of the highlighted word in each of the following sentences.

16. Her remarks about market trends were **apropos** because we are considering a major change in our marketing approach.

    A. pertinent   B. spooky   C. positive

17. We can **avert** future disaster only by taking precautions against accidents now.

    A. predict   B. lessen   C. prevent

18. I **ascribe** our poor sales last month to consumer uncertainty about the economy.

    A. assume   B. credit   C. report

19. We should not purchase any business until we **audit** its books.

    A. examine   B. read   C. hear

20. All Persian carpets from the House of Nasseri are **authentic**.

    A. original   B. genuine   C. high quality

Select one of these words to complete each of the following sentences, and write the word in the space provided.

    anticlimax   **antipathy**   **antithesis**   **apathy**   **attrition**

21. Because of his _____ toward office work, he has decided on a career that will seldom require him to sit behind a desk.

22. Her _____ may infect the other programmers, who might then lose their enthusiasm for the project.

23. The _____ of right is wrong.

24. After all the talk about changing store operations, the minor change in store hours seems an

    _____.

25. She doesn't like to fire anybody, so she'll whittle her staff through _____.

Follow-up Word Study   Check your answers at the end of this chapter. In the spaces below, write the words that you spelled or used incorrectly. (Use a separate piece of paper if you missed more than five words.) Then look up each word in your dictionary, and carefully study its spelling, pronunciation, definition, and history (etymology). Finally, to help fix the word in your memory, write it in a sentence.

Word   Sentence

_____   _____

_____   _____

_____   _____

_____   _____

_____   _____

CHECK YOUR ANSWERS

Master Key Concepts

I. nonverbal
  A. time and space
  B. listening
	IV. barriers
	  A. filtering
	  B. specific and accurate
	  C. complexity
	  D. media richness

I. nonverbal
  A. time and space
  B. listening

II. repeating
  A. sender
  B. encoding
  C. channel, medium
  D. decoding
  E. feedback

III. A. formulating

IV. barriers
  A. filtering
  B. specific and accurate
  C. complexity
  D. media richness

V. A. perception
  B. credibility
  C. control

VI. A. audience
  B. key points

Quiz Yourself

1. The six main types of nonverbal messages are facial expressions and eye behavior, gestures and postures, vocal characteristics, personal appearance, touching behavior, and use of time and space. (pp. 32–33)

2. The five phases involved in the communication process are
   a. The sender has an idea.
   b. The idea becomes a message.
   c. The message is transmitted.
   d. The receiver gets the message.
   e. The receiver reacts and sends feedback to the sender. (p. 37)

3. The final step, when the receiver sends feedback to the source, is what allows you to evaluate the effectiveness of your message. (p. 37)

4. Three common problems that may occur when a message is being developed are
   a. Indecision about the message content
   b. Lack of familiarity with the situation or the audience
   c. Difficulty in expressing ideas (p. 38)

5. To overcome poor listening, you can
   a. Paraphrase what you've understood
   b. Empathize with the speaker
   c. Resist jumping to conclusions (pp. 40–41)

6. Every message contains both a *content* meaning, which deals with the subject of the message, and a *relationship* meaning, which suggests the nature of the interaction between the sender and the receiver. (p. 41)

7. Business messages are complex in a number of ways:
   a. The sender of the message may not always completely agree with the ideas that have to be expressed or may be emotionally reluctant to send the message.
   b. The subject is often inherently dry or difficult to explain. (pp. 42–43)

8. To overcome competition barriers, you can try the following:
    a. Avoid making demands on a receiver who doesn't have the time to pay attention.
    b. Make written messages visually appealing and easy to understand.
    c. Deliver oral messages by speaking directly to your receiver. (p. 43)

9. Here are some of the things you can do to create your message carefully:
    a. Learn about your audience.
    b. Tell your audience what to expect.
    c. Use concrete, specific language.
    d. Keep your audience focused.
    e. Connect new information to information the audience is already familiar with.
    f. In concluding the message, review the key points. (pp. 47–48)

10. Feedback can be made more useful if you
    a. Plan how you want to obtain feedback and choose an appropriate method of transmission.
    b. Listen to and value the feedback you get.
    c. Encourage people to be open with you.
    d. Use feedback to revise your message in order to overcome misunderstandings. (p. 49)

Develop Your Word Power

1. advertise	6. *C*	11. A	16. A	21. antipathy
2. anxious	7. allowable	12. E	17. C	22. apathy
3. analyze	8. apologize	13. D	18. B	23. antithesis
4. annual	9. analysis	14. C	19. A	24. anticlimax
5. *C*	10. advisable	15. B	20. B	25. attrition

Chapter 3

Communicating Interculturally

The main point of Chapter 3 is that communication with people who are from other cultures and other countries requires special sensitivity and enhanced skills. As you read the chapter, think about not only the language barriers that often exist but also the cultural barriers that affect communication. When you finish reading, seek opportunities to communicate with people from cultures other than your own and take note of the accommodations you must make to communicate well.

MASTER KEY CONCEPTS

Use the following terms to fill in the blanks in the outline. All terms are used, but none is used more than once.

advertisements	direct	flexible	pronunciation
complexity	ethical	intercultural	status
context	ethnocentrism	judgment	subculture
cultural diversity	exports	persistent	trade barriers
culture			

I. Whether communicating across national borders or across language and cultural barriers at home, _____ (p. 56) communication requires special skills.
   A. International business communication has increased because of increasing _____ (p. 56), relaxing _____ (p. 56), and increasing foreign competition in domestic markets.
   B. The _____ (p. 56) in the United States has resulted from immigration trends, differing ethnic backgrounds, active hiring of more ethnic minorities, and common differences such as gender, age, physical ability, and educational background.

II. We all belong to many different cultures.
   A. A _____ (p. 58) is a shared system of symbols, beliefs, attitudes, values, expectations, and norms for behavior; a cultural group that exists within a major culture is called a _____ (p. 58).
   B. Cultures vary in social values, roles and _____ (p. 61), decision-making customs, concepts of _____ (p. 62), concepts of personal space, cultural _____ (p. 62), body language, social behavior and manners, and legal and _____ (p. 63).

III. When you deal with people who don't speak your language at all, you have three options: learn their language, use a translator, or teach them your language.
   A. Although many international business letters are written in English, many other forms of communication must be translated, including _____ (p. 65), warranties, maintenance manuals, product labels, policy and procedure manuals, and reports.
   B. Several sources of confusion in oral communication are _____ (p. 65), the way people use their voices, and idiomatic expression.

IV. The tendency to judge all other groups according to one's own group's standards, behaviors, and customs is called _____ (p. 67).

V. Tips for developing intercultural communication skills include taking responsibility for communication, withholding _____ (p. 69), showing respect, empathizing, tolerating ambiguity, looking beyond the superficial, being patient and _____ (p. 70), recognizing your own cultural biases, being _____ (p. 70), emphasizing common ground, sending clear messages, increasing your cultural sensitivity, dealing with the individual, and learning when to be _____ (p. 71).

Check your answers at the end of this chapter.

QUIZ YOURSELF

1. Briefly describe four ways cultures and subcultures differ.

2. List the nine areas of cultural differences that can give rise to misunderstanding in international business communication.

3. Give an example of how the U.S. focus on efficiency and productivity might be inappropriate in another culture.

4. Give an example illustrating how a gesture that is meaningful in one country can be misconstrued by a person from another culture.

5. Describe a situation in which it might be practical for an organization to overcome language barriers by teaching other people to speak English.

6. Which forms of written communication from U.S. firms to foreign countries are most likely to require translation?

7. What language barriers might you encounter in a conversation with a person for whom English is a second language?

8. Briefly discuss the implications of ethnocentrism.

9. Explain several factors that could cause problems when negotiating with someone from another culture.

10. Give some tips on how to achieve clarity in letters written in English to people from other cultures.

Check your answers at the end of this chapter.

BUILD YOUR SKILLS: PLAN YOUR BUSINESS TRIP ABROAD

Your boss has asked you to spend two weeks scouting for business opportunities in a foreign country. Your assignment is to find a good location for a new resort hotel. Where you go is up to you, so pick a country that you have never seen before and plan your two-week trip. Make a list of all the things you will need to do or learn before you go.

EXPAND YOUR KNOWLEDGE: THE GO-BETWEENS

Relatively few American businesspeople are fluent in the languages of the countries with which they do business. Therefore, they must often conduct their intercultural transactions with the aid of translators (written communication) and interpreters (spoken communication). Vic Petrelli, who spent six years as an overseas project manager with Aramco, has had plenty of firsthand experience with these go-betweens.

Vic negotiated contracts for electric-power projects in Saudi Arabia. "That meant that I had to deal with Saudi Arabian contractors and government bureaucrats, as well as Pakistani engineers," Vic recalls. "Usually the Pakistanis served as interpreters, because they could speak better English than the people I had to negotiate with. Most of the world's engineering students learn English as a base language."

But schooling in the English language is not always enough. "Head and hand movements and facial expressions are quire different from culture to culture," Vic notes. "Some quite expensive problems arose from those differences. I was in Al-Hasa, the world's largest oasis. The electric-power system was being run by a group of Pakistani engineers. My job was to get a transmission line strung through the oasis to serve 62 villages. I explained to the Pakistanis how we could save about six months of work and a lot of money, and they seemed to agree that they would put some wire aside for the project.

"The Pakistanis have a side-to-side head movement that looks to a Westerner like a sign that they understand. But what it really means is maybe. Pakistanis will never say anything negative to a Westerner, true or not true. I was getting this head movement from the Pakistanis and thought everything was ready to go. But when we showed up to start work, 22 miles of wire was missing. I though we had fully communicated, but because of cultural differences we had not."

You might think that written communication would present fewer problems. But such was not the case, according to Vic: "All of our contracts had to be translated from English into Arabic. Well, almost all. The technical passages were in English, preceded by a statement something like this: `Due to the technical nature of this contract, the following passage won't be translated into Arabic.' There are simply no Arabic words for many of the technical terms.

"We also ran into problems with some of the general paragraphs because of cultural differences. The connotations of our words just could not be properly translated into Arabic. Also, U.S. businesspeople expect contract language to be precise, but in most Middle Eastern cultures, nothing is laid on the table. They like to see as much remain in the gray area as possible to reduce the possibility of losing face if something goes wrong. That can cause some huge problems, especially when you're trying to manage the contract after it has been signed. You might be trying to say that `According to Paragraph X, you're supposed to be doing this,' but what the other people are seeing in the Arabic contract is 'You don't necessarily have to do this.'"

As if learning to communicate with people from Pakistan and Saudi Arabia wasn't enough, Vic also had to interact with people from Germany, the Philippines, and Japan. So he has learned a few things about the world of translation and interpretation: "Most managers and salespeople involved in international business speak English; in some countries, English is taught in school as the language of business. But the more technical the subject, the more necessary it is to have an interpreter. The sales department of an international company usually has someone who can interpret—especially into English, maybe into several other languages.

"The best quality for an interpreter to have is to really like people and to be good at working with them. To overcome cultural differences, an interpreter has to 'read' everything—the words themselves, gestures, eye movements, everything. Engineers tend to be a bit introverted, which further impedes communication—unless the interpreter is adept at reading nonverbal cues. The broader the interpreter's background knowledge, of course, the better off he or she is, because a good general background helps the interpreter put things in perspective. And the more the interpreter knows about what is being talked about, the easier it is to explain in two languages."

Vic has a few simple tips for those who work with interpreters. First, he says, "speak in as many one- and two-syllable words as possible. Using legalistic phrases and flowery speech will do nothing but confuse the interpreter. At the same time, you have to present a clear picture of what you want. The interpreter may actually be able to help you organize your thinking to make communication easier."

Vic's second suggestion is to ask the interpreter to repeat every passage in English before passing it on in another language. "If the interpreter summarizes the idea for you—'Is this what you mean?'—everybody benefits."

The third suggestion applies more to your own behavior: "Be careful not to offend the other party. Be as open and as friendly as possible. Any gruffness of manner or stern look can be interpreted in many different ways, depending on the culture. People tend to start talking to the interpreter and forget that the other person over there is the one receiving the message. Most Westerners also tend to have too strong a personality. They come on like they're handling a large meeting. But with that stern, heavy look about them, they intimidate people from many other cultures into not really conversing.

"I was in a meeting with an Arab contractor who could read only the Arabic portion of the contract. . . . A Lebanese interpreter . . . went to the meeting with us. It was extremely important . . . that both parties understand what was going to have to be done. I tried to keep my explanations to the interpreter as simple as possible and to paint as clear a picture as possible. Then the interpreter summarized for me his understanding of each passage before explaining it in Arabic to the contractor. Then he would ask if there were any questions and translate those. This back-and-forth process was slow and tedious, but it was the only way to be sure that the Arabic contractor and I were talking about the same thing."

1. How could Vic Petrelli have avoided the problem of the missing 22 miles of wire?

2. How difficult is it to become an interpreter? What is the typical background of people in this profession? Does the job pay well? To answer these questions write to some of the organizations that employ interpreters: Peace Corps, United Nations, and U.S. State Department. Ask about the qualifications and compensation of interpreters.

DEVELOP YOUR WORD POWER

Spelling Challenge   Identify the misspelled word in each of the following sentences, and spell it correctly in the space provided. If all the words in a sentence are spelled correctly, write *C* in the space.

_____   1. Seize the opportunity to profit from others' mistakes!

_____   2. The most sensable course is to build slowly.

_____   3. These serviceable tablecloths will give you many years of wear.

_____   4. Our sales representatives receive a strait commission.

_____   5. Compare the strenth of Grit detergent with that of your current brand.

_____   6. This policy supercedes your old one.

_____   7. Donna desperately wants to succede in sales.

_____   8. The replacement we are sending is similar to the umbrella you bought.

_____   9. Keep yesterday's receipts seperate from today's.

_____   10. Each day has a certain rythem from start to finish.

Vocabulary Challenge   Match the words in the first column with the definitions in the second column.

_____ 11. tacit   A. implied

_____ 12. tedious   B. succinct

_____ 13. tenacious   C. persistent

_____ 14. terse   D. hackneyed

_____ 15. trite   E. monotonous

Circle the best definition of the highlighted word in each of the following sentences.

16. Be careful not to **subvert** your own authority by appearing too playful.

  A. undermine   B. increase   C. mock

17. Five temporary clerks will be **sufficient** during the holidays.

  A. enough   B. employed   C. absent

18. Professor Buckalew will be one of the panelists at the **symposium**.

  A. inquiry   B. trade show   C. conference

19. This move will require us to **synchronize** many people and things.

  A. weed out   B. coordinate   C. notify

20. Include a **synopsis** at the beginning of the report.

  A. outline   B. introduction   C. summary

Select one of these words to complete each of the following sentences, and write the word in the space provided.

superficial   superfluous   susceptible   symbolic   synonymous

21. Unfortunately, our sophisticated new equipment is _____ to breakdown.

22. See if you can flesh out this _____ analysis.

23. The name Pearson's is _____ with value.

24. The statue in front of the building is _____ of our role in the world of health care.

25. Jane already realizes her mistake; your criticism is _____.

Follow-up Word Study   Check your answers at the end of this chapter. In the spaces below, write the words that you spelled or used incorrectly. (Use a separate piece of paper if you missed more than five words.) Then look up each word in your dictionary, and carefully study its spelling, pronunciation, definition, and history (etymology). Finally, to help fix the word in your memory, write it in a sentence.

<u>Word</u>   <u>Sentence</u>

_____   _____

_____   _____

_____   _____

_____   _____

_____   _____

CHECK YOUR ANSWERS

Master Key Concepts

I. intercultural
   A. exports, trade barriers
   B. cultural diversity

II. A. culture, subculture
   B. complexity, status, context, ethical

III. A. advertisements
   B. pronunciation

IV. ethnocentrism

V. judgment, persistent, flexible, direct

Quiz Yourself

1. Cultures and subcultures vary in their
   a. Stability—the amount and speed of change
   b. Complexity—how accessible information is
   c. Composition—homogeneity or heterogeneity of the culture
   d. Acceptance—how outsiders are treated (p. 59)

2. Misunderstandings are especially likely to occur because of differences in
   a. Social values
   b. Roles and status
   c. Decision-making customs
   d. Concepts of time
   e. Concepts of personal space
   f. Cultural context
   g. Body language
   h. Social behavior and manners
   i. Legal and ethical behavior (pp. 61–64)

3. The U.S. belief that modern, labor-saving methods are superior to old-fashioned, labor-intensive methods is inappropriate in a country where unemployment is an extremely serious problem. In such a country, the method that requires the most workers may well be the most beneficial to society. (p. 61)

4. Here are two examples that illustrate how a gesture that is considered meaningful in one country can be misconstrued by a person from another culture:
   a. A U.S. executive crosses his legs so that the sole of his shoe is showing, unaware that this gesture is viewed as an insult by an Egyptian businessperson.
   b. A U.S. saleswoman thinks nothing of it when an Arab businessperson runs his hand backward across his hair. She fails to recognize the gesture as a romantic invitation. (p. 63)

5. Many multinational companies offer English-language training programs for their foreign employees. Tenneco, for example, instituted an English-language training program for its Spanish-speaking employees in a New Jersey plant. The classes concentrated on practical English for use on the job. According to the company, these classes were a success: accidents and grievances declined. and production improved. (p. 65)

6. The following types of written communication are likely to require translation:
   a. Advertisements
   b. Warranties
   c. Repair and maintenance manuals
   d. Product labels
   e. Policy and procedure manuals and benefit plans used by foreign subsidiaries of U.S. companies
   f. Reports passed between foreign subsidiaries and U.S. headquarters (p. 65)

7. When conversing with someone for whom English is a second language, barriers arise from pronunciation problems, speech patterns, idiomatic expressions, and variations in the meaning of some words and phrases. (pp. 65–67)

8. Ethnocentric people are prone to stereotyping and prejudice. They generalize about entire groups of people on the basis of sketchy evidence, and then develop biased attitudes toward the group. As a consequence, they fail to see people as they really are. They ignore the personal qualities of individuals. (p. 67)

9. When negotiating with someone from another culture, you're likely to encounter a number of differences.
   a. Your approach to negotiation may differ (such as preferring an impersonal or a more sociable atmosphere).
   b. Your tolerance for disagreement may differ.
   c. Your problem-solving techniques may differ.
   d. Your protocol may differ.
   e. Your attitudes about schedules may differ.
   f. Your decision-making methods may differ. (pp. 72–73)

10. When writing letters to people from other cultures
    a. Use short, precise words.
    b. Rely on specific terms; avoid abstractions.
    c. Stay away from slang, jargon, buzzwords, idioms, acronyms, and North American product names.
    d. Use shorter and simpler sentences than usual.
    e. Use short paragraphs.
    f. Use many transitional devices.
    g. Use numbers, visual aids, and preprinted forms. (p. 73)

Develop Your Word Power

1. *C*	6. supersedes	11. A	16. A	21. susceptible
2. sensible	7. succeed	12. E	17. A	22. superficial
3. *C*	8. similar	13. C	18. C	23. synonymous
4. straight	9. separate	14. B	19. B	24. symbolic
5. strength	10. rhythm	15. D	20. C	25. superfluous

Chapter 4

Communicating through Technology

The main point of Chapter 4 is to emphasize how important it is for today's businesspeople to understand, use, and adapt to technological tools of communication. The chapter emphasizes how technology affects communication, offers guidance about when it's appropriate to use various technological tools, introduces the ways technology can help produce messages, and introduces proper formats for various technological media.

MASTER KEY CONCEPTS

Use the following terms to fill in the blanks in the outline. All terms are used, but none is used more than once.

audience expectations	E-mail	networks	teleconferencing
boilerplates	electronic	overload	time
cost	fax	presentation	voice mail
databases	graphics	scanner	word processors
desktop publishing	nature	spell checkers	work-life
dictation system			

I. Because technology keeps changing, no prescriptive rules dictate when it's appropriate to use a particular technological tool for communicating. The decision is based on four guidelines:
   A. _____ (p. 82) determine the methods that are acceptable to the people who will receive your message.
   B. Often the biggest factor in your technology choice is _____ (p. 82), although _____ (p. 82) will also have an impact, not only on how much you can afford to spend but also on how much is appropriate for the situation.
   C. What you need to say in the document, the _____ (p. 82) of the message, determines what technological tool you will choose.
   D. Your _____ (p. 83) needs dictate how you will send your message, whether you will use typeset printing and color graphics or electronic mail.

II. The dominant tools for creating printed documents are _____ (p. 83). Of course, you can use group authoring tools (sometimes called groupware) when two or more people are working together on a document.
   A. To computerize the process of assembling finished pages, _____ (p. 83) software was created.
   B. _____ (p. 84) are collections of facts ranging from financial figures to the text of reports.
   C. Many executives dictate messages and documents, whether to an assistant or into a _____ (p. 86).
   D. Prewritten text often used in business messages can range from standard blocks of text called _____ (p. 87) to already printed versions of material that you want to enter into your computer using a device known as a _____ (p. 88).
   E. The software for creating business visuals falls into two basic groups: presentation software and _____ (p. 89) software.

28

F. _____ (p. 90) are handy tools for catching typos, but they cannot replace strong spelling skills.

G. Using regular phone lines, you can transmit an exact reproduction of a document from one _____ (p. 93) machine to another.

III. An increasing number of documents are never placed on paper, being written on computer, transmitted along telephone lines or other connections, and read on computer. These _____ (p. 94) documents can save the amount of paper a business uses.

A. Documents created, transmitted, and read entirely on computer are called _____ (p. 94).

B. _____ (p. 94) connect people within a single company, across town, across the country, and around the world.

IV. Technology can also improve oral communication between individuals and groups.

A. Similar to E-mail in concept, _____ (p. 97) doesn't require each user to have a computer, only a touch-tone phone, letting you send, store, and retrieve spoken messages.

B. Through _____ (p. 97) and videoconferencing, you can conduct meetings via phone lines and satellite with people who are scattered around the world.

V. Technology can speed the exchange of information, improve teamwork, overcome organizational structure, and decrease communication costs; however, it can also lead to information _____ (pp. 97–98), burden people with unwanted messages, isolate some people from employment opportunities, and blur the line between _____ (p. 98) and home-life.

Check your answers at the end of this chapter.

QUIZ YOURSELF

1. When might it be a good idea to send your message on videotape?

2. Give two examples of external databases you might want to use when planning a business document.

3. What is a CD-ROM? Give two examples of this recent technology.

4. Name two functions that help you revise your document, and explain what these functions do.

5. What are some limitations of a grammar checker?

6. In what three ways can a word processor and desktop publishing software help you produce a business document?

7. Explain what mail merge can do for document distribution.

8. What two benefits can fax machines provide businesspeople?

9. What presentation tools might you use in a large meeting?

10. Why doesn't technology solve all our business communication problems?

Check your answers at the end of this chapter.

BUILD YOUR SKILLS: SUPPOSE YOU WERE EQUIPPING AN OFFICE ...

Let's say that you have decided to go into business for yourself by opening a one-person real estate office in your hometown. You have rented space in a new building. Now you must obtain the furnishings, equipment, and supplies you need to get started. Make a list of all the items you need. Remember, you're on a tight budget.

EXPAND YOUR KNOWLEDGE: WHEN YOUR OFFICE ISN'T
AT THE OFFICE ANYMORE

The electronic tools of business communication are allowing people to get out of the traditional office. This phenomenon is called *telecommuting* if you're a salaried or hourly employee who works at home; *teleworking* if you're a salaried or hourly employee who works on the road or in customers' offices (perhaps from a cellular phone or a notebook computer); or simply *working at home* if you're an independent contractor, a free-lancer, or an entrepreneur.

As telecommuting becomes more common, a growing number of companies are giving this new approach a try. Although small businesses are more likely to have employees who work at home, large companies like J. C. Penney, The Travelers Companies, and Pacific Bell are finding out that with home-based employees, they can save office space, cut down on office expenses, and increase worker productivity by as much as 25 percent.

Pacific Bell started its pilot program to avoid freeway congestion during the 1984 Summer Olympics and has been impressed with the results. Du Pont has more than 1,000 employees teleworking and has noted improvement in productivity, improvement in morale, and a new competitive edge. Other companies see the option of working at home as an inexpensive way to recruit and retain valued workers. After the 1994 earthquake in Los Angeles, many people in that city began looking into telecommuting, both to stay closer to home and to avoid the freeways where bridges had collapsed.

An increasing number of workers aren't waiting for employers to come around; they're starting up and operating full-time businesses from their homes. Andrew Pearson conducts his financial-services business from his home in Edgewood, Rhode Island. He keeps up with the markets on his computer, and he keeps up with his customers on his telephone and fax machine.

Without question, home-based workers run into some pitfalls:

- Home-based entrepreneurs earn about 70 percent of what their in-office, salaried counterparts make.
- Home-based entrepreneurs put in long hours (to build and keep the business going) with few or no vacations.
- Home-based workers may find that their jobs begin to consume their lives (and to survive, they must consciously plan activities away from home).
- Burnout can occur faster at home (because working at home can mean never getting a break). David Shay is director of quality and productivity for KPMG Peat Marwick, and he complains that, "With modems, faxes, telephones, and voice mail, I'm finding that home is no longer the place to go to get away from it all. Interruptions follow me home."
- Some home-based workers are bedeviled by hostile zoning boards.
- Parents who think they can work at home and care for their kids alone get a rude awakening.
- Telecommuting can be hazardous to your career (because your face isn't being seen, it's easier for management to leave you out of decisions).
- Some cost-cutting corporations sometimes try to turn telecommuters into unprotected contract workers (who have no employee benefits or insurance).
- Some home-based workers begin to feel lonely and anxious, missing the social interaction of the "downtown" office.

Still, those who love the electronic life claim that it can be liberating, and they cite the absence of commuting time, the added time available for families, the lack of office politics, the ability to set individual hours, the feeling of independence, and the increase in productivity. The corporate office will probably never disappear completely, but thanks to the electronic tools of business communication, the flexibility of working at home can no longer be ignored.

1. Who do you think works at home? Make a list of as many occupations as you can think of that could be readily pursued at home.

2. If telecommuting is so great, why don't more companies try it?

DEVELOP YOUR WORD POWER

Spelling Challenge   Identify the misspelled word in each of the following sentences, and spell it correctly in the space provided. If all the words in a sentence are spelled correctly, write *C* in the space.

_____ 1. Reserve the meeting room for next Wensday.

_____ 2. For a long report, a table of contents is useful.

_____ 3. A deposit is unecessary for orders under $50.

_____ 4. This year our researchers discovered a twelfth-century townsite.

_____ 5. While I'm on the road, you can reach me threw the main office.

_____ 6. Midday tempratures are in the high 70s.

_____ 7. The store needs a through, floor-to-ceiling cleaning.

_____ 8. We are truly sorry for any inconvenience you have experienced.

_____ 9. After only a week, the thermometer is no longer useable.

_____ 10. Store your valuables in our security vaults.

Vocabulary Challenge   Match the words in the first column with the definitions in the second column.

_____ 11. ulterior   A. one-sided

_____ 12. uncompromising   B. firm

_____ 13. unilateral   C. unparalleled

_____ 14. unprecedented   D. sophisticated

_____ 15. urbane   E. concealed

Circle the best definition of the highlighted word in each of the following sentences.

16. After working with Richard for five years, I have learned to cope with his **vagaries**.

    A. abstractions   B. bad moods   C. whims

17. The **vicissitudes** of the restaurant business parallel the state of the general economy.

    A. ups and downs   B. facts   C. truths

18. Before our new product line comes out, we will be **vulnerable** to the competition.

    A. bothersome   B. attractive   C. defenseless

19. Many of our customers are **wary** because they have been disappointed.

    A. combative   B. tired   C. on guard

20. Many new inspectors are overly **zealous**.

    A. sensitive   B. diligent   C. trained

Select one of these words to complete each of the following sentences, and write the word in the space provided.

vacillating   vapid   versatile   vigilant   vindictive

21. Protect your home with a _____ watchdog.

22. We have enough specialists; let's try to find someone who is _____.

23. Don't be in a hurry to write up a contract for a _____ client; his mind will change before the ink is dry.

24. A _____ commercial is unlikely to build anyone's enthusiasm.

25. Julia is _____ and will not hesitate to pay you back for insulting her.

Follow-up Word Study   Check your answers at the end of this chapter. In the spaces below, write the words that you spelled or used incorrectly. (Use a separate piece of paper if you missed more than five words.) Then look up each word in your dictionary, and carefully study its spelling, pronunciation, definition, and history (etymology). Finally, to help fix the word in your memory, write it in a sentence.

Word   Sentence

_____   _____

_____   _____

_____   _____

_____   _____

_____   _____

CHECK YOUR ANSWERS

Master Key Concepts

I. A. audience expectations
    B. time, cost
    C. nature
    D. presentation

II. word processors
    A. desktop publishing
    B. databases
    C. dictation system
    D. boilerplates, scanner
    E. graphics

    F. spell checkers
    G. fax

III. electronic
    A. E-mail
    B. networks

IV. A. voice mail
    B. teleconferencing

V. overload, work-life

Quiz Yourself

1. You might want to send your message on videotape when you need to convey emotion and excitement but you don't have the time to visit every member of your audience. (p. 82)

2. Examples of external databases include Econbase, a database of economic forecasts and projects, and Tax Notes Today, which explains all recent government actions regarding federal and state taxes. (p. 84)

3. A CD-ROM is a type of compact disk that can be read by special computer equipment. Examples include Microsoft Bookshelf (a collection of seven references including a dictionary, a thesaurus, and an atlas), back issues of *The Wall Street Journal*, the names and addresses of business executives, and government trade statistics. (p. 84)

4. When revising a document, *cut and paste* is a function that allows you to cut a block of text out of one section and paste it in somewhere else. The *search and replace* function helps you track down words or phrases and change them if you need to. (p. 90)

5. Since the computer doesn't have a clue about what you're trying to say, determining whether you've said it correctly is difficult. Moreover, even if you've used all the rules correctly, a grammar checker still can't tell whether your document communicates clearly. (p. 91)

6. A word processor and desktop publishing software can help you produce business documents in the following ways:
    A. Adding a first-class finish (by providing attractive typefaces or by adding color graphics)
    B. Managing document style (by insuring consistency with such features as style sheets)
    C. Generating supporting elements (such as footnotes, endnotes, index, or table of contents). (pp. 92–93)

7. Mail merge automatically combines a standard version of a document with a list of names and addresses. It will produce one copy for each person on your mailing list, saving you the trouble of inserting the name and address each time. (p. 93)

8. Fax machines offer businesspeople two distinct advantages: overcoming the delay problems of regular mail and overcoming the time-zone problems of trying to contact someone by phone. (p. 93)

9. Technology provides an array of presentation tools for large meetings.
    A. Overhead transparencies are clear sheets of plastic with images printed on them, which can be projected onto a screen for viewing.
    B. 35 mm slides are just like the slides you can produce with a camera, which can be projected onto a screen.
    C. A computer driven presentation transfers the computer's display to a large-screen television.
    D. Group decision support systems can connect everyone through computers whether to vote or consider a decision from various points of view. (p. 97)

10. Even though technology helps people communicate with more people more efficiently, it adds to the complexity of the situation, requiring businesspeople to learn how to use new tools at their disposal. Technology is also expensive, requiring companies to spend more money for speed and efficiency. Finally, technology cannot do the thinking, planning, or communicating, so all communication efforts are only as good as the people sending and receiving them. (pp. 97–98)

Develop Your Word Power

1. Wednesday	6. temperatures	11. E	16. C	21. vigilant
2. *C*	7. thorough	12. B	17. A	22. versatile
3. unnecessary	8. truly	13. A	18. C	23. vacillating
4. twelfth	9. usable	14. C	19. C	24. vapid
5. through	10. *C*	15. D	20. B	25. vindictive

PART TWO

THE WRITING PROCESS

Chapter 5

Planning Business Messages

The main point of Chapter 5 is that the most effective business messages are planned. As you read the chapter, think about why it is important to have a clear purpose when you communicate and why it is important to keep your audience's needs in mind. When you finish reading, think about some written and oral messages you have sent that would have benefited from greater advance planning.

MASTER KEY CONCEPTS

Use the following terms to fill in the blanks in the outline. All terms are used, but none is used more than once.

accurate	channel	idea	practical
audience	collaborating	information	purpose
brainstorming	content	motivational	reaction

I. The composition process consists of three main steps: planning, composing, and revising.

II. The first step in planning a business message is defining your _____ (p. 106).
   A. You need a clear purpose to decide whether to proceed, to respond to the audience, to focus the _____ (p. 107), and to establish the channel and medium.
   B. There are three general purposes to business communication: informing, persuading, and _____ (p. 107) with the audience; within the general purpose, a message also has a specific purpose.
   C. A message should not be sent if the purpose is not realistic, the timing isn't right, you are not the right person to deliver the message, or the purpose is not acceptable to the organization.

III. The second step in planning a business message is analyzing the _____ (p. 109).
   A. Developing an audience profile involves asking several questions: What is the size and composition of the audience? Who is the primary audience? What is the audience's probable _____ (p. 109)? What is the audience's level of understanding? What is your relationship with the audience?
   B. To satisfy the audience's _____ (p. 112) needs, you need to find out what the audience wants to know, anticipate unstated questions, provide all the required information, be sure the information is _____ (p. 113), and emphasize ideas of greatest interest to the audience.

35

  C. To satisfy the audience's _____ (pp. 114–115) needs, you need to use either a rational or an emotional approach or a combination of the two.

  D. To satisfy the audience's _____ (p. 115) needs, you need to make the information easy to grasp.

IV. The third step in planning a business message is establishing the main _____ (p. 115).

  A. One way to come up with a main idea is to use _____ (pp. 116–118) techniques, such as the storyteller's tour, the random list, the FCR worksheet, the journalistic approach, and the question-and-answer chain.

  B. Limit the scope of your message to three or four major points, no matter what the message length.

V. The fourth step in planning a business message is selecting the _____ (p. 118) and the medium.

  A. Use oral communication if your purpose is to collaborate with the audience.

  B. The most common types of written communication used in business are letters, memos, reports, and proposals.

Check your answers at the end of this chapter.

QUIZ YOURSELF

1. What are the three main steps involved in preparing business messages?

2. Give four reasons why it is important to have a clear purpose for your business messages.

3. What are the three general purposes common to business communication?

4. What four questions should you ask yourself to test your purpose?

5. What five steps can you take to develop an audience profile?

6. When trying to satisfy your audience's information needs, what five steps should you take?

7. What can you do to minimize mistakes in the information you provide?

8. What is the difference between the topic of a message and the main idea of a message?

9. List and briefly describe five brainstorming techniques.

10. List five situations in which an oral message would be more appropriate than a written one.

Check your answers at the end of this chapter.

BUILD YOUR SKILLS: DEVELOPING AUDIENCE PROFILES

For each of the following communication situations, develop an audience profile (probable size and composition, probable reaction to the message, likely level of understanding):

a. A speech to seniors at a large inner-city high school about careers in accounting
b. A speech to business majors at a large state university about careers in accounting
c. A letter to all persons who bought a Mercedes in Palm Springs last month, urging them to purchase a service contract
d. A letter to all persons who bought a television set at a discount TV warehouse in East Los Angeles last month, urging them to purchase a service contract

EXPAND YOUR KNOWLEDGE: WINNING FRIENDS AND INFLUENCING PEOPLE

Much business communication is meant to win people over. You may want to change their opinions or behavior or just accomplish your goals while maintaining their goodwill. Dale Carnegie, a long-acknowledged master of human relations and communication, recommended 12 rules for winning people to your way of thinking:

1. *The only way to get the best of an argument is to avoid it.* Suppose that you win a verbal battle. Is the person you've argued with going to like you more for winning? Undoubtedly not! You're better off either avoiding a confrontation or conceding, especially on the smaller, less important points. And remember: you could lose an argument.

2. *Show respect for other people's opinions; never tell them that they are wrong.* Even is a person is actually wrong, saying "You're wrong, and I'm going to tell you why" will never influence her or him to admit the error. Instead, say something like this: "I might be mistaken in my opinions, but I disagree with you. Can we talk about our differences?"

3. *If you are wrong, admit your error quickly and emphatically.* An odd thing happens when you criticize yourself before someone else does. Frequently, the other person forgets all about blaming you and defends you instead.

4. *Begin in a friendly way.* If someone steams toward you and begins yelling, will you listen? Probably not. In fact, you will be either too scared to listen or so offended that you will go out of your way to thwart the person. You will be much more likely to go along with someone who seems to understand you and like you. Other people react the same way.

5. *Get other people saying "yes, yes" immediately.* As much as you can, make statements that the other person can agree with—especially at the beginning. Try to emphasize the similarities in your goals and characterize your differences as relating only to methods. Once people have said no, they don't want to back down.

6. *Let other people do a great deal of the talking.* Many a salesperson tells a tale like this: "I had a presentation to make but couldn't talk. So I let my client talk, and he (or she) convinced himself." The reasons? First, people would rather talk about themselves than hear about you. Second, by listening, you learn about needs you may never have guessed.

7. *Let other people feel that the idea is theirs.* Would you rather get credit for a great idea or achieve the results intended by the idea? If you are more interested in results, plant suggestions in people's minds or ask them for advice.

8. *Try honestly to see things from other people's point of view.* People usually have a comprehensive set of reasons for their actions or beliefs. If you take the time to learn their reasons, you will encourage them to try to see your point of view too.

9. *Be sympathetic with other people's ideas and desires.* When blocked by seemingly petty complaints or strivings, try this approach: "I don't blame you for feeling the way you do. If I were you, I would undoubtedly feel the same way."

10. *Appeal to the nobler motives.* Most people want to be—and want to be thought of as—honest, fair, sincere, truthful, and so on. If you act on the assumption that they do embody all these noble ideals, you will usually reap positive results.

11. *Dramatize your ideas.* Unfortunately, plain facts—even the most relevant, important facts—are often not enough. But facts in the form of demonstrations, illustrations, examples, even vivid turns of speech do get people's attention. And once people are paying attention, they are open to the influence of facts.

12. *Throw down a challenge.* People want to excel and feel important. Therefore, they can often be motivated by an opportunity to show that they are winners.

These ideas, first published in 1936 in a book filled with anecdotes proving their value, have stood the test of time.

1. Dale Carnegie's ideas have been popular for over 50 years. Why do you suppose this is so?

2. How might you let someone feel that an idea is his or hers instead of yours?

DEVELOP YOUR WORD POWER

Spelling Challenge   Identify the misspelled word in each of the following sentences, and spell it correctly in the space provided. If all the words in a sentence are spelled correctly, write *C* in the space.

_____ 1. How large is the balance in my account?

_____ 2. The applicant was an outstanding athelete in high school.

_____ 3. Would you please handle the arangements for the pen house?

_____ 4. Mr. Blevins apreciates loyalty.

_____ 5. There were no apparent cracks in the housing.

_____ 6. Patrick's carries an extensive line of fine apparrel for men.

_____ 7. All applible equal opportunity laws will be observed during the hiring process.

_____ 8. Avoid arguements with all customers.

_____ 9. Her decision was based on the assumtion that Louise is retiring.

_____ 10. See how well the applicants handle akward encounters.

Vocabulary Challenge   Match the words in the first column with the definitions in the second column.

_____ 11. blasé   A. obvious

_____ 12. blatant   B. inclusive

_____ 13. cogent   C. unimpressed

_____ 14. comprehensible   D. understandable

_____ 15. comprehensive   E. to the point

Circle the best definition of the highlighted word in each of the following sentences.

16. They will accept any **bona fide** offer for the company.

   A. high   B. from the loyal   C. genuine

17. Take the criticisms of a **chronic** complainer with a grain of salt.

   A. timely   B. grouchy   C. habitual

18. We answer letters in **chronological** order.

   A. customary   B. by time   C. haphazard

19. Only the most **circumspect** middle managers should be given a copy of this report.

   A. discreet   B. overweight   C. around for a long time

20. The expression "What goes up must come down" is a **cliché**.

   A. puzzle   B. trite saying   C. metaphor

Select one of these words to complete each of the following sentences, and write the word in the space provided.

capitulate	chide	circumvent	compel	compromise

21. If we insist, they will eventually _____ to our demands.

22. We cannot _____ any employee to contribute to this fund drive.

23. Attendance at that meeting will _____ your reputation for objectivity.

24. You can _____ health and safety regulations for only so long before a serious accident occurs.

25. Do not _____ your employees if they fail to read your mind.

Follow-up Word Study   Check your answers at the end of this chapter. In the spaces below, write the words that you spelled or used incorrectly. (Use a separate piece of paper if you missed more than five words.) Then look up each word in your dictionary, and carefully study its spelling, pronunciation, definition, and history (etymology). Finally, to help fix the word in your memory, write it in a sentence.

<u>Word</u>   <u>Sentence</u>

_____   _____

_____   _____

_____   _____

_____   _____

_____   _____

CHECK YOUR ANSWERS

Master Key Concepts

II. purpose
 A. content
 B. collaborating

III. audience
 A. reaction
 B. information, accurate
 C. motivational
 D. practical

IV. idea
 A. brainstorming

V. channel

Quiz Yourself

1. The three main steps in preparing a business message are planning, composing, and revising. (p. 104)

2. You need a clear purpose to
   a. Decide whether to proceed with producing the message
   b. Respond to your audience's needs
   c. Focus the content of the message
   d. Choose a channel for the message and a medium within that channel (pp. 106–107)

3. The three general purposes of messages are to inform, to persuade, and to collaborate. (p. 107)

4. To test your purpose, ask yourself
   a. Is the purpose realistic?
   b. Is this the right time?
   c. Is the right person delivering the message?
   d. Is the purpose acceptable to the organization? (p. 108)

5. When developing an audience profile,
   a. Determine the size and composition of the audience?
   b. Identify the primary audience?
   c. Estimate the audience's probable response?
   d. Gauge the audience's level of understanding?
   e. Define your relationship with the audience? (pp. 109–110)

6. The steps you need to take to satisfy the audience's information needs are
   a. Find out what the audience needs to know.
   b. Anticipate unstated questions.
   c. Provide all the required information.
   d. Be sure the information is accurate.
   e. Emphasize ideas of greatest interest to the audience. (pp. 112–114)

7. Among the steps you can take to minimize mistakes are
   a. Check to make certain your organization can meet any commitments you make.
   b. Check for any errors in your facts or logic.
   c. Make sure any outside sources consulted are up-to-date and reliable.
   d. Double-check mathematical for financial calculations.
   e. Double-check all dates and schedules.
   f. Examine your assumptions and conclusions to be certain they are valid. (p. 113)

8. The topic is the broad subject of the message, such as "company health clubs." The main idea makes a statement about the topic that provides a rationale and explains the purpose of the message in terms the audience can accept, such as "The costs of providing a company health club would be more than offset by gains in productivity and reductions in insurance costs." (p. 116)

9. Brainstorming techniques include
   a. Storyteller's tour—talking into a tape recorder, pretending you are giving an overview of your message to someone you run into on the street
   b. Random list—making a list of everything that pops into your head pertaining to your message
   c. FCR worksheet—dividing a sheet of paper into three columns, one each for findings, conclusions, and recommendations
   d. Journalistic approach—answering the questions of who, what, when, where, why, and how
   e. Question-and-answer chain—following a chain of questions your audience might ask and coming up with replies for them (pp. 117–118)

10. An oral message is more appropriate when
    a. You want immediate feedback from your audience.
    b. Your message is relatively simple and easy to accept.
    c. You do not need a permanent record.
    d. You can assemble the audience conveniently and economically.
    e. You want to encourage interaction to solve a problem or reach a decision. (pp. 119–120)

Develop Your Word Power

1. *C*	6. apparel	11. C	16. C	21. capitulate
2. athlete	7. applicable	12. A	17. C	22. compel
3. arrangements	8. arguments	13. E	18. B	23. compromise
4. appreciates	9. assumption	14. D	19. A	24. circumvent
5. *C*	10. awkward	15. B	20. B	25. chide

Chapter 6

Composing Business Messages

The main point of Chapter 6 is that any message has more impact when the facts and ideas have been carefully organized. As you read the chapter, think about the various purposes of business messages and the organizational patterns that are most effective for each purpose. When you finish reading, see whether you can classify the business messages you receive according to their organizational patterns.

MASTER KEY CONCEPTS

Use the following terms to fill in the blanks in the outline. All terms are used, but none is used more than once.

company	evidence	polite	tone
credibility	goodwill	positive	understand
direct	indirect	purpose	"you"
disorganized	outline	sequence	

I. Good organization is a hallmark of good communication.
   A. Messages seem _____ (p. 128) when the sender takes too long to get to the point, includes irrelevant information, gets ideas mixed up, or leaves out necessary information.
   B. Good organization can be achieved by ensuring that the subject and _____ (p. 129) are clear, relating all information in the message to the subject and purpose, grouping ideas in a logical way, and including all necessary information.
   C. Good organization is important because it helps the audience _____ (pp. 130–131) the message, helps the audience accept the message, saves the audience's time, and simplifies the communicator's job.

II. Good organization is a two-step process: defining and grouping the ideas, and establishing the _____ (p. 132) of ideas through organizational plans.
   A. An _____ (p. 133) is a systematic way of grouping ideas; an organization chart can also be used to identify the main idea, the major points, and the supporting _____ (p. 133).
   B. There are two approaches for sequencing the main ideas in a message: _____ (p. 135), in which the main idea is placed first and followed by the evidence, and _____ (p. 135), in which the evidence is first and the main idea is later.
   C. The four basic plans for short messages are those for direct requests; routine, good-news, and _____ (pp. 136–140) messages; bad-news messages; and persuasive messages.
   D. Longer messages may follow an informational or analytical pattern, depending on the purpose of the message.

III. When preparing the first draft of a message, try to establish the appropriate style and tone, depending on the nature of your message and your relationship with the reader.
   A. The first step toward getting the right _____ (p. 142) is to think about the relationship you want to establish with your audience.
   B. Project the _____ (p. 145) attitude by talking in terms of the audience's interests and referring when possible to the audience instead of yourself.

    C. Emphasize the _____ (p. 146) by focusing on opportunities for improvement instead of criticizing or trying to assess blame.

    D. Establish your _____ (pp. 147–149) by showing that you understand the other person's situation, are competent, can back up your claims with evidence, and are confident.

    E. The best tone for business messages is almost always a _____ (p. 150) one.

    F. In addition to writing for the reader, you are also writing for the _____ (p. 151), so be sure that your words are acceptable to the organization and that your style is compatible with the image it wants to project.

Check your answers at the end of this chapter.

QUIZ YOURSELF

1. What are four common sources of disorganization in business communication?

2. What are the four basic advantages of a well-organized document?

3. List six types of details that can be used to present evidence in a report.

4. Describe the four basic types of letters, memos, and other brief messages and explain how the audience is likely to react to each. Which basic organizational approach (direct or indirect) is best for each?

5. What is the best way to begin a bad-news message?

6. How does the choice of organizational pattern for a longer message relate to the purpose?

7. What are five specific things to avoid if you want to establish a businesslike tone?

8. Name five specific things you can do to emphasize the positive aspects of your message.

9. List four ways you can exhibit courtesy in business communications.

10. Discuss what it means to "write for the company."

Check your answers at the end of this chapter.

BUILD YOUR SKILLS: HOW SHOULD THESE MESSAGES BE ORGANIZED?

For each of the messages described below, select one of the following four organizational plans:

a. Direct approach for direct requests
b. Direct approach for routine or good-news messages
c. Indirect approach for bad-news messages
d. Indirect approach for persuasive messages

Here are the situations that require some sort of communication. How should each message be organized?

1. You are the manager of a restaurant. A disgruntled customer has complained about the slow service at dinner on a recent evening. You are assuring the customer that you are concerned about the complaint and have taken appropriate action.
2. You are a market-research analyst who has been assigned to study the hospital-products industry. You are asking hospital administrators to allow you to interview them.
3. You are a buyer for a large department store. You are complaining to one of your suppliers about the quality of the last shipment of merchandise you received.
4. You're a stock broker, and you have recently moved from one brokerage firm to another. You are letter your clients know of the change and encouraging them to continue doing business with you at your new firm.
5. You have opened a gift store in a new shopping mall. Because your initial sales have been below expectations, you are unable to pay your rent on time. You are asking the shopping-center owner for an extension.
6. As the shipping clerk for a building-supply company, you are informing a customer that her order has been received and that her merchandise is being shipped according to her instructions.
7. You are making arrangements with a resort hotel for your firm's annual sales convention.
8. You have been asked to speak at a luncheon meeting of a professional association, but you are unable to accept and are declining the invitation.

EXPAND YOUR KNOWLEDGE: HOW TO TAP YOUR CREATIVITY

The greatest untapped resource in the world of business is the underused creative energy of the people in it. Most people use only about one-fifth of their creativity. Yet creative thinking brings about the changes most beneficial to society and to us all. Fortunately, you can learn to think more creatively in only minutes—just by understanding how the creative process works.

What is the creative process? It's just new ideas to solve problems, primarily by recombining the known into something original and different. Whether the creative breakthrough is a poem, a painting, a business concept, or a scientific discovery, new ideas come about through a typical sequence. The creative act involves these five steps, or "stages of thought":

1. Exploring the problem and gathering data on it
2. Reading and absorbing this information
3. Letting your unconscious mind consider the problem, review the data, and synthesize the solution

4. Giving birth to the new idea—"Eureka, I have it!"
5. Shaping and developing the idea to practical usefulness

Creative ability is not limited to a chosen few. We all have it—or *can*, once we learn how to put these five steps to use.

Now that you understand the creative process, the following guidelines will help you put it to work:

- Write down the problem. Do not rely on memory.
- Translate the problem into clear, simple language.
- If possible, translate the problem into figures, graphs, charts, or mathematical symbols.
- Search published sources for additional related data.
- Take notes and develop files on these data.
- Discuss the problem and possible solutions with others.
- Expand your thinking by using a checklist of things to think about.
- For a new perspective, try turning the problem upside down.
- If you feel frustrated, don't worry. Relax. Turn your attention to other matters. Rest your mind. Sleep.
- Take time to be by yourself. Shut out interruptions. Free yourself of trivial work and concerns.
- When the new idea is born, write it down.

1. Here is a test of your creativity. Suppose that you are going into the food business. Your idea is to sell canned oranges preserved in juice, much like canned peaches or pears. Design a system for peeling the oranges, packing them in cans, labeling the cans, and packing the cans in cartons for shipment to grocery stores.

2. Creativity involves recombining the known into something new and different. To expand your creativity, develop a paragraph that logically ties together these apparently unrelated phrases:

> Animal noises
> A shoe factory
> A little boy in fancy clothes
> The scent of roses in the air

DEVELOP YOUR WORD POWER

Spelling Challenge   Identify the misspelled word in each of the following sentences, and spell it correctly in the space provided. If all the words in a sentence are spelled correctly, write *C* in the space.

_____   1. The problem is basicly one of quality.

_____   2. Please send a broshure on your kitchen lighting fixtures.

_____   3. We can make your bisness more profitable.

_____   4. Mark January 15 on your calender.

_____   5. When you practice your speech, strive to make it believeable.

_____   6. Schedule a meeting to unveil the new advertising campain.

_____   7. He has 12 years' experience as a bookeeper.

_____   8. Jason has a strong belief in himself.

_____ 9. Another course in personnel management would be benefical.

_____ 10. How have you benefited from the program?

Vocabulary Challenge   Match the words in the first column with the definitions in the second column.

_____ 11. concede   A. to approve

_____ 12. concur   B. to squeeze

_____ 13. condone   C. to discuss

_____ 14. confer   D. to agree

_____ 15. constrict   E. to admit

Circle the best definition of the highlighted word in each of the following sentences.

16. This job requires the ability to **conceptualize**.

    A. form a mental image   B. agree with others   C. convince others

17. Annette has **concocted** another excuse for skipping the meeting.

    A. conspired   B. rejected   C. devised

18. Ms. Starr will serve as the **conduit** for all suggestions from the staff.

    A. recorder   B. judge   C. channel

19. **Conjecture** about Dr. Drandall's successor is premature.

    A. gossip   B. uninformed guesses   C. strong feeling

20. He is a **consummate** speaker and much in demand.

    A. superb   B. exciting   C. bawdy

Select one of these words to complete each of the following sentences, and write the word in the space provided.

    compulsive   **compulsory**   **concise**   **conducive**   **contemporary**

21. I will need only five minutes to present a _____ overview of the year's accomplishments.

22. The _____ family consists of two breadwinners and one or two children.

23. Attendance at Monday's staff meeting is _____ for all clerks.

24. Brian has _____ need to correct everyone's grammar.

25. A supportive atmosphere is _____ to creativity and initiative.

Follow-up Word Study   Check your answers at the end of this chapter. In the spaces below, write the words that you spelled or used incorrectly. (Use a separate piece of paper if you missed more than five words.) Then look up each word in your dictionary, and carefully study its spelling, pronunciation, definition, and history (etymology). Finally, to help fix the word in your memory, write it in a sentence.

Word   Sentence

_____   _____

_____   _____

_____   _____

_____   _____

_____   _____

CHECK YOUR ANSWERS

Master Key Concepts

I. A. disorganized
    B. purpose
    C. understand

II. sequence
    A. outline, evidence
    B. direct, indirect
    C. goodwill

III. A. tone
    B. "you"
    C. positive
    D. credibility
    E. polite
    F. company

Quiz Yourself

1. Business writing seems disorganized when the writer
    a. Takes too long to get to the point
    b. Includes irrelevant material
    c. Groups ideas in a confusing way
    d. Leaves out necessary information (pp. 128–129)

2. A well-organized document
    a. Helps the audience understand the message
    b. Helps the audience accept the message
    c. Saves the audience time
    d. Simplifies the communicator's job (pp. 130–131)

3. Type of details that can be used to present evidence in a report include
    a. Facts and figures
    b. Examples or illustrations
    c. Description
    d. Narration
    e. Reference to authority
    f. Visual aids (p. 135)

4. Here are the four most common types of brief messages, the reader's most likely reaction to each, and the best organizational approach for each:
    a. A direct request is a simple, routine inquiry. The recipient is likely to be interested and willing. Use the direct approach.
    b. A routine, good-news, or goodwill message provides basic, everyday information. The audience is likely to be neutral, interested, or pleased. Use the direct approach.
    c. A bad-news message conveys disappointing information. The audience is likely to be displeased. Use the direct approach.
    d. A persuasive message asks the audience to do something that will benefit the sender. The audience may be uninterested in complying or unwilling to comply. Use the indirect approach. (p. 140)

5. Begin a bad-news message by putting the sincere explanation before the refusal to focus attention on your reasons. (p. 139)

6. When the purpose of a long message is to inform, the major points are based on a natural order, with the main idea presented first and then the subtopics. When the purpose of a long message is to persuade or collaborate, the organizational pattern should be analytical, focusing either on the conclusions and recommendations or on logical arguments. (p. 141)

7. To achieve a businesslike tone
    a. Don't be too familiar.
    b. Don't be excessive in your use of humor.
    c. Don't flatter the audience.
    d. Don't preach to the audience.
    e. Don't brag. (p. 144)

8. To emphasize the positive aspects of your message
    a. Stress what is or will be, not what isn't or won't be.
    b. In offering criticism or advice, emphasize what the other person can do to improve.
    c. Point out how the reader will benefit from your message.
    d. Avoid words with negative connotations.
    e. Avoid superlatives and exaggerations. (pp. 146–147)

9. You can demonstrate your courtesy in the following ways:
    a. Use tactful language rather than blunt terms.
    b. Adjust your language so it is appropriate to the relationship between you and the reader.
    c. Do or say something special to demonstrate your person interest in the reader.
    d. Be prompt in your correspondence. (p. 150)

10. Writing for the company means that you must handle your correspondence in a way that is compatible with the interests and style of the organization. Your own personality and views should be adjusted to project an image that is acceptable to the company, and your way of expressing yourself should conform to the company's wishes. (pp. 151–152)

Develop Your Word Power

1. basically	6. campaign	11. E	16. A	21. concise
2. brochure	7. bookkeeper	12. D	17. C	22. contemporary
3. business	8. *C*	13. A	18. C	23. compulsory
4. calendar	9. beneficial	14. C	19. B	24. compulsive
5. believable	10. *C*	15. B	20. A	25. conducive

Chapter 7

Revising Business Messages

The main point of Chapter 7 is that making an effort to revise and refine your messages helps your audience understand what you mean, exactly in the way you mean it. As you read the chapter, think about the ways the readability of your message is affected by word choice, sentence construction, paragraph development, design decisions, and accuracy of mechanics. When you finish reading, analyze the weaknesses in your own writing style and develop an approach to revising your written messages.

MASTER KEY CONCEPTS

Use the following terms to fill in the blanks in the outline. All terms are used, but none is used more than once.

beginning	dependent	modifiers	pronoun
classification	ending	nouns	topic
compound	functional	obsolete	transitional
content	illustration	predicate	verbs

  I. When revising your document, plan to go over it three times: once for content and organization, once for style and readability, and once for mechanics and format.
   A. When evaluating content and organization, see what might be added or cut, and pay special attention to the _____ and the _____ (p. 159).
   B. When reviewing style and readability, check your vocabulary and sentence structure, and apply a readability formula if necessary.
   C. When assessing word choice, pay attention to correctness, even though the rules of grammar are constantly changing.

 II. In the United States, plain English is a way of helping your audience understand your meaning.
   A. _____ (p. 162) words (conjunctions, prepositions, articles, and pronouns) are used to express relationships; _____ (p. 162) words (nouns, verbs, adjectives, and adverbs)—whether connotative or denotative, concrete or abstract—carry meaning.
   B. In business writing, the best words to use are those that are strong (meaning _____ and _____) (pp. 163–164), familiar, short, and uncamouflaged by unneeded suffixes.
   C. Avoid biased language that might offend the audience.

III. Words do not achieve their full meaning until they are assembled into sentences, which must have a least a subject (noun or pronoun) and a _____ (p. 169).
   A. Effective writing mixes the three types of sentences: simple, consisting of one subject-predicate set; _____ (p. 169), consisting of two or more independent clauses joined by such words as *and, but,* or *or;* and complex, consisting of one main independent clause and a _____ (p. 169) clause, which cannot stand alone.
   B. The most readable writing has many short sentences, is in the active voice, has no unnecessary words or phrases, avoids _____ (p. 173) and pompous language, takes a moderate tone, and does not string together sentences that should be separate. It makes firm statements whenever possible instead of hedging, minimizes indefinite _____ (p. 174) starters, expresses parallel ideas in parallel form, reduces awkward pointers to a

minimum, eliminates dangling _____ (p. 175), avoids long sequences of nouns, keeps subject and predicate close together, and emphasizes key thoughts.

IV. A paragraph is a series of sentences related to a single thought.
   A. The typical paragraph consists of a _____ (p. 177) sentence, related sentences that develop the topic, and _____ (p. 178) words and phrases.
   B. Of the many ways paragraphs can be developed, these five are most common: by _____ (p. 178), by comparison or contrast, by discussion of cause and effect, by _____ (p. 179), and by discussion of problem and solution.
   C. Paragraphs are most effective when they stick to one point, are relatively short (about 100 words), and are varied in structure and length.

Check your answers at the end of this chapter.

QUIZ YOURSELF

1. What is the Fog Index, and how is it calculated?

2. Conjunctions, prepositions, articles, and pronouns are all _____ words.

3. An _____ word stands for a concept, quality, or characteristic instead of a thing you can touch or see.

4. A _____ sentence contains two or more independent thoughts of equal importance joined by *and, but,* or *or.*

5. Explain what active voice is.

6. Relative pronouns such as _____, _____, and _____, are frequently sources of wordiness.

7. What is a hedging sentence?

8. Give an example of a dangling modifier.

9. What is a paragraph?

10. Identify five of the most common ways that paragraphs can be developed.

Check your answers at the end of this chapter.

BUILD YOUR SKILLS: ELIMINATE THE LEGALESE, PLEASE!

The following excerpt from a standard contract issued by a moving and storage company is replete with legal terms. Try your hand at rewriting this passage in plain English:

> No liability shall be provided for the mechanical or electrical derangements of pianos, radios, phonographs, clocks, refrigerators, television sets, automatic washers, or other instruments or appliances unless evidence is provided of external damage to such equipment, or unless said articles or appliances are serviced as provided in subparagraph (1) below. The carrier reserves the right to inspect these articles or appliances to determine whether they are in good working order before accepting them for shipment. Carrier assumes no liability whatsoever for returning, refocusing, or other adjustments of television sets unless such services were made necessary due to carrier's negligence.
>
> 1. Upon request of shipper, owner, or consignee of the goods, carrier will, subject to the provisions of subparagraph (2) below, service and unservice such articles as stoves, automatic washers, and dryers at origin and destination. Such servicing does not include removal or installation of articles secured to the premises or plumbing, electrical, or carpentry services necessary to disconnect, remove, connect, and install such articles and appliances.
>
> 2. If carrier does not possess the qualified personnel to properly service and unservice such articles or appliances, carrier, upon request of shipper or consignee or as agent for them, shall engage third persons to perform the servicing and unservicing. When third persons are engaged by the carrier to perform any service, the carrier will not assume responsibility for their activities or conduct; amount of their charges; nor the quality or quantity of service furnished.

BUILD YOUR SKILLS: CAN THIS LETTER BE IMPROVED?

This letter from a bank manager is designed to interest checking-account customers in opening an Individual Retirement Account (IRA) with the bank. Rewrite the letter so that it has stronger words, more effective sentences, and more coherent paragraphs.

Dear Valued Customer:

As a highly esteemed and valued customer of this financial establishment, I know that you appreciate it whenever we are able to offer you an opportunity to earn a higher return on your financial investments. For this reason, I would like to inform you of the benefits that can be obtained by making an investment in an Individual Retirement Account (IRA) with American Atlantic Bank and Trust.

It is possible to move closer to achieving your financial goals by opening an IRA, which enables you to obtain the protection of your income dollars from taxes, while at the same time giving you earnings growth and a cushion of financial comfort for impending retirement years.

The mechanism that affords you this valuable opportunity is simple. The full amount of your financial contribution to your IRA in a given tax year can be deducted from your taxable income in that year. In addition, the interest earned on your investment accumulates on a tax-exempt basis until such time as you withdraw it after your retirement. At the time of your retirement, most people who rely on earned income for the bulk of their working years are in a lower tax bracket. Hence, the interest earned on the IRA, as well as the principal withdrawn, are taxed at a lower rate than they would have been had they been declared as income during the wage-earning years.

We at American Atlantic Bank and Trust are able to offer you IRA terms that are attractive. For example, did you know that you are allowed to invest up to 100 percent of your annual earnings or a maximum of $2,000, whichever is higher, in an IRA? Furthermore, if your wife doesn't work and if you file jointly, you can contribute up to $2,250. And if both you and your wife are employed, as much as $4,000 can be invested on your behalf in a jointly held IRA each and every year in which both of you are employed.

Opening an IRA at American Atlantic Bank and Trust is truly easy. If you must make a withdrawal before you reach age 50, the amount you withdraw will be subject to an Internal Revenue Service tax penalty; however, the penalty does not apply if the withdrawal of funds is necessitated by death or by permanent disability.

Just complete the enclosed document at your earliest convenience and return it to me, the undersigned. By taking a few moments to complete the enclosure at this time, you will make your retirement appreciably more secure and vastly more comfortable in the long run. Isn't it worth it?

Do not delay! Act now!

Very truly yours,

Jocelyn Burkhardt

EXPAND YOUR KNOWLEDGE: READABILITY = EASE + INTEREST

Making your letters, memos, and reports easy to read is one thing, but making them interesting is quite another. What makes a written document interesting? To a large extent, "personal words" and "personal sentences" are the elements that involve readers, according to Dr. Rudolf Flesch. He has developed a method for measuring human interest:

1. Count the number of words in a writing sample.
2. Count the personal words:
   - All pronouns, except *it, its, itself* and *them, their, theirs, themselves* when referring to things rather than to people
   - All words, singular and plural, that refer to men or to women, such as *John Jones, Mary, father, sister, actress*—not common-gender words like *teacher, doctor, employee, assistant, spouse*
   - All group words *people* (with the plural verb) and *folks*
3. Divide the total number of personal words by the total number of words in the sample and multiply by 100 to get the number of personal words per 100 words.
4. Count the number of sentences in the sample.
5. Count the personal sentences:
   - Spoken sentences, marked by quotation marks or otherwise, often including speech tags like "he said," set off by colons or commas (such as *We told him: "You can take it or leave it"*)
   - Questions, commands, requests, and other sentences directly addressed to the reader (such as *Does this sound impossible?* or *It means a lot to people like you and me*)—but not sentences that are only indirectly or vaguely addressed to the reader (*This is typical of our national character* or *You can never tell*)
   - Exclamations
   - Grammatically incomplete sentences whose full meaning has to be inferred from the context (such as *Well, he wasn't* or *The minute you walked out*)

6. Divide the total number of personal sentences by the total number of sentences in the sample and multiply by 100 to get the number of personal sentences per 100 sentences.
7. Multiply the number of personal words per 100 words by 3.635.
8. Multiply the number of personal sentences per 100 sentences by 0.314.
9. Add the figures from steps 7 and 8 to get the human-interest score, which indicates the percentage of personal words and sentences in the sample. If the human-interest score is 0, your sample has no human interest; if the score is 100, the sample is full of human interest.

In the following passage from Dr. Flesch's *The Art of Readable Writing*, all personal words are in capital letters and all personal sentences are italicized:

> *SCHOPENHAUR said: "The first rule for a good style is to have something to say; in fact, this in itself is almost enough." The British diplomat HAROLD NICOLSON wrote: "The first essential is to know what one wishes to say; the second is to decide to whom on wishes to say it." And the Hungarian mathematician GEORGE POLYA came up with this one: "The first rule of style is to have something to say. The second rule of style is to control YOURSELF when, by chance, YOU have two things to say; say first one, then the other, not both at the same time."*
>
> *No doubt NICOLSON and POLYA made valuable additions; but, as YOU see, SCHOPENHAUER'S first rule still stands.* It is likely to be put in first place by anybody else who may want to draw up rules of style.
>
> *But, YOU will say, that doesn't help much.* That just passes the buck back to the person who wants to know how to write. *"Have something to say"* sounds much like saying *"Be smart"* or *"Have a mind of YOUR own."*
>
> *In the main, that's true.* But having something to say also means having a good stock of facts; and there are ways and means of getting at facts and keeping them handy. Most PEOPLE who do any writing (without being professional writers) are handicapped by simply not knowing how to collect THEIR material.
>
> *Let ME tell YOU a little story: It was a Sunday evening.* I was putting the finishing touches on a research report I was working on. Suddenly I realized that I didn't have certain figures on magazine circulation that I had meant to use. If I couldn't get these figures at once I would miss MY deadline. I was on the spot.
>
> The solution was a simple as can be: I called the public library and had MY information within two minutes.

The human-interest score of this passage is about 45. Compare the scores that Dr. Flesch computed for a variety of magazines:

Description of Style	Percentage of Personal Words	Percentage of Personal Sentences	Human-Interest Score	Typical Magazine
dull	2 or less	0	0 to 10	scientific
mildly interesting	4	5	10 to 20	trade
interesting	7	15	20 to 40	digest
highly interesting	10	43	40 to 60	*New Yorker*
dramatic	17 or more	58 or more	60 to 100	fiction

Before you try to boost the human-interest level in everything you write, remember that some business documents must remain impersonal. However, personal words and personal sentences do help readers pay attention to your message.

1. Both the Fog Index and the Flesch human-interest score are methods for measuring writing effectiveness. How do they differ?

2. How useful are such methods of measuring readability as the Fog Index and the human-interest score? What's good about them? What's not so good?

DEVELOP YOUR WORD POWER

Spelling Challenge   Identify the misspelled word in each of the following sentences, and spell it correctly in the space provided. If all the words in a sentence are spelled correctly, write *C* in the space.

_____ 1. How many commitee members are from Purchasing?

_____ 2. Add the colum of figures twice to make sure the total is right.

_____ 3. Mr. Nguyen's choise is the brown chair.

_____ 4. All your purchases are chargible when you have King credit.

_____ 5. He is certanly going to ask for a raise.

_____ 6. I would put it in the business category.

_____ 7. Current conditions are very changable.

_____ 8. Quality products are not cheep!

_____ 9. A new office manager has already been choisen.

_____ 10. I turned over all my comercial accounts to Suzanne.

Vocabulary Challenge   Match the words in the first column with the definitions in the second column.

_____ 11. conviction   A. believability

_____ 12. credence   B. formal introduction

_____ 13. credential   C. standard of judgment

_____ 14. criterion   D. evidence of authority

_____ 15. debut   E. fixed belief

Circle the best definition of the highlighted word in each of the following sentences.

16. Melissa **contends** that none of the sites is acceptable.

    A. believes   B. asserts   C. suggests

17. See whether you can hold your **contentious** staff together long enough to finish the project.

    A. quarrelsome   B. prize-winning   C. unmotivated

18. Paul's conclusions were **contradictory**.

    A. stubborn   B. inconsistent   C. unacceptable

19. The jute pad was installed **contrary** to our wishes.

    A. in accordance with   B. beyond   C. against

20. You have bought a **counterfeit** microchip that we did not produce.

    A. ready-made   B. fake   C. printed

Select one of these words to complete each of the following sentences, and write the word in the space provided.

continual   continuous   credible   creditable   cursory

21. The _____ roar of the air conditioners drowns out casual conversations.

22. The district attorney cannot prosecute unless a _____ witness is found.

23. A _____ reading of the letter yielded no new information, so she reread it.

24. The team's fans formed a _____ line in front of the stadium, forcing delivery crews to detour to a side gate.

25. Considering your lack of experience, you have done a _____ job.

Follow-up Word Study   Check your answers at the end of this chapter. In the spaces below, write the words that you spelled or used incorrectly. (Use a separate piece of paper if you missed more than five words.) Then look up each word in your dictionary, and carefully study its spelling, pronunciation, definition, and history (etymology). Finally, to help fix the word in your memory, write it in a sentence.

Word   Sentence

_____   _____

_____   _____

_____   _____

_____   _____

_____   _____

CHECK YOUR ANSWERS

Master Key Concepts

I. A. beginning, ending

II. A. functional, content
   B. nouns, verbs

III. predicate
   A. compound, dependent
   B. obsolete, pronoun, modifiers

IV. A. topic, transitional
   B. illustration, classification

Quiz Yourself

1. The Fog Index measures the readability of a document. To calculate the Fog Index, choose several 100-word writing samples. For each sample, count the number of words in each sentence, the number of sentences, and the number of words with three or more syllables. Calculate the average number of words per sentence and the percentage of words with three or syllables. Add these two numbers, and then multiply by 0.4. The resulting number is the Fog Index. For a general business audience, a level of 8 to 11 is about right. (p. 160)

2. Conjunctions, prepositions, articles, and pronouns are all *functional* words. (p. 162)

3. An *abstract* word stands for a concept, quality, or characteristic instead of a thing you can touch or see. (p. 162)

4. A *compound* sentence contains two or more independent thoughts of equal importance joined by *and, but,* or *or.* (p. 169)

5. The active voice places the subject of a sentence before the verb, and the object of the sentence follows it. Active voice produces shorter, stronger sentences than passive voice. (pp. 170–171)

6. Relative pronouns such as *who, that,* and *which* are frequently sources of wordiness. (p. 171)

7. A hedging sentence is one that tries too hard to avoid stating a judgment as a fact. Hedging sentences frequently include words like *may* and *seem.* (p. 174)

8. Here are some examples of dangling modifiers—phrases with no real connection to the subject of the sentence:
   a. Walking to the office, a red sports car passed him.
   b. Going down in the elevator, the office seemed to be in a different world.
   c. Working as fast as possible, the budget soon was ready. (p. 175)

9. A paragraph is a cluster of sentences all related to the same general topic. It is a unit of thought, often separated from other units of thought by the typographical device of indenting the first line. (p. 177)

10. Five of the most common ways to develop a paragraph are
   a. Illustration
   b. Comparison or contrast
   c. Cause and effect
   d. Classification
   e. Problem and solution (pp. 178–179)

Develop Your Word Power

1.	committee	6.	*C*	11.	E	16.	B	21.	continual
2.	column	7.	changeable	12.	A	17.	A	22.	credible
3.	choice	8.	cheap	13.	D	18.	B	23.	cursory
4.	chargeable	9.	chosen	14.	C	19.	C	24.	continuous
5.	certainly	10.	commercial	15.	B	20.	B	25.	creditable

PART THREE

LETTERS, MEMOS, AND OTHER BRIEF MESSAGES

Chapter 8

Writing Direct Requests

The main point of Chapter 6 is that direct requests are most likely to yield the desired result and to leave the desired impression on the audience when they are organized according to the direct plan. As you read the chapter, observe how a single pattern—main idea, explanation, courteous close—can effectively be applied to many situations. When you finish reading, try to apply the direct plan to some of the direct requests that you make.

MASTER KEY CONCEPTS

Use the following terms to fill in the blanks in the outline. All terms are used, but none is used more than once.

adjustment	credit	memo	recommendation
advertisement	direct	middle	reference
appreciation	invitations	purchase	routine
confidential			

I. _____ (p. 196) requests are meant to elicit some action or information from an interested and willing audience.
   A. Begin with a clear statement of the most important question or idea, specifying the exact mature and scope of your request.
   B. Use the _____ (p. 197) section to explain why you are making the request, couching your explanation in terms that show how the audience will benefit by complying.
   C. Conclude with a courteous expression of _____ (p. 198) and a specific request for action, complete with any time limits that apply.

II. For placing orders, the direct plan takes on many of the characteristics of a well-designed order form: an offer to _____ (p. 199) the goods, a complete description of the goods being ordered, a delivery and billing address, payment details, and a courteous close that suggests some future reader benefit.

III. Even a request for _____ (p. 201) information or action may have a significant effect on an organization's relationship with customers, clients, suppliers, and shareholders.
   A. Requests for action from someone within the organization may be written in _____ (p. 201) format but should still make the desired action clear, appealing, and easy.

    B. Requests to other businesses may be in response to an _____ (p. 203) or may simply be inquiries about products.

    C. People outside the organization are often asked to do something—attend a meeting, return an information card, endorse a document, confirm an address, supplement information on an order; a brief form letter is sometimes adequate for this purpose.

IV. A request for a minor, matter-of-course claim or _____ (p. 206) may follow the direct plan as long as the tone is positive and unemotional and sufficient detail is provided.

V. The direct approach is used for routine _____ (pp. 210–211) requests, although a standardized application form is sometimes used by the creditor; in addition, businesses applying for credit should supply a financial statement and perhaps a balance sheet.

VI. When requesting a _____ (p. 212–213) for a job, promotion, scholarship, club membership, or credit card you may also follow the direct plan.

    A. Before using someone's name as a _____ (p. 212), write a direct request seeking permission to do so; remind the reader of the connection between you.

    B. A letter requesting information about an applicant should follow the direct plan; however, to protect against legal problems, you should be careful to ask about only those characteristics related to the job or credit being sought and to reassure the reader that the information will be kept _____ (p. 214).

VII. The direct plan, in standard letter or memo format, may be used to issue _____ (pp. 215–216), which may also be laid out more imaginatively.

Check your answers at the end of this chapter.

QUIZ YOURSELF

1. When is it most appropriate to use the direct plan for a request?

2. Briefly explain the organizational plan for a direct request.

3. What type of information should be included in the middle section of a direct request?

4. In placing an order for goods, what basic facts should you include?

5. When an inquiry is written in memo format to employees of the company, how should it be organized?

6. List some of the reasons a business might request routine action from customers or other people outside the company.

7. What type of information could you include to document a claim or a request for adjustment?

8. What information do businesses supply when applying for credit?

9. How would you organize a letter asking a former professor for a recommendation?

10. What details should be included in an invitation?

Check your answers at the end of this chapter.

BUILD YOUR SKILLS: WHAT'S WRONG WITH THIS DIRECT REQUEST?

Someone representing the publisher of a free monthly bulletin for educators has drafted this letter. What could he do to make it more effective as a direct request?

May 7, 1991

Ms. Betty Morrison
17 Meadow Lane
Bridgewater, MA 02324

Dear Ms. Morrison:

As a reader of *Know-It-Now*, you can take advantage of varied articles on current trends and events in education. Right now we are updating our mailing list; we hope that you'll be able to take time to help us in this important endeavor. It should not be too time consuming.

If we are to keep sending you our publication each month, we must ask you to fill out the enclosed card. Please mail it to us relatively soon.

Sincerely,

Jason Bettancourt
Circulation Department

JB/ta

EXPAND YOUR KNOWLEDGE: THE MEEK PERSON'S GUIDE
TO ASKING FOR HELP

Nobody is self-sufficient. In the world of business, checking references, requesting routine action, filing claims and adjustments, and inquiring about people, products, or services all qualify as asking others for help. But maybe asking others for help is difficult for you. Do any of the following views sound like yours? If so, read the internal dialogs that come after them to learn how you can assert yourself—and ask for help without guilt or discomfort.

- *If I ask someone for a favor, I am imposing on him or her.* Not true. I am imposing only if I believe that the person doesn't have the right to deny my request for help—or if I do not allow him or her to do so. I am also imposing if my request represents an undue inconvenience. As long as I know the other person has the freedom to say no, and as long as my request isn't overly inconveniencing, I have the right to make it.

- *If I ask for help, the other person will not be able to say no even if he or she wants to.* People are likely to act in their own best interests. If I am not sure that another person really wants to help me, I can always ask whether he or she prefers that I ask someone else. If I expect to behave assertively in making requests, I must assume that others can assertively refuse my requests if they want to.

- *If I ask for help, the other person should realize that I really need it—and should help me.* People are free to grant or to refuse my requests. They are not obligated to help me. All I can do is ask for help and indicate why I need it. If they say no, I may indicate my disappointment, but I should not try to pressure them to comply.

- *If I ask for and receive a favor from another, I will be obligated to do him or her an equal or greater favor in the future.* A favor is granted or refused freely. If I feel obligated, it is probably because I think I am not deserving or because I regard favors as social requirements that are not given freely. I may feel grateful to one who does a favor for me, and I may want to do him or her a favor in return. But in most cases, obligation is not written into a favor when it is granted.

1. Like everything else, asking for help is easier if you have a little experience. Try these role-playing exercises with your classmates to refine your skill in asking for favors:
   a. You are a market-research representative who is studying consumer preferences in buying frozen waffles. Your job is to call households to ask an adult resident to answer a series of questions about his or her attitudes toward frozen waffles. Try to persuade prospective interviewees (members of your class) go give you 15 minutes of their time.
   b. Your college or university has asked you to participate in a fundraising drive for the school. You have been given a list of alumni to call and ask for contributions. Practice your call.
   c. You have decided to run for political office. It is six months before the election, and you are trying to build a campaign organization by calling members of your political party and asking for their help. What do you say? Practice your appeal.
   After completing these exercises, are you any better at asking for help? Does it become easier to face the possibility of rejection after you've talked with a few people? Do you feel more confident in posing your request? Does the content of your appeal become more effective?

2. Some people are reluctant to ask for favors because they don't want to appear weak or dependent. Are they being silly, or does asking for help actually make you more helpless? Do people gain power over you when they grant you favors? Discuss.

DEVELOP YOUR WORD POWER

Spelling Challenge   Identify the misspelled word in each of the following sentences, and spell it correctly in the space provided. If all the words in a sentence are spelled correctly, write C in the space.

_____ 1. A compitent secretary is an asset to any company.

_____ 2. I cannot conceive of any product that everyone would buy.

_____ 3. Be slow to condem and quick to praise.

_____ 4. Is he concious of how poorly educated he sounds?

_____ 5. Enthusiasm is contageous.

_____ 6. I brought in a sample of their lotion for comparisen.

_____ 7. We are compleatly out of that model but can get another one soon.

_____ 8. How can you concentrate with all this construction going on?

_____ 9. My consciense will not allow me to quit without two weeks' notice.

_____ 10. Her work is consistant although not outstanding.

Vocabulary Challenge   Match the words in the first column with the definitions in the second column.

_____ 11. defer   A. to put off

_____ 12. deplete   B. to scatter

_____ 13. deride   C. to misrepresent

_____ 14. dispel   D. to scoff at

_____ 15. distort   E. to decrease

Circle the best definition of the highlighted word in each of the following sentences.

16. Jack is a **deft** typist.

    A. hard of hearing   B. daffy   C. skillful

17. It is time to edit all the **defunct** policies out of the employee manual.

    A. awkward   B. sanitized   C. extinct

18. My position on opening a branch office is **diametrically** opposed to yours.

    A. in some measure   B. directly   C. firmly

19. It is hard to see the point in a report this **diffuse**.

    A. wordy   B. mild   C. different

20. Her **disdain** for the junior accountants has created ill feeling in the office.

    A. admiration   B. extra work   C. scorn

Select one of these words to complete each of the following sentences, and write the word in the space provided.

demise   dexterity   diagnosis   dilemma   dissonance

21. She was faced with the _____ of resigning or being fired.

22. The _____ with which you closed to deal was admirable.

23. The report is based on Hawkes & Associates' _____ of the company's ills.

24. A workplace characterized by _____ creates stress.

25. The _____ of our department left 20 people scrambling for jobs.

Follow-up Word Study   Check your answers at the end of this chapter. In the spaces below, write the words that you spelled or used incorrectly. (Use a separate piece of paper if you missed more than five words.) Then look up each word in your dictionary, and carefully study its spelling, pronunciation, definition, and history (etymology). Finally, to help fix the word in your memory, write it in a sentence.

Word   Sentence

_____   _____

_____   _____

_____   _____

_____   _____

_____   _____

CHECK YOUR ANSWERS

Master Key Concepts

I. direct
   B. middle
   C. appreciation

II. purchase

III. routine
   A. memo
   B. advertisement

IV. adjustment

V. credit

VI. recommendation
   A. reference
   B. confidential

VII. invitations

Quiz Yourself

1. The direct plan should be used for a request when you can assume that your audience will be interested in what you have to say or at least be willing to cooperate with you. (p. 196)

2. Direct requests have three basic parts:
   a. An opening that states the request or presents the main idea
   b. A middle section that explains the request or idea in more detail so the reader knows how to respond correctly
   c. A cordial closing that clearly states the desired action (p. 196)

3. The middle section of a direct request should include any information that suggests a reader benefit. In addition, this section should cover facts about the subject of your request and your reason for making it. (pp. 197–198)

4. When placing an order for goods, include
   a. The date the order is placed
   b. A clear statement that you want to buy the merchandise
   c. A complete description of the items you want, including catalog number, quantity, name or brand, color, size, price, and total amount due
   d. The address where the goods should be shipped
   e. The billing address (if different from the shipping address)
   f. The method of shipment desired
   g. Payment details (p. 199)

5. Inquiries in memo format follow the same direct plan as a letter. They begin with a statement of the purpose of the inquiry, followed by an explanation of the request and a final reminder of the desired action. (p. 201)

6. Businesses might make a routine request to customers or other outsiders for any of the following reasons:
   a. To invite them to attend a meeting
   b. To encourage them to return an information card
   c. To ask them to endorse a document
   d. To request that they confirm their address
   e. To ask them to provide additional information about an order (pp. 204–205)

7. To document your claim or request for adjustment, you could send a copy of your canceled check, the sales slip or receipt, dated correspondence, a description of the merchandise, and any other relevant document. (p. 207)

8. To obtain credit, businesses supply such information as the company name, the length of time in business, the name of the company's bank, and addresses of businesses where credit has already been established. (p. 210)

9. Use the direct approach when you are writing to ask a former professor for a recommendation. Begin by stating the request, refreshing the professor's memory about your association. Explain why you are making the request and provide information about yourself that the professor can use to support a recommendation. Close with an expression of appreciation, as well as details about where the information should be sent. If appropriate, enclose a resume and a stamped, preaddressed envelope. (p. 213)

10. An invitation should include the following details:
    a. Nature of the event
    b. Date and time
    c. Location (perhaps with directions or a map)
    d. Sponsor or host of the event
    e. Additional facts that might be helpful to the guests, such as cost, attire, schedule, and so on (p. 215)

Develop Your Word Power

1. competent	6. comparison	11. A	16. C	21. dilemma
2. *C*	7. completely	12. E	17. C	22. dexterity
3. condemn	8. *C*	13. D	18. B	23. diagnosis
4. conscious	9. conscience	14. B	19. A	24. dissonance
5. contagious	10. consistent	15. C	20. C	25. demise

Chapter 9

Writing Routine, Good-News, and Goodwill Messages

The main point of Chapter 9 is that the direct plan—often augmented by resale and sales-promotion material—can be used to organize routine, good-news, and goodwill messages. As you read the chapter, think about all the kinds of messages that fall into this category. When you finish reading, practice weaving subtle resale and sales-promotion material into your messages.

MASTER KEY CONCEPTS

Use the following terms to fill in the blanks in the outline. All terms are used, but none is used more than once.

action	congratulations	goodwill	positive
adjustment	customer	greeting	resale
benefits	details	grudging	sales promotion
condolence	direct	main	

I. Understanding how _____ (p. 230) messages are organized allows you to compose excellent examples quickly.
   A. By opening with a clear statement of the _____ (p. 230) point, you prepare the reader to understand the message.
   B. The middle and longest section of the message explains the _____ (p. 231) while reinforcing the positive aspects of the message.
   C. The final section summarizes the main point, courteously indicates what should happen next, and highlights reader _____ (p. 232).

II. When responding positively to an inquiry, order, or request, use the _____ (p. 232) plan.
   A. An acknowledgment of an order, which provides an opportunity to build customer goodwill, should assure the reader that the order is being filled, clarify all details of the transaction, and do a bit of selling through _____ (pp. 232–233) or sales promotion.
   B. When responding to requests for information or _____ (pp. 234–235) when no sale is involved, the main goal is to answer all the questions fairly and honestly and to create a positive impression of the organization; when a potential sale is involved, an added goal is to emphasize the customer benefits of making a purchase and to close with a specific suggestion that will move the customer one step closer to the sale.

III. When responding favorably to a request of _____ (p. 236), you have the opportunity to build customer loyalty.
   A. When the organization is at fault, avoid a _____ (p. 238) tone, and avoid blaming any particular person or division; instead, emphasize that your organization tries to do a good job.
   B. When the _____ (p. 240) is at fault, courteously state that you will resolve the problem to the customer's satisfaction, but politely explain what went wrong so that the customer will not inadvertently repeat his or her error and thus again be disappointed; be objective and avoid blame, so that the customer will do business with you again.

C. When a third party is at fault, the best solution is usually to honor the claim but to offer at least a partial explanation of the problem to avoid giving the impression that your negligence caused it.

IV. Letters approving credit mark the beginning of a relationship with a customer, so they build goodwill and offer resale or _____ (p. 245) information as well as explain the terms of credit.

V. Use the direct approach when conveying positive information about people, such as recommendation letters or good news about employment.

VI. Because both directives and instructions are routine messages, they should follow the direct plan.

VII. Good-news messages about products and operations include letters to customers and press releases.

VIII. A _____ (p. 250) message is a friendly, unexpected note with no direct business purpose; it focuses on the recipient, not the sender.
   A. Letters of _____ (p. 251) tell readers you have noticed their accomplishments and are happy about their success.
   B. Letters of appreciation document the contributions of employees and other business associates.
   C. Letters of _____ (pp. 253–254) help ease the stress of someone who is suffering from health or business problems or the loss of a loved one.
   D. Newcomers and long-time customers all appreciate letters of _____ (p. 255).

Check your answers at the end of this chapter.

QUIZ YOURSELF

1. Describe the basic organizational plan for routine, good-news, and goodwill messages.

2. What should you include in the middle section of a favorable reply to an order?

3. What are the three main goals in replying to a request for information if a potential sale is involved?

4. What are the two main goals in replying to routine requests if no sale is involved?

5. What general impression would you try to convey when responding to claims if your company is at fault?

6. What details should be included in the middle section of a routine approval of a request for credit?

7. What information should be included in a letter of recommendation?

8. What is the appropriate tone for a goodwill message, and what are some ways of achieving this tone?

9. Discuss some of the dos and don'ts of writing letters of condolence.

10. What approach should a company with a limited budget take toward seasonal greetings to customers?

Check your answers at the end of this chapter.

BUILD YOUR SKILLS: WHAT'S WRONG WITH THIS GOOD-NEWS LETTER?

Someone representing the publisher of mass-market paperbacks has drafted this letter. What could she do to make it more effective as a good-news message?

August 16, 1995

Mr. Fernando Hidalgo
The Readers' Nook Bookstore
28900 Alameda Way
Phoenix, AZ 85018

Dear Mr. Hidalgo:

This is in response to your query about advertising expenses and local promotion efforts. Our usual policy is to share advertising expenses on a 40–60 basis.

Our new line of Unicorn Romances debuts this month. It would be in your best interest to display the entire line in a large rack on the counter by the cash register. We believe that customers will be attracted to our books by a new display. This display features a beam of light bouncing against the ceiling on what look like clouds. It's an expensive display and hard to install, but we believe that it's worth it.

As far as your local promotion efforts go, they should get some assists from our national TV and radio campaign. That's about the best we can offer, although for a short time we will participate in the local efforts you mentioned. Making a rare exception, we will share expenses for this local campaign on a 50–50 basis.

Call us soon to set up the details for this campaign.

Sincerely,

Kathy Walker Reaban
Promotion Director

KWR/opp

BUILD YOUR SKILLS: WHAT'S WRONG WITH THIS GOODWILL LETTER?

A representative of a computer company has drafted this letter. What could he do to make it more effective as a goodwill message?

February 18, 1995

Mr. Ralph Teagarden
Chief of Program Design
Interdata Software
100 Ives Dairy Road
Chapel Hill, NC 27514

Dear Mr. Teagarden:

This letter is to inform you that the recent reception given by you for our programmers was well received. They liked Interdata Software and the Speedit Editor, which was developed by you.

You will, I trust, accept our appreciation for this assistance.

Cordially yours,

Gerald MacKenzie
Vice-President, Systems

GMK/bn

EXPAND YOUR KNOWLEDGE: A "MAGIC" FORMULA FOR BUSINESS SUCCESS

Joe Girard has sold more new cars and trucks, for 11 years running, than any other human being. In fact, in a typical year Joe sells more than twice as many vehicles as anybody else. When asked about his success, Joe responded, "I send out over 13,000 cards every month."

Joe's magic is the same magic employed by many successful companies. It is simply service, overpowering service, especially after-sales service. Joe notes, "I do something that a lot of salespeople don't and that's believe that the sale really begins *after* the sale—not before. The customer isn't even out the door, and my son has already made up a thank-you note." A year later, Joe might intercede personally with the service manager on behalf of his customer. Meanwhile, he keeps the communications flowing.

Joe's customers won't forget him once they buy a car from him; he won't let them! Every month throughout the year, they get a letter from him. It arrives in a plain envelope, always a different size or color. "It doesn't look like direct mail. And they open it up and the front of it reads, `I like you.' Inside it says `Happy New Year from Joe Girard.'" He sends a card in February to wish customers a "Happy George Washington's Birthday." In March it's "Happy St. Patrick's Day." They love the cards, Joe boasts: "You should hear the comments I get on them."

Out of context, Joe's 13,000 cards sound like just another sales gimmick. But like the top companies, Joe seems genuinely to care. Says Joe: "The great restaurants in the country have love and care coming out of their kitchens, and when I sell cars, my customers are going to leave with the same feeling they'll get when they walk out of a great restaurant. My customers are not," he says, "an interruption or pain in the neck. They are my bread and butter."

1. How could you use Joe Girard's technique in your intended career?

2. Sending 13,000 cards every month is an expensive proposition, even though the cost is deductible as a business expense. Do you think that Joe could achieve the same effect by sending the cards less frequently?

DEVELOP YOUR WORD POWER

Spelling Challenge   Identify the misspelled word in each of the following sentences, and spell it correctly in the space provided. If all the words in a sentence are spelled correctly, write *C* in the space.

_____ 1. How well do your figures corellate with theirs?

_____ 2. A curteous attitude helps maintain goodwill.

_____ 3. Their debt may exceed their ability to repay.

_____ 4. Do not be decieved by their expressions of friendship.

_____ 5. With prior permission, you can conduct a controled burn.

_____ 6. When you finish typing today's correspondance, file these.

_____ 7. He gets angry whenever he hears any critisism.

_____ 8. All final desicions on marketing are made by Beth Bryant.

_____ 9. Please make an appointment for a time convenent to you.

_____ 10. I will take complete responsibility for any dificiency.

Vocabulary Challenge   Match the words in the first column with the definitions in the second column.

_____ 11. divert   A. to trespass

_____ 12. emit   B. to deflect

_____ 13. emulate   C. to try to equal or excel

_____ 14. encroach   D. to intensify

_____ 15. enhance   E. to send forth

Circle the best definition of the highlighted word in each of the following sentences.

16. Investors and farmers should **diversify** to minimize risk.

   A. branch out   B. insure themselves   C. plan

17. The **diversity** of the audience made analysis of their needs difficult.

   A. restlessness   B. hostility   C. heterogeneity

18. The "just-in-time" inventory system aims to increase **efficiency**.

   A. profits   B. morale   C. effectiveness

19. Rick's **elan** is an asset to his sales career.

   A. dash   B. luxury automobile   C. good looks

20. The office staff turned out **en masse** to wish her good luck in her new job.

   A. in a party mood   B. after work   C. as a group

Select one of these words to complete each of the following sentences, and write the word in the space provided.

   divisive   dogmatic   dynamic   efficacious   eloquent

21. Jane's _____, energetic presentation generated enthusiasm for the new selling season.

22. The federation's _____ appeal conveyed powerful images of human suffering.

23. Try to avoid being _____ in meetings; let others share their opinions too.

24. Promoting from within is sometimes _____ but sometimes beneficial.

25. Terry Lee's group is well known for its _____, results-oriented approach.

Follow-up Word Study   Check your answers at the end of this chapter. In the spaces below, write the words that you spelled or used incorrectly. (Use a separate piece of paper if you missed more than five words.) Then look up each word in your dictionary, and carefully study its spelling, pronunciation, definition, and history (etymology). Finally, to help fix the word in your memory, write it in a sentence.

Word   Sentence

_____   _____

_____   _____

_____   _____

_____   _____

_____   _____

CHECK YOUR ANSWERS

Master Key Concepts

I. positive
   A. main
   B. details
   C. benefits

II. direct
   A. resale
   B. action

III. adjustment
   A. grudging
   B. customer

IV. sales promotion

VIII. goodwill
   A. congratulations
   C. condolence
   D. greeting

Quiz Yourself

1. The basic organizational plan for routine, good-news, and goodwill messages is to
   a. Give a clear statement of the main idea
   b. Provide necessary details
   c. Close courteously (pp. 230–232)

2. The middle section of a favorable reply to an order provides a clear, accurate summary of the transaction: when the delivery may be expected; the cost of the merchandise, shipping, and taxes; and an explanation of problems that may have arisen. This section might also include a summary of your credit terms, plus resale or sales-promotion information. (pp. 232–233)

3. The three main goals in replying to a request for information if a sale is involved are to
   a. Respond to the immediate request
   b. Encourage a sale
   c. Convey a good impression of you and your firm (pp. 234–235)

4. The two main goals in replying to a request for information if no sale is involved are to
   a. Respond to the request
   b. Leave a favorable impression of your company or foster good working relationships (pp. 235–236)

5. When replying to claims when your company is at fault, try to restore the customer's faith in the firm. Instead of shifting the blame or offering excuses, emphasize the company's efforts to do a good job and imply that the error was unusual. (p. 238)

6. The middle section of a letter approving credit should include a full statement of the credit arrangements: the upper limit of the account, dates that bills are sent, possible arrangements for partial monthly payments, discounts for prompt payments, interest charges for unpaid balances, and due dates. (p. 242)

7. A letter of recommendation should include
   a. The name of the candidate
   b. The job or benefit that the candidate is seeking
   c. An indication of whether the writer is answering a request or taking the initiative
   d. The nature of the relationship between the writer and the candidate
   e. Facts relevant to the position or benefit sought
   f. The writer's overall evaluation of the candidate's suitability for the job or benefit sought (p. 244)

8. Goodwill messages should have a warm, sincere, and friendly tone. To achieve this tone, adopt the "you" attitude, focusing on the audience's feelings and interests rather than on your own. Generally, you should keep the message short and relatively casual. Avoid exaggeration, and back up any compliments with specific points that demonstrate your sincerity. (p. 250)

9. When writing letters of condolence
   a. Keep reminiscences brief.
   b. Write in your own words.
   c. Be tactful.
   d. Take special care to spell names correctly and to be accurate with your facts.
   e. Write about special qualities of the deceased.
   f. Write about special qualities of the bereaved person.
   g. Don't let fear of saying something wrong keep you from saying anything at all. (p. 254)

10. A company on a limited budget should send its seasonal greetings when they will have the greatest impact. In general, the company might want to avoid sending messages during the winter holidays, when people receive many other cards. A note at Easter or the Fourth of July might have more impact. If possible, the greeting should be tied in with a holiday that relates to the company's products or services. For example, a florist might send greetings around Valentine's Day, and a stationery store might send messages in April to coincide with National Secretary's Week. (p. 255)

Develop Your Word Power

1. correlate	6. correspondence	11. B	16. A	21. dynamic
2. courteous	7. criticism	12. E	17. C	22. eloquent
3. C	8. decisions	13. C	18. C	23. dogmatic
4. deceived	9. convenient	14. A	19. A	24. divisive
5. controlled	10. deficiency	15. D	20. C	25. efficacious

Chapter 10

Writing Bad-News Messages

The main point of Chapter 10 is that bad-news messages are most likely to be accepted when they follow the indirect plan. As you read the chapter, think about how embedding the bad news within positive buffers helps make it more acceptable. When you finish reading, think about the bad news you have had to convey and how using the indirect approach might have helped ease the pain.

MASTER KEY CONCEPTS

Use the following terms to fill in the blanks in the outline. All terms are used, but none is used more than once.

accusation	buffer	indirect	rationale
action	fair	positive	routine
alternatives	impersonal	promises	substitute
back order			

I. When presenting bad news, you have three objectives: to make the reader aware that the bad news is a firm decision, to convince the reader that your decision is _____ (p. 268) and reasonable, and to leave the reader with a _____ (p. 268) attitude toward you and your organization.
   A. The indirect plan is a roundabout approach consisting of a _____ (p. 269) that introduces the subject of the letter, establishes rapport with the reader, and provides a transition to the next section; a statement of the reasons supporting the negative decision; a statement of the bad news itself, couched in positive and _____ (p. 269) language; and a positive close that is neither apologetic nor insincere.
   B. The direct plan, which emphasizes the bad news itself, may be used when the bad news is _____ (p. 273), when you want to convey a forceful message, or when you know that the audience prefers candor.

II. When conveying bad news about an order, try to promote an eventual sale along the lines of the original order, make instructions and additional information as clear as possible, and keep the customer from losing interest by maintaining a positive tone.
   A. When replying to an unclear order, either in writing or over the phone, the _____ (p. 274) approach allows you to confirm the original order and bolster the sale before explaining the problem.
   B. When an ordered item is temporarily out of stock, you must _____ (p. 275) it for a customer. You can either begin with the good news that part of the order is en route or begin by confirming the sale and commenting enthusiastically on the product before explaining why you are unable to ship the order; in either case, close on an upbeat note that reinforces the sale.
   C. When you must _____ (p. 275) another product for the one ordered, write a letter that "sells" the alternative and gives the customer simple directions for ordering; if the

substitute is more expensive, you must also convince the customer that it is better than the original item.

    D. When you cannot fill the order at all, your goal is to say no but to be as helpful as possible.

III. When conveying negative answers and information, say no clearly, but be sure you fulfill any _____ (p. 279) you make; for this, the indirect plan is usually most effective, although the direct plan may also be used.

    A. If bad news about products or services is routine and will not have an emotional impact on the reader, the direct approach is more efficient; but if the news will seriously affect the reader, it is better to state the _____ (p. 280) before the bad news.

    B. When declining to cooperate with routine requests, you may use either the direct plan or the indirect plan—with reasons before the bad news.

    C. In declining invitations and requests for favors, the indirect plan is better for communicating with acquaintances and strangers; the direct plan, for communicating with friends.

IV. When refusing adjustment of claims and complaints, your job is to avoid accepting responsibility and yet avoid making an _____ (p. 284) that involves the customer.

V. Refusing to extend credit is always a sensitive matter, so the best approach is to use the indirect plan to soften the bad news; be careful, however, to use as positive a tone as possible, to avoid writing anything that may be construed as a personal attack, and to emphasize the positive _____ (p. 287) that remain—such as the possibility that credit can be granted at some time in the future, the benefits of paying cash, and the attractive goods and services that your organization offers to all customers.

VI. Use the indirect plan for conveying unfavorable news about people—such as refusals to write recommendations, rejection of job applicants, negative performance reviews, and termination notices—because the reader will almost certainly be emotionally involved.

VII. When you must release bad news about company operations or performance, it is best to briefly explain the bad news in the context of a positive thought—whether using the direct or indirect plan.

Check your answers at the end of this chapter.

QUIZ YOURSELF

1. What are the four parts of a bad-news letter organized according to the indirect plan?

2. What are the characteristics of an effective buffer?

3. When presenting reasons for your negative decision, what two common evasive tactics should you avoid?

4. What are some of the techniques you might use to end a bad-news letter on a positive note?

5. When you are trying to convince a potential customer to buy a substitute product that is more expensive than the original item, what approach should you use?

6. Discuss when you should use the direct versus the indirect plan in turning down a routine request.

7. Briefly explain what your goal should be when writing a refusal to make an adjustment or to honor a complaint.

8. How would you vary a letter refusing to extend credit to two candidates—one with a long record of delinquent payment and one who is just starting out professionally and lacks a sufficient credit history to meet your requirements?

9. What three goals do you have when writing a termination letter?

10. What three types of situations require bad-news letters about company operations or performance?

Check your answers at the end of this chapter.

BUILD YOUR SKILLS: WHAT'S WRONG WITH THIS BAD-NEWS LETTER?

Someone representing the distributor of lawn-care equipment has drafted this letter. What could he do to make it more effective as a bad-news message?

April 28, 1995

Mr. Luther Dodge
814 South Pinewood Drive
Kansas City, MO 64108

Dear Mr. Dodge:

We regret to inform you that the 22-inch Kleen-Kut mower and grass catcher is unavailable at this time.

However, we do expect to receive a shipment of mowers in a short time. When they arrive, we'll send one off to you.

These mowers are excellent products, and we are sorry that you are unable to buy one right away. Please accept our countless apologies for this delay.

While you're waiting for your lawn mower, you might want to flip through our catalog, available at any local hardware store. Or ask us to send you one. At any rate, nearly all of our catalog items are in stock and can usually be ordered easily.

Sincerely,

Michael Flynn
Customer Relations

MF/eg

EXPAND YOUR KNOWLEDGE: HOW TO SAY "OOPS" GRACEFULLY

Alas, even the best-intentioned companies sometimes make obvious mistakes. If so, their best course is to try to maintain the trust of customers—by being honest. Common sense tells you, however, that it is possible to minimize the bad news by presenting it in as favorable a light as possible.

For example, through an error in its computer programming, the Moody State Bank has not kept separate records of tax-free and taxable interest in IRA and Keogh accounts. On January 31, forms with the wrong information were sent to customers. Some customers have called, so the bank's officers have decided to send out a letter explaining the error:

The interest income that you earn from your Individual Retirement Account (IRA) or from your Keogh account is not taxable until you begin drawing from these accounts. Many of our customers have called in to ask why their IRA and Keogh interest income was included along with regular taxable interest on the 1099 forms sent to them—a good question.	The buffer is informative and cooperative.
In an effort to process your accounts as efficiently as possible, Moody State Bank recently purchased a Compuplex-199 computer. It should enable us to give you even faster, more accurate service than before.	The source of the error is introduced in terms of how the change will benefit customers.
But we goofed! In our effort to get your 1099 form to you in January, we rushed the programming of the new computer. The result is that taxable and nontaxable interest income were erroneously combined and listed as a single figure.	The error is admitted in a positive context.
We (and the Compuplex-199) are working full speed to get your corrected 1099 form to you within a week.	The three-paragraph close details the action that is being taken to correct the error and offers help.
Meanwhile, if you have an IRA or a Keogh account, DO NOT declare as taxable interest the amount listed on the 1099s that you received from us last week. You will have your corrected figures in ample time to prepare your tax returns.	
If you have any questions about this matter, you're welcome to call us at 675-2028. We will be glad to provide any further information you need.	The final paragraph assures the reader of direct, personal attention.

Although this letter contains negative news, the general tone is objective and supportive. The writer admits the bank's error but does not dwell on an apology. Most readers are likely to place as much confidence in the bank as ever.

1. Although saying "oops!" may occasionally be necessary, the cost of doing so is often considerable. To get an idea of the magnitude of how much it can cost to make and correct a simple mistake, consider the case of the Moody State Bank. Suppose that the bank has 750 customers with IRA and Keogh accounts. Roughly how much do you suppose it cost to send these customers the correct information on tax-free and taxable interest, assuming that three letters were eventually mailed to each account holder?

2. Try your hand at writing an "oops" letter, using the following situation as a point of departure. You are the marketing manager for a line of tricycles designed for three- to five-year-old children. After shipping a new lot of the trikes to 1,500 retail outlets around the country, you have discovered that the entire lot was packaged without pedals. Write a letter to the retail store managers explaining the situation and outlining your solution.

DEVELOP YOUR WORD POWER

Spelling Challenge   Identify the misspelled word in each of the following sentences, and spell it correctly in the space provided. If all the words in a sentence are spelled correctly, write C in the space.

_____   1. They are definetly planning to attend the meeting on the 9th.

_____   2. We are dependant on a small distributor for supplies of that item.

_____   3. Our deluxe vacation package includes a stay at one of the most desireable resorts.

_____   4. You will not be dissappointed with your purchase.

_____   5. The last quarter was disasterous, but sales are improving.

_____   6. I have no dout that Hal will do a good job.

_____   7. After deducting operating expenses, you are left with a defecit.

_____   8. Read the discription of all available modifications on page 3.

_____   9. Every office worker should have access to a dictionery.

_____   10. Our goal is to limit the number of disatisfied customers.

Vocabulary Challenge   Match the words in the first column with the definitions in the second column.

_____ 11. enumeration   A. front

_____ 12. esprit de corps   B. copy

_____ 13. extrovert   C. sense of union

_____ 14. facade   D. list

_____ 15. facsimile   E. outgoing person

Circle the best definition of the highlighted word in each of the following sentences.

16. The most **expedient** course is simply to repackage the unsold items.

    A. speediest   B. least expensive   C. advantageous

17. Gretchen **expended** a lot of energy putting out the first issue of the company newsletter.

    A. spent   B. wasted   C. invested

18. Can we somehow **exploit** our reputation for social responsibility?

    A. publicize   B. take advantage of   C. abuse

19. Her delivery of **extemporaneous** speeches is excellent.

    A. about current events   B. long and complicated   C. with few or no notes

20. His behavior can partially be excused on the basis of **extenuating** circumstances.

    A. a long list of   B. mitigating   C. embarrassing

Select one of these words to complete each of the following sentences, and write the word in the space provided.

equable   **equitable**   **esoteric**   **facetious**   **fallacious**

21. Peter's _____ disposition makes him a pleasure to work with.

22. The staff will prosecute because Royal's solicitors made _____ statements.

23. Leave the more _____ references out of the bibliography for general readers.

24. The attorneys will negotiate _____ solutions to these disputes.

25. A serious meeting is no place for _____ remarks!

Follow-up Word Study   Check your answers at the end of this chapter. In the spaces below, write the words that you spelled or used incorrectly. (Use a separate piece of paper if you missed more than five words.) Then look up each word in your dictionary, and carefully study its spelling, pronunciation, definition, and history (etymology). Finally, to help fix the word in your memory, write it in a sentence.

<u>Word</u>   <u>Sentence</u>

_____   _____

_____   _____

_____   _____

_____   _____

_____   _____

_____

CHECK YOUR ANSWERS

_____

Master Key Concepts

I. fair, positive
   A. buffer, impersonal
   B. routine

II. A. indirect
   B. back order
   C. substitute
   E. action

III. goodwill
   A. rationale

IV. accusation

V. alternatives

Quiz Yourself

1. The four parts of a bad-news letter organized according to the indirect plan are
   a. A buffer
   b. Reasons supporting the negative decision
   c. A clear, diplomatic statement of the negative decision
   d. A helpful, friendly, positive close (p. 269)

2. An effective buffer accomplishes several things:
   a. It starts the message pleasantly with a point agreeable to the reader.
   b. It introduces the subject of the letter.
   c. It expresses neither a yes nor a no.
   d. It provides a smooth transition to the second paragraph. (p. 270)

3. When presenting reasons for your negative decision, try to avoid these evasive tactics:
   a. Hiding behind company policy
   b. Apologizing needlessly (p. 271)

4. To end a bad-news letter on a positive note, you might conclude with
   a. An attainable solution
   b. Off-the-subject resale information
   c. A suggestion for action (p. 272)

5. Send a letter "selling" the substitute product (but avoid the term *substitute*), and organize it to follow the indirect plan. Give simple directions for ordering. The section containing reasons should show that the more expensive substitute can do much more than the originally ordered item and is therefore worth a higher price. (p. 275)

6. When turning down a routine request, use the direct plan if the reader will not be emotionally involved with your response. However, follow the indirect plan if you believe the reader may react emotionally to your refusal to grant the request. (p. 279)

7. When refusing to make an adjustment or honor a complaint, your objective as a writer is to avoid accepting responsibility for the unfortunate situation and yet avoid blaming or accusing the customer. In the long run, your objective is to retain the customer's goodwill. (p. 284)

8. The letter refusing credit to the chronically delinquent candidate should not offer any hope for future credit approval, whereas the letter to the young professional should point to the possibility of future credit business. (p. 286)

9. When writing a termination letter, you have three goals:
   a. To present the reasons for the termination
   b. To avoid statements that might involve the company in legal action
   c. To leave the relationship between your company and the terminated employee as favorable as possible (p. 290)

10. These three situations might require bad-news letters about company operations or performance:
    a. A change in company policy that has a negative effect on the reader
    b. Performance problems in the company
    c. Controversial or unpopular company operations (p. 290)

Develop Your Word Power

1. definitely	6. doubt	11. D	16. C	21. equable
2. dependent	7. deficit	12. C	17. A	22. fallacious
3. desireable	8. description	13. E	18. B	23. esoteric
4. disappointed	9. dictionary	14. A	19. C	24. equitable
5. disastrous	10. dissatisfied	15. B	20. B	25. facetious

Chapter 11

Writing Persuasive Messages

The main point of Chapter 11 is that persuasive messages require a special form of the indirect plan—attention, interest, desire, action (AIDA)—and particular attention to the needs of the audience. As you read the chapter, think about how reader needs, benefits, and appeals are linked in persuasive messages. When you finish reading, analyze the strengths and weaknesses of some of the persuasive messages you have received and then try improving those that are weak.

MASTER KEY CONCEPTS

Use the following terms to fill in the blanks in the outline. All terms are used, but none is used more than once.

AIDA	consumer	influencing	result
beginning	credibility	notification	selling
benefits	defensive	reminder	ultimatum
collection	fair		

I. Persuasion is _____ (p. 306) an audience by informing them and by aiding their understanding. The audience is free to choose.
   A. Before you can write a persuasive message, ask yourself what you're writing about, who you're writing to, and what you want to _____ (p. 306) from the message.
   B. The task of motivating an audience requires you to understand people's needs, to enlist their emotions and logic, to convey _____ (p. 306), and to choose words that convey what you mean without arousing any undesirable emotions.
   C. The _____ (p. 309) plan, a form of indirect plan used specifically for persuasive messages, begins with a statement that grabs the audience's attention, develops interest by stressing how your information benefits the audience, builds desire by providing evidence directly related to your point, and ends by urging some easy, beneficial action.

II. Because the recipient of a persuasive request may receive nothing tangible in return, these letters are particularly difficult to write. Take special care to highlight the direct and indirect _____ (p. 310) of complying with your request.

III. When making a claim or request for adjustment to someone you suspect will be hostile or skeptical, use the AIDA plan; take special care to be calm, logical, and cordial, and assume that the recipient will want to do the _____ (p. 312) thing.

IV. A systematic approach is most useful in writing sales letters.
   A. The three steps involved in planning a sales letter are to determine the _____ (p. 315) points (most attractive features) and _____ (pp. 315–316) benefits of your product, to define the demographic (socioeconomic) and psychographic (psychological) characteristics of the audience, and to plan the format and approach you should take.
   B. Several special techniques are used when preparing the copy for sales letters: getting attention by making the audience think about needs you might be able to fulfill; emphasizing the central selling point (the point that most distinguishes your product from that of the competition while still meeting the needs of potential buyers); highlighting the consumer benefits of buying your

product by referring to them at the _____ (p. 319) and close of the letter; using action words; emphasizing price if it's one of your strong selling points or de-emphasizing a relatively high price; supporting your claims with sufficient evidence; and motivating action by being specific about the action you desire and making action easy.

    C. To enhance their effect, most sales letters are part of a carefully coordinated package of materials, and they are sent to a carefully selected list of potential customers.

V. Most people are interested in settling their debts as quickly as possible, but because credit is such an emotional area, _____ (p. 323) messages must be prepared with all the care lavished on other persuasive messages.

    A. People who cannot pay their bills generally feel _____ (p. 325); therefore, you must first try to neutralize their defensiveness by appealing to their better nature and then, if that approach doesn't bring results, turn to a negative appeal that points up the consequences of not acting.

    B. Collection letters are sent in an escalating sequence of messages, typically beginning with a _____ (p. 327), proceeding to a routine _____ (p. 327), then a more personal inquiry, then a more demanding "urgent notice," and finally a businesslike _____ (p. 328) that avoids malicious or defamatory statements.

Check your answers at the end of this chapter.

QUIZ YOURSELF

1. What is the "hierarchy of needs," and how does it pertain to the creation of persuasive messages?

2. Persuasive writers use many different plans to organize their messages, but the best known is the

_____ plan: _____, _____,

_____, and _____.

3. Briefly discuss the contents of the final section of a persuasive message.

4. When writing a persuasive request, you must take special care to highlight

_____ and _____ benefits. _____ benefits might include a premium for someone who responds to a survey or a free membership to someone

who makes a donation to an organization. _____ benefits might include the prestige of, say, giving free workshops to small businesses.

5. When writing a persuasive claim or request for adjustment, what tone should you take?

6. _____ are the most attractive features of a product or service;

   _____ are the particular advantages that buyers realize from those features.

7. What are some techniques that can be used in a sales letter to motivate action?

8. One type of direct-mail list is the _____, which is compiled by the company from the rolls of previous customers and even those who have inquired about the company's products or services.

9. What are five legal actions you might take against someone who fails to respond to a series of collection letters?

10. The final step in the collection series is the _____.

Check your answers at the end of this chapter.

BUILD YOUR SKILLS: WHAT'S WRONG WITH THIS PERSUASIVE LETTER?

A business student has drafted this letter. What could she do to make it more effective as a persuasive message?

> 544 Collins Avenue
> Apartment 6-G
> Houston, TX 77077
>
> January 10, 1995

Ms. Michelle Jacobs
Jacobs Consulting Agency
2366 Bakerfield Boulevard, Suite 608
Houston, TX 77079

Dear Mr. Jacobs:

Could you please tell me how I might obtain a copy of the results of the study of male executives' attitudes toward female executives? In a recent talk you gave, as you'll probably remember, that study was mentioned.

I need this study for a term paper I'm writing. Please send the information to the above address fairly soon. If you know of any other such pertinent data, perhaps you could enclose that as well.

By the way, I really enjoyed your talk. Thanks for all your help.

Sincerely,

Liz Raphael

EXPAND YOUR KNOWLEDGE: HOW TO INCREASE YOUR CREDIBILITY

Business writing is effective only if the audience believes what you say. How credible are you? To find out, answer the following questions. Give yourself one point if your answer is *never*, two points for *seldom*, three points for *sometimes*, four points for *usually*, and five points for *always*.

- Do you promise to do something, and then let it slide by?
- Do you find yourself complaining a lot to others?
- Do you have difficulty getting others to pay attention to you?
- Do you focus on your own interests and point of view when presenting information to others?
- Do you make statements and later find out that some of your information is incorrect or write something before you are sure of all the facts?
- When something goes wrong, is your main response to apologize?

If your score is between 6 and 17, you are exceptionally credible. Keep up the good work. But if your score is between 18 and 30, you probably will find that you can improve with a little effort.

To increase your credibility, observe these basic rules:

a. Organize and word your message so that it flows smoothly from point to point, projecting an image of strength and composure.

b. Inspire trust from the start by citing personal experiences and illustrations that underscore your character and competence.

c. Avoid not only outright falsehoods but also clever deceptions—statements that are literally true but misleading.

d. Convey a message that not only is true but also sounds true, as if you really believe in and care about what you are saying. One way to achieve this goal is to understate rather than overstate your case.

e. Support your arguments with facts, which carry more weight than opinions. Then audience members can make up their own minds.

f. Admit your mistakes. Nothing enhances your credibility more than a reputation for owning up when you are wrong.

g. Target your message to the audience's needs, emotions, values, and goals. Write to their point of view.

h. Use crisp, direct words and phrases that impart power and persuasiveness to your writing.

i. Avoid scare tactics and negativity. Instead, when presenting a problem, offer one or more possible solutions.

1. Name five public figures who have credibility and inspire confidence. Why have you selected these people?

2. Is credibility a constant factor, or does an individual's credibility depend on the occasion and the audience?

DEVELOP YOUR WORD POWER

Spelling Challenge   Identify the misspelled word in each of the following sentences, and spell it correctly in the space provided. If all the words in a sentence are spelled correctly, write *C* in the space.

_____   1. Please send either a chrome or a brass easel.

_____   2. Dr. Mueller empasized the importance of good employee relations.

_____   3. We are equipt to serve all your ecological needs.

_____   4. Yours is the eigth request for a commercial energy audit.

_____   5. BASIC is one of the elementery programming languages.

_____   6. How can we enhance the engineers' envirement?

_____   7. Please elimenate all references to egg salad from the new menu.

_____   8. We have just spent $1 million on new hospital equipment.

_____   9. Their goal is apparently to embarass us at the annual meeting.

_____   10. The emphisis in the brochure should be on elegance and style.

Vocabulary Challenge   Match the words in the first column with the definitions in the second column.

_____ 11. fastidious   A. unprovoked

_____ 12. formidable   B. demanding

_____ 13. fortuitous   C. supposed

_____ 14. gratuitous   D. fortunate

_____ 15. hypothetical   E. intimidating

Circle the best definition of the highlighted word in each of the following sentences.

16. The other employees resented her tendency to **flaunt** her promotion.

   A. mock   B. brag about   C. be dissatisfied with

17. So far, Ken has **floundered** in his position.

   A. prospered   B. struggled   C. failed

18. If she continues to **flout** the new rules, she will be fired.

   A. scoff at   B. enforce   C. complain about

19. Our efforts to market the new product were **hampered** by a lack of funds.

   A. aided   B. harmed   C. impeded

20. I will not **hinder** your efforts to reorganize the department.

   A. make fun of   B. second-guess   C. obstruct

Select one of these words to complete each of the following sentences, and write the word in the space provided.

   gaffe   **gamut**   **harangue**   **hyperbole**   **hypertension**

21. The flower seeds we offer run the _____, from alyssum to zinnia.

22. We cannot afford another _____ like the one Barbara committed during the negotiations yesterday.

23. He suffers from _____ and should not work so hard.

24. Your sales letter will be much more convincing if you eliminate some of the

   _____.

25. The staff is demoralized and should not be subjected to another _____.

Follow-up Word Study   Check your answers at the end of this chapter. In the spaces below, write the words that you spelled or used incorrectly. (Use a separate piece of paper if you missed more than five words.) Then look up each word in your dictionary, and carefully study its spelling, pronunciation, definition, and history (etymology). Finally, to help fix the word in your memory, write it in a sentence.

Word   Sentence

_____   _____

_____   _____

_____   _____

_____   _____

_____   _____

CHECK YOUR ANSWERS

Master Key Concepts

I. influencing
    A. result
    B. credibility
    C. AIDA

II. benefits

III. fair

IV. A. selling, consumer
    B. beginning

V. collection
    A. defensive
    B. notification, reminder, ultimatum

Quiz Yourself

1. The "hierarchy of needs" is a psychological concept for analyzing people's motivations. The theory is that people must satisfy basic, lower-level needs before they can concentrate on higher-level needs. The most fundamental needs are physiological (air, food, water, sleep, shelter). When these needs have been met, a person moves to the next level, the need for safety and security. These needs are followed by social needs for affection, friendship, and group ties. Once the social needs have been satisfied, a person becomes motivated by a need for esteem and status. At the final level of motivation, the person is driven by a need for self-actualization (creative, wisdom, vocation, fulfillment).

    Because audiences have different needs, different appeals are used to motivate them to take a desired action. For example, people who are struggling financially might be motivated by an appeal that emphasizes savings or a product's durability. A more affluent audience might respond better to an appeal that emphasizes beauty, distinctiveness, or status. (pp. 305–306)

2. Persuasive writers use many different plans to organize their messages, but the best known is the AIDA plan: *attention, interest, desire,* and *action.* (p. 309)

3. The final section of a persuasive message is an appeal for a specific action. This section should remind the audience of the benefit of taking the desired action and make the action easy to take. (p. 310)

4. When writing a persuasive request, you must take special care to highlight *direct* and *indirect* benefits. *Direct* benefits might include a premium for someone who responds to a survey or a free membership to someone who makes a donation to an organization. *Indirect* benefits might include the prestige of, say, giving free workshops to small businesses. (p. 310)

5. When pressing your claim, you want to persuade—not just complain. Focus on the benefits of solving the problem rather than on the horrors of neglecting your complaint. (p. 312)

6. *Selling points* are the most attractive features of a product or service; *consumer benefits* are the particular advantages that buyers realize from those features. (p. 315)

7. To motivate action in a sales letter, offer an incentive for making an immediate decision. For example, you might guarantee delivery by a certain date or offer a discount for orders received within a certain time period. If there is no particular reason to act quickly, you might provide other incentives:
    a. Prizes or special offers for early responses
    b. Convenient payment terms
    c. Free trial periods
    d. Product guarantees
    e. Convenient, no-strings request cards for additional information. (p. 321)

8. One type of direct-mail list is the *house list*, which is compiled by a company from the rolls of previous customers and even those who have inquired about the company's products or services. (p. 323)

9. Here are five actions legally available to unpaid creditors:
    a. Reporting the delinquent customer to a credit agency
    b. Repossessing the purchased item
    c. Demanding the surrender of collateral put up to secure the loan
    d. Turning the account over to a collection agency
    e. Engaging the services of a lawyer and taking the matter to court (p. 326)

10. The final step in the collection series is the *ultimatum*. (p. 328)

Develop Your Word Power

1. *C*	6. environment	11. B	16. B	21. gamut
2. emphasized	7. eliminate	12. E	17. B	22. gaffe
3. equipped	8. *C*	13. D	18. A	23. hypertension
4. eighth	9. embarrass	14. A	19. C	24. hyperbole
5. elementary	10. emphasis	15. C	20. C	25. harangue

PART FOUR

EMPLOYMENT MESSAGES

Chapter 12

Writing Résumés and Application Letters

The main point of Chapter 12 is that a properly prepared résumé and application letter are essential to your search for a job. As you read the chapter, think about how both the résumé and the application letter are constructed to "sell" you to potential employers. When you finish reading, analyze your own career preferences and then write a résumé and a model application letter that can help you get the job you want.

MASTER KEY CONCEPTS

Use the following terms to fill in the blanks in the outline. All terms are used, but none is used more than once.

accurate	job-inquiry	references	targeted
application	midsection	résumé	updates
attention-getter	objective	selling	work content
education	performance	solicited	

I. Before you apply for a job, you should think about the career you want.
   A. Begin by analyzing what you have to offer—your marketable skills, educational background, work experience, and personal characteristics.
   B. The second step is to determine what you want—your _____ (p. 349) goals (the skills you want to use in your work), your personal _____ (p. 349) goals (those that will help you to get ahead on the job), and your work environment preferences (the kind of company, industry, and geographical area you want to work in).
   C. The next step is to make a list of companies that might be interested in your qualifications and that would enable you to accomplish your goals.

II. A _____ (p. 353) is a brief account of your qualifications in a special format; its purpose is to interest employers in giving you a personal interview.
   A. The opening section summarizes your identity, your job or career _____ (pp. 354–356), and your qualifications and date of availability.
   B. The body of the résumé describes your _____ (p. 356), work experience, relevant skills, activities and achievements, personal data, _____ (pp. 358–359), and support data that are available (such as transcripts and work samples); in selecting and organizing this information, your goal is to emphasize your strongest qualifications.

92

C. The organization of a résumé depends on your background and goals; it could be chronological, functional, or _____ (p. 359).

D. The "perfect" résumé is the one that convinces the employer to grant you a personal interview.

III. Your _____ (p. 363) letter tells what you can do for the company and why you believe you are qualified for the job.

A. If your application letter has been _____ (p. 364) (if you are sending it in response to an announced job opening), begin with a simple statement of how you know about the job and why you qualify for the position; if you are sending an unsolicited letter (one to a company that has not announced an opening), you should open with an _____ (p. 365) of some sort, as in a sales letter, and a statement of your reason for writing.

B. The _____ (p. 367) of your application letter should highlight your strongest selling points and indicate how they can benefit the potential employer.

C. In the final paragraph, request an interview and make it easy to arrange; close by referring to your strongest _____ (p. 368) point.

D. The "perfect" application letter achieves the simple purpose of getting you a personal interview.

IV. A job search may require three other types of written messages.

A. A _____ (p. 369) letter—a direct request for an application form—should include enough information to show that you are a reasonable candidate.

B. If you are asked to fill out a standard application form, be complete, _____ (pp. 369–370), and neat.

C. If you have not received a response to your application letter within a month or so, follow up with another letter that _____ (p. 371) your application with any recent job-related information and ask the organization to keep your name in its active file.

Check your answers at the end of this chapter.

QUIZ YOURSELF

1. What is the difference between a "work-content" and a "performance" goal?

2. What are some sources you might use to locate employment opportunities?

3. What six general types of information should you present after the opening section of your résumé?

4. When writing your résumé, should you present your educational qualifications or your work experience first? Discuss.

5. What are some of the most common criticisms expressed by people who read résumés?

6. What organization plan would you use for an application letter?

7. The contents of the opening paragraph of your application letter depend on whether it is

    _____ or _____ . A _____ application

    letter is one set in regard to an announced job opening. An _____ , or
    "prospecting," letter is one sent to a company that has not announced an opening.

8. What does the midsection of an application letter accomplish?

9. What would you try to accomplish in the closing paragraph of an application letter?

10. What is the purpose of a job-inquiry letter?

Check your answers at the end of this chapter.

BUILD YOUR SKILLS: WHAT'S WRONG WITH THIS RÉSUMÉ?

A college student has drafted this résumé. What could she do to make it more effective?

RÉSUMÉ

Alicia Suarez
2348 Tigertail
Miami, Florida 33133
Telephone (315) 376-3636

<u>Career Objective</u>: I have always aspired to a management position in a growing firm because I'm good with numbers and love to sell just about any product.

SALARY RANGE: $25,000 plus with good benefits, preferably a company car.

Education

Right now I'm working on a bachelor's degree in business administration. My courses are wide-ranging and include Western Civ., Speech, and various courses in finance and marketing. I expect to graduate next spring, from the University of Miami at Coral Gables. I also attended Miami-Dade Junior College for one year.

<u>Experience</u>

JUNIOR ACCOUNTANT. In this position I prepared and processed important financial documents for Pan American Importers, Inc. In addition, my job included running the computers. (No secretarial work was involved, although I can type 40 wpm.) Part-time, while in school.

<u>Sales Rep</u>. For MCI, Inc. I handled a large territory and scored many successes with a range of clients. The dollar volume of my territory climbed considerably while I was there. 1992.

Volunteer Work at South Miami Hospital.

<u>Activities</u>

Treasurer for Delta Gamma Sorority at U of M.

Volleyball Team

Involved in Campus Entrepreneurs Society.

Workshops—This fall I attended a workshop on "Honing Your Persuasive Speaking Skills." It was sponsored by the Miami Chapter of IABC.

Achievements

Bilingual
Rotary Club Scholarship

Personal Data: 5'2", 140 lbs., recently married

Hobbies—Water Skiing

BUILD YOUR SKILLS: WHAT'S WRONG WITH THIS APPLICATION LETTER?

A young career woman has drafted this application letter. What could she do to make it more effective?

208 East 83 St.
New York, NY 10028
March 20, 1995

Mr. Alan Frankel, President
Frankel Merchandising, Inc.
11 East 53 St.
New York, NY 10022

Dear Mr. Frankel:

Please consider me for the position in your accounting department that was recently advertised in a trade journal.

I am hardworking, enthusiastic, and have a lot of experience in this field. My co-workers have always said that I was a star-quality team player. Just take a look at my résumé and you'll see exactly what I mean. My education also provides valuable preparation for employment in your company.

I hope that we can have an interview soon, although you should keep in mind that Thursday afternoon is the only time I'm available to discuss future employment at this point. Never-the less, after we speak, I think you'll be convinced that I'm the best applicant for the job!!

Sincerely,

Vanessa Rossetti

EXPAND YOUR KNOWLEDGE: PUTTING YOUR BEST FOOT FORWARD

The job market is highly competitive, and so naturally you want every advantage available to you. Linda Wells, president of Darland-Wells Associates, a Connecticut firm specializing in management recruiting, describes what she does to give her applicants the edge: "To maintain my own reputation, I have to send out only the best candidates. It seems superficial to say so, but appearances are very important. A person who doesn't look right for a job won't get past the front door in a lot of companies. So I always talk with my applicants face to face. I give them little bits of advice on what to wear, what questions to ask, what points in their backgrounds to emphasize."

Charlotte Stier also heads her own placement firm, Car & Associates, in Washington. Stier estimates that she has seen thousands of résumés since she entered the field in 1970. "The more work experience an applicant has," she laughs, "the shorter the résumé seems to be. People who don't have much to say generally end up saying too much." Stier recommends that you don't try to be all things to all people. You're better off zeroing in on one or two performance areas where you're really good. That way you can write a brief résumé—preferably one page but no more than two—and still provide lots of details, which employers want to see."

Another way to focus your résumé is to spell out your goals. Stier recommends that job seekers state at the top of their résumés both the immediate position they want and their long-range goals. "An employer should know where you've set your sights."

Once you've stated these goals, you can begin to list your qualifications. "If you've held jobs," Stier suggests, "try to present yourself in terms of the skills they involved rather than detailing your job responsibilities. Organizational skills, analytical skills, creative skills, managerial skills—these are what employers understand and look for.

"Be totally honest," she adds. And be specific. For example, when listing past jobs, say how long you worked at each one, from month/year to month/year."

But what if you're just getting out of school? "Mention the skills you've developed there, such as business writing or accounting. And list your most relevant courses and how you've done in each one, assuming you've done well." Stier also recommends emphasizing the work experience that recent graduates may have had while in school. "Even if it was selling shoes or working in a fast-food restaurant, part-time job experience says that you have discipline. It says that you want to make something of yourself."

Another problem many résumés have is their style—or lack of it. Stier has seen too many résumés filled with "I did this" and "I did that." She shakes her head. "That's amateurish. And it adds unnecessary words. Be brief," she cautions. "And go with action verbs—not pronouns like *I, me,* and *my.*"

Even more important: "Don't build yourself up beyond believability. I've seen résumés for people who answered the phones for a week while the boss was away and then listed themselves as assistant manager. And the honors you list must relate to the career field you want to enter. Scholastic honors are important—but not the fact that you won a campus pie-eating contest."

When it comes time to type your résumé, be careful about spelling. "When I see a résumé with misspellings and an awkward style, I assume that the applicant's verbal skills are equally weak, and so will an employer. Before sending out a résumé, check every word for spelling errors. Check punctuation, too."

What skills does Stier believe will give you an edge in job hunting? "The work picture is changing," she says. "It's hard to know what abilities will be in demand several years down the road. But communication skills are essential now—and always will be. Being able to communicate effectively can be your single most marketable asset."

Suppose that you are Charlotte Stier and that Caleb Green is your client. How would you advise him to modify his résumé?

CALEB M. GREEN

2632 Hesby Avenue   Age: 30
North Hollywood, CA 91434   Married
Phone: (213) 990-6110   2 children

EXPERIENCE

Product Manager, Health Systems, Inc., Burbank, Calif., 1992-1995
I am in charge of a line of respiratory-care products that are sold to hospitals. My job is to plan the production, pricing, and marketing strategy for this line, which is sold by our sales force.

Design Engineer, Health Systems, Inc., Burbank, Calif., 1989-1992
As an engineer, I was involved in designing respiratory-care products, such as inhalation machines and nebulizers.

Associate Engineer, Vortex, Encino, Calif., 1983-1989
At Vortex, I worked on designing all sorts of plastic devices for use with hospital products. Most of these items used tubing, valves, and connectors that had to meet high heat tolerances, since they were usually sterilized repeatedly by hospitals.

EDUCATION

Pepperdine University, Malibu, Calif., 1989-1992
I got an M.B.A. at night school at Pepperdine while I was working full time for Health Systems. I graduated with a B average and a major in Marketing.

California Institute of Technology, Pasadena, Calif., 1985-1989
I have a B.S. degree in mechanical engineering. My grades were excellent. I was on the dean's list six semesters, and Cal Tech is a tough school, as perhaps you know. I lived in the dorm and worked part time in the school cafeteria. I was also on the swim team.

PERSONAL BACKGROUND

I was born and raised in Kentucky, but my parents moved to California when I was in high school, and I've been hear ever since. I don't ever want to leave, because my hobby is surfing.

DEVELOP YOUR WORD POWER

Spelling Challenge   Identify the misspelled word in each of the following sentences, and spell it correctly in the space provided. If all the words in a sentence are spelled correctly, write *C* in the space.

_____   1. Amy excells at writing collection letters.

_____   2. We are extremally grateful for all your help.

_____   3. A fascinating program has been scheduled for Febuary.

_____   4. Ye Olde Pet Shoppe is no longer in existance.

_____   5. Before you incur any additional expence, talk to us.

_____   6. Yes, I am familar with your financial services.

_____   7. A full-fledged investigation is feasable but unnecessary.

_____   8. I am especialy pleased with your latest recruiting trip.

_____   9. The cost of supplies for the Boise office should not exceed $900.

_____   10. With your expiriense, you should do well here.

Vocabulary Challenge   Match the words in the first column with the definitions in the second column.

_____   11. incessant   A. rambling

_____   12. incipient   B. beginning

_____   13. incoherent   C. not noticeable

_____   14. incongruous   D. not harmonious

_____   15. inconspicuous   E. without interruption

Circle the best definition of the highlighted word in each of the following sentences.

16.   Even after a day of work, his desk was immaculate.

    A. spotless   B. buried   C. polished

17.   His talent as a supervisor is to **impel** people to do their best.

    A. allow   B. urge   C. shame

18.   In a crowded office, it is all too easy to **impinge** on another's right to privacy.

    A. encroach   B. presume upon   C. take advantage of

19. From the **inception** of this program, Pat has taken an active role.

    A. formulation   B. outcome   C. beginning

20. You will **incur** Mr. Crane's displeasure if you lobby too hard for your own ideas.

    A. bring about   B. increase   C. face

Select one of these words to complete each of the following sentences, and write the word in the space provided.

impending   impenetrable   impertinent   impervious   impulsive

21. She has a strong ego that is _____ to their insults.

22. With Ms. Cartwright guarding the door, Dr. Hruska's office is _____.

23. Would it be _____ of me to suggest that you try a larger size?

24. The point of using this appeal is to motivate _____ buying on the part of those standing in line.

25. An _____ audit will keep me from taking a vacation next week.

Follow-up Word Study   Check your answers at the end of this chapter. In the spaces below, write the words that you spelled or used incorrectly. (Use a separate piece of paper if you missed more than five words.) Then look up each word in your dictionary, and carefully study its spelling, pronunciation, definition, and history (etymology). Finally, to help fix the word in your memory, write it in a sentence.

Word   Sentence

_____   _____

_____   _____

_____   _____

_____   _____

_____   _____

CHECK YOUR ANSWERS

Master Key Concepts

I. B. work content, performance

II. résumé
   A. objective
   B. education, references
   C. targeted

III. application
   A. solicited, attention-getter
   B. midsection
   C. selling

IV. A. job-inquiry
   B. accurate
   C. updates

Quiz Yourself

1. Work content goals are related to the skills you want to use in your work. For example, if you are a good communicator, your work content goal might be to find a job in which you can use your writing and speaking skills.

   Performance goals are related to the level of achievement you want to attain. These goals might be stated in terms of the organizational level you hope to reach, the amount of money you want to make, and the speed at which you want to advance. (pp. 349–350)

2. The best way to look for a job is to explore as many pathways as possible, taking advantage of the normal recruiting process and looking for opportunities on your own. Sources to explore include
   a. On-campus interviews
   b. Advertisements placed by employers in newspapers, professional journals, and other publications
   c. Placement agencies run by private companies, government, and trade associations
   d. Referrals from friends (pp. 350–353)

3. The main body of your résumé should present six key elements:
   a. Career objective or summary of qualifications
   b. Education
   c. Work experience
   d. Relevant skills
   e. Activities and achievements
   f. Personal data (pp. 356–359)

4. Your résumé should present your strongest qualifications first. If you are still in school and have held only part-time or summer jobs, your educational qualifications will probably be your best selling point and should be given prominence. If you have been out of school for several years and have held responsible, full-time jobs related to the position you seek, you should discuss your work experience before describing your education. (p. 359)

5. People who read résumés complain about these common faults in the résumés they receive:
   a. Too long
   b. Too short or sketchy
   c. Hard to read
   d. Wordy
   e. Too slick
   f. Amateurish
   g. Poorly reproduced

h. Misspelled and ungrammatical throughout
i. Lacking a career objective
j. Boastful
k. Dishonest
l. Gimmicky (p. 363)

6. Application letters are persuasive sales messages. They are organized according to the direct plan—more specifically, the AIDA plan, to develop attention, interest, desire, and action. (p. 363)

7. The contents of the opening paragraph of your application letter depend on whether it is *solicited* or *unsolicited*. A *solicited* application letter is one sent in regard to an announced job opening. An *unsolicited*, or "prospecting," letter is one sent to a company that has not announced an opening. (pp. 364–367)

8. The midsection of an application letter should
   a. Summarize your qualifications that are directly related to the job (or mentioned in an employment ad)
   b. Show how you have put your qualifications to use
   c. Provide evidence of desirable personal qualifications
   d. Tie salary requirements (if requested) to the benefits of hiring you
   e. Refer to your résumé (pp. 367–368)

9. In the closing paragraph of an application letter, ask for an interview and make the interview easy to arrange. (pp. 368–369)

10. The purpose of a job-inquiry letter is to request an application form. (p. 369)

Develop Your Word Power

1. excels	6. familiar	11. E	16. A	21. impervious
2. extremely	7. feasible	12. B	17. B	22. impenetrable
3. February	8. especially	13. A	18. A	23. impertinent
4. existence	9. *C*	14. D	19. C	24. impulsive
5. expense	10. experience	15. C	20. A	25. impending

Chapter 13

Interviewing for Employment and Following Up

The main point of Chapter 13 is that a job interview gives the company a chance to evaluate you and gives you a chance to evaluate the company. As you read the chapter, think about the attitudes and preparation that contribute to a successful interview. When you finish reading, rehearse a job interview, either mentally or with a friend, until you feel that you can handle any type of interview you may encounter.

MASTER KEY CONCEPTS

Use the following terms to fill in the blanks in the outline. All terms are used, but none is used more than once.

acceptance	compatible	resignation	thank-you
bad-news	directed	screening	two
capabilities	questions	stress	warm-up

I. A good job interview enables the interviewer to find the best person for the job and helps the applicant find the job best suited to her or his _____ (p. 380).
   A. Most employers conduct two or three interviews before making a job offer. The typical sequence includes: a preliminary _____ (p. 381) to eliminate unqualified applicants, an initial evaluation by a personnel or recruiting employee, and a final interview by the supervisor or department manager. An applicant may encounter interviews that are _____ (pp. 382–383) (structured by a checklist or series of prepared questions), open-ended (involving broad, open-ended questions), or designed to produce _____ (p. 383) (as a test of the applicant's ability to cope with pointed questions, hostility, and criticism).
   B. Employers want to hire people who are suitable for the job and who will fit into the organization.
   C. An interview gives the applicant a chance to find out whether the people, the organization, and the work itself are _____ (p. 385) with his or her skills, interests, and goals.
   D. To reduce the natural tension that accompanies a job interview, take steps in advance to handle it successfully: investigate the company and the job, evaluate what you have to offer, develop answers to likely questions, think ahead about _____ (p. 387) to ask, bolster your confidence for the interview, polish your interview style, plan to look good, and be ready when you arrive.
   E. The way you handle an interview depends on whether it is at the screening, selection, or final stage; nevertheless, all interviews have three stages: the _____ (p. 393), the question-and-answer stage, and the close.

II. Your job search may require you to write other kinds of messages to employers.
   A. Within two days of each interview, send a _____ (p. 398) message that expresses appreciation, conveys your continuing interest, and asks for a decision.
   B. If you have not heard from the interviewer within _____ (p. 399) weeks, send a note of inquiry based on the assumption that the delay doesn't imply an outright rejection.
   C. If you receive a job offer while you still have interviews scheduled with other companies, write an enthusiastic note requesting more time to make your decision.

D. Within five days of a job offer that you want to take, send a letter of _____ (p. 401); bear in mind that such a letter is a legally binding contract.

E. If you receive a job offer that you do not want to accept, send a tactful and sincere letter following the _____ (p. 401) plan; try to leave the door open for future contact in case the job you do accept doesn't work out.

F. If you must quit one job in order to take another, send a letter of _____ (p. 402) that follows the bad-news plan; try to sound positive so that your former employer will willingly supply recommendations in the future.

Check your answers at the end of this chapter.

QUIZ YOURSELF

1. Briefly describe the three steps in the typical interview process.

2. Interviews take various forms, depending on what the recruiter is attempting to discover about the applicant. Explain the differences between directed and open-ended interviews, and name one advantage of each.

3. What two things are employers looking for in potential employees?

4. How can you find out whether you are likely to be compatible with your potential co-workers?

5. Before you go to an interview, what facts should you try to find out about the prospective employer and job?

6. Staging mock interviews with a friend can help overcome flaws in your interview style. What are five common weaknesses in personal style that interviewers notice?

7. Give some general pointers on how to discuss salary during a job interview.

8. What organizational plan should you use in writing a thank-you note to a job interviewer?

9. If, after the interview, you are not advised of the decision by the promised date or within two weeks, you might send a _____.

10. How should your organize a letter of acceptance?

Check your answers at the end of this chapter.

BUILD YOUR SKILLS: ARE YOUR QUESTIONS READY?

When interviewing for a job, you have two objectives: to create a good impression and to determine whether the job and the organization are right for you. The questions you ask help you achieve both objectives. To prepare yourself, make a list of 15 or 20 questions that you would like answered during a typical job interview.

BUILD YOUR SKILLS: WHAT'S WRONG WITH THIS FOLLOW-UP LETTER?

A job applicant has drafted this follow-up letter. What could he do to make it more effective?

1906 Bentley Avenue
Sharon, PA 16146
June 12, 1995

Ms. Elizabeth Monroe
Director of Human Resources
Pennsylvania Power and Light
600 Claremont Boulevard
Sharon, PA 16146

Dear Ms. Monroe:

Talking with you was a real pleasure. It's exciting to know that even people in large corporations have outside interests like scuba diving and backpacking. If I'm hired, I look forward to joining you on some of the Sierra Club outings we chatted about.

Please keep me in mind for the position we discussed. Hope to hear from you soon.

Sincerely yours,

Al Giordano

EXPAND YOUR KNOWLEDGE: THE ASSERTIVE INTERVIEWEE

Everybody knows that the point of an interview is to give the prospective employer a chance to evaluate the prospective employee. But you should do more in an interview than just meekly answer questions. For one thing, employers usually don't want to hire people who seem to think too little of themselves. For another, the point of an interview is also to give you a chance to evaluate the company.

How can you talk to a prospective employer without seeming to be too wishy-washy? Begin by going into the interview with the right attitude. If you go in thinking that you won't get the job, you probably won't. Negative assumptions can undermine and defeat you. So develop a positive outlook instead: Believe that you will succeed.

You can boost your confidence by preparing as thoroughly as you can for the interview: putting résumé, supporting materials, and your appearance all in order and practicing your interviewing technique over and over. With those basics under control, you can be confident of handling almost anything that arises. After all, an interview is a fairly standard event. If something does come up that you are not prepared for, just do your best—and be yourself. You don't know what specific qualities the interviewer is looking for, and so it makes no sense to try remolding your personality to fit the interviewer's ideal. Instead of worrying about the competition for a job, look on the interview as a chance to make your own unique qualities known.

In your job search, you will eventually have an interview that seems to be bearing fruit; the interviewer will start talking as if you will definitely be joining the company. Many people get so excited by the prospect of a serious job offer that they lose all rationality at this point and leave the interview in a haze of goodwill and eager anticipation. Instead, they should start asking questions that will help them evaluate the job objectively. Here are some questions that you can reasonably ask the interviewer when the job appears to be within your reach:

- What happened to the last person who had this job?
- May I talk to someone who is doing what I will be doing?
- What is this company like as a place to work?
- Is the company growing, and where is the growth coming from?
- How and by whom will my performance be measured?
- How will the company help me meet the goals we agree on?
- What is the salary range for similar jobs in this organization?
- What other compensation is the company willing to offer?
- If relocation is involved, how much will the company help?
- What will I get in writing?

Don't fear being direct when an interview seems to be going well; most employers will appreciate your hard-headed approach. Those that don't may have personality or organizational problems that will make the job difficult for you. And you are better off asking questions before you take the job. The alternative may be looking for a new one a few months down the road.

1. Can you think of any specific "symptoms" that might indicate a company is not for you? What are they?

2. Asserting yourself when the interview is going well is one thing. Taking control when things are going badly is another. What can you do if you and the interviewer seem to be on different wavelengths?

DEVELOP YOUR WORD POWER

Spelling Challenge   Identify the misspelled word in each of the following sentences, and spell it correctly in the space provided. If all the words in a sentence are spelled correctly, write *C* in the space.

_____   1. We communicate with our foriegn offices via Telex.

_____   2. Sandra Hayes is the fourth factory representative we have had.

_____   3. Take a vacation that fulfils all your dreams!

_____ 4. In the annual report, you can generalise about our problems.

_____ 5. Can you garantee delivery by May 1?

_____ 6. This photograph was taken from a heighth of 200 feet.

_____ 7. Over fourty people have applied for the clerical position.

_____ 8. Your new camera is frajel, so treat it gently.

_____ 9. The federal goverment requires us to subject several reports.

_____ 10. Guard against auto theft with a Lookout alarm.

Vocabulary Challenge   Match the words in the first column with the definitions in the second column.

_____ 11. induce   A. to provoke

_____ 12. infuse   B. to mediate

_____ 13. instigate   C. to insert

_____ 14. intercede   D. to cause

_____ 15. interject   E. to instill

Circle the best definition of the highlighted word in each of the following sentences.

16. When I think of summer, I have an **indelible** image of blue and white.

   A. strong   B. inappropriate   C. unerasable

17. We might be able to stop the **innuendo** by making a public statement.

   A. indirect criticism   B. competition   C. investigation process

18. Mr. Billings spends an **inordinate** amount of time on the telephone.

   A. excessive   B. unmeasurable   C. unauthorized

19. Can **insipid** conclusions support strong recommendations?

   A. faulty   B. bland   C. brilliant

20. We are **insolvent** and cannot meet our obligations.

   A. inebriated   B. puzzled   C. bankrupt

Select one of these words to complete each of the following sentences, and write the word in the space provided.

      ingenious   **ingenuous**   **insatiable**   **interminable**   **intermittent**

21. Because she is so sincere and _____, she is able to calm angry people.

22. An _____ beep is probably more effective than a steady tone.

23. New DinnerTime frozen entrees are big enough for even _____ appetites.

24. She came up with an _____ solution to the problem that I had never thought of.

25. His _____ quest for a "hot deal" is finally beginning to irritate me.

Follow-up Word Study   Check your answers at the end of this chapter. In the spaces below, write the words that you spelled or used incorrectly. (Use a separate piece of paper if you missed more than five words.) Then look up each word in your dictionary, and carefully study its spelling, pronunciation, definition, and history (etymology). Finally, to help fix the word in your memory, write it in a sentence.

<u>Word</u>   <u>Sentence</u>

_____

_____

_____

_____

_____

CHECK YOUR ANSWERS

Master Key Concepts

    I. capabilities
        A. screening, directed, stress
        C. compatible
        D. questions
        E. warm-up

    II. A. thank-you
          B. two
          D. acceptance
          E. bad-news
          F. resignation

Quiz Yourself

1. The typical interview process consists of three steps:
   a. A preliminary screening (often held on campus) that enables the company to eliminate unqualified applicants
   b. An initial visit to the company, designed to give the personnel officer or department manager an opportunity to narrow the field a little further
   c. A final interview that gives the supervisor a chance to decide whether a particular candidate is the right person for the job (pp. 381–382)

2. The directed interview is planned from start to finish by the interviewer. He or she poses a series of prepared questions within a specific time period and makes note of the interviewee's responses. An open-ended interview has a less structured and more relaxed format. The interviewer poses broad, general questions and encourages the interviewee to talk freely. Directed interviews are useful for gathering facts; open-ended interviews are useful for bringing out the interviewee's personality. (pp. 382–383)

3. Employers are looking for
   a. Evidence that the person can handle the job (suitability)
   b. Evidence that the person will fit in with the organization (p. 384)

4. To find out whether you are likely to be compatible with potential co-workers, do some research about the company and its personnel. Arrange to talk with an employee if you can. Analyze the people you meet during your interviews to determine whether you have similar values, interests, and backgrounds. (p. 385)

5. Before going to a job interview, try to find out these facts about the employer:
   a. Company name
   b. Location(s)
   c. Company age
   d. Products and services
   e. Position in the industry
   f. Earnings
   g. Growth
   h. Organization

   Try to find out these facts about the job:
   a. Job title
   b. Job functions
   c. Job qualifications
   d. Career path
   e. Salary range
   f. Travel opportunities
   g. Relocation opportunities (p. 386)

6. Five common weaknesses in personal style that interviewers notice are
   a. Poor personal appearance
   b. Overbearing, "know-it-all" attitude
   c. An inability to articulate ideas clearly
   d. A lack of knowledge and/or experience
   e. A passive or indifferent attitude (p. 391)

7. Don't make money a major point of discussion. Try to avoid the subject until late in the interview, and let the company representative bring up the topic. If you are asked directly about your salary

expectations, say that you would expect to receive the standard salary for the job. If the interviewer doesn't mention salary, you can simply ask what the position pays, but do not inquire about fringe benefits until you have a firm job offer. (pp. 396–397)

8. A thank-you message to a job interviewer should be organized like a routine message, using the direct plan. The main idea (your gratitude for the interview) should come first. (p. 398)

9. If, after the interview, you are not advised of the decision by the promised date or within two weeks, you might send a *note of inquiry*. (p. 399)

10. A letter of acceptance should follow the good-news plan. Begin by accepting the position and expressing thanks. Identify the job you are accepting. Cover any necessary details in the middle section of the letter, and then conclude by saying that you look forward to reporting for work. (p. 401)

Develop Your Word Power

1. foreign	6. height	11. D	16. C	21. ingenuous
2. *C*	7. forty	12. E	17. A	22. intermittent
3. fulfills	8. fragile	13. A	18. A	23. insatiable
4. generalize	9. government	14. B	19. B	24. ingenious
5. guarantee	10. *C*	15. C	20. C	25. interminable

PART FIVE

REPORTS AND PROPOSALS

Chapter 14

Using Reports and Proposals as Business Tools

The main point of Chapter 14 is that many types of reports and proposals are used in business and that organization and format reflect their purpose. As you read the chapter, think about the way that function influences format. When you finish reading, look for examples of business reports and proposals and try to classify them in the categories outlined in the chapter.

MASTER KEY CONCEPTS

Use the following terms to fill in the blanks in the outline. All terms are used, but none is used more than once.

dislikes	plans	receptive	tailored
elaborate	policies	regulatory	unsolicited
justification	position papers	solicited	verifiable
needs	proposals		

I. A good business report tells readers what they need to know—no more, no less.
   A. Regardless of what medium you use for your message, try to keep the likes and _____ (p. 410) of your readers in mind. As you make decisions about the content, format, style, and organization of your report, the readers' _____ (p. 410) should be your main concern.
   B. A report can be _____ (pp. 410–411) according to who originates it, what subject it covers, when it is prepared, where it is sent, why it is prepared, and how _____ (p. 411) the audience is.

II. Reports provide a formal, _____ (p. 411) link among people, places, and times.
   A. Reports for monitoring and controlling operations—_____ (p. 413), operating reports, and personal activity reports—summarize what is happening and help managers plan the future; they are generally standardized in organization and format, and they are distributed to upper-level management on a routine, recurring basis.
   B. Reports for implementing _____ (p. 416) and procedures—lasting guidelines and _____ (p. 417)—enable managers to communicate the organization's standards and general rules to all employees; to some extent, they follow a standard format, and they may be collected in a special book and updated periodically.
   C. Reports for complying with the requirements of _____ (p. 418) agencies explain what an organization is doing to respond to the rules imposed by various government

110

agencies; they follow a standard format dictated by the agency and are often recurring, periodic documents.

D. _____ (p. 421) for obtaining new business range from simple letters to multivolume manuscripts and may be presented in a format dictated by the potential client or lender; proposals may be _____ (p. 421) (prepared at the request of clients) or _____ (p. 422) (initiated by the company without special invitation from the client).

E. Reports for documenting client work—interim progress reports and final reports—keep clients informed about the status of work on a contract; the interim reports are relatively informal, but the final report is more _____ (p. 424), designed to serve as a permanent record of the contract.

F. Reports for guiding decisions—research reports, _____ (p. 427) reports, and troubleshooting reports—provide managers with a written analysis of the pros and cons of alternatives; they are prepared in response to unique, nonrecurring situations and may be organized according to either the direct or the indirect plan, depending on the audience's probable reaction to their conclusions and recommendations.

Check your answers at the end of this chapter.

QUIZ YOURSELF

1. What is a business report?

2. What are six specific questions you should ask yourself before you decide on the format, style, and organization of your report?

3. _____ reports, prepared on your own initiative, require more detail and support

   than _____ reports, which are prepared at the request of another person.

4. What are the six most common categories of business reports?

5. What is a personal activity report? Give a few typical examples.

6. Give some general guidelines on the style that should be used for policy/procedure reports.

7. Briefly summarize the characteristics of compliance reports.

8. _____ vary in length and complexity, but all are basically attempts to get products, services, or projects accepted by outside business or government clients.

9. Briefly describe the differences between interim progress reports and final reports.

10. What are three of the most common decision-oriented reports?

Check your answers at the end of this chapter.

BUILD YOUR SKILLS: CAN YOU ANALYZE THESE REPORTS?

Take a look at the four reports outlined below, and then analyze each in terms of these six factors:

a. Who (initiated the report)?
b. What (subject does it cover)?
c. When (is it being prepared)?
d. Where (is it being sent)?
e. Why (is it being prepared)?
f. How (receptive is the reader)?

If the outline does not provide enough information to enable you to make a decision, use your best judgment and common sense to deduce the answer.

Report 1: Instrument Division—Monthly Update

  I. Summary of monthly activities
      A. New orders
      B. Shipments
      C. Profits

 II. Sales by product line
      A. Analytical instruments
          1. New orders
          2. Shipments
      B. Industrial monitoring equipment
          1. New orders
          2. Shipments
      C. Audiometers
          1. New orders
          2. Shipments

III. Problems
      A. Design problems with the Omega system
      B. Production delays in liquid scintillation system

IV. Next month's forecast

Report 2: Observations on the U.S. Rubber Industry

   I. Basic supply-demand characteristics
     A. Dependence on motor vehicle industry
     B. Competition from foreign suppliers
     C. Increasing importance of long-life radials

  II. The outlook for tire rubber
     A. Original equipment
     B. Replacement market

 III. The outlook for nontire rubber
     A. Basic segments
     B. Five-year forecast
     C. Long-term outlook

 IV. Growth opportunities for innovators
     A. Run-flat tires
     B. One-piece integral tires and rims
     C. Twin-tire concept
     D. Liquid-injection molded tires

Report 3: Optimizing the Organization Structure

   I. Statement of the problem
     A. Changes in the nature of the company
     B. Need for changes in the company's structure

  II. Scope of work
     A. Design of an optimum organizational structure
     B. Implementation of structure over time

 III. Issues for analysis
     A. Strengths and weaknesses of current structure
       1. What functions must be performed?
       2. How well does the present organization accommodate these functions?
     B. Centralization versus decentralization
     C. Organizational alternatives
       1. Line/staff structure
       2. Functional organization
       3. Project-management organization
       4. Matrix organization
     D. Informal organization and corporate "culture"

 IV. Methods and procedures
     A. Review of company operations
     B. Interviews with company managers and employees

  V. Work plan and schedule
     A. Phase I: Define requirements
     B. Phase II: Analyze alternatives and select optimum structure
     C. Phase III: Implement new structure

VI. Qualifications
   A. Related experience
   B. Staff qualifications

VII. Projected costs

Report 4: Illegal and Improper Activities

I. Purpose of policy

II. Prohibited transactions
   A. Illegal political contributions
   B. Bribes, payoffs, and kickbacks
   C. Violations of customs law
   D. Violation of tax law
   E. Violations of laws of business conduct
      1. Monopolies or unfair competition
      2. Registration of securities
      3. Labor negotiations
   F. Payment of excessive fees or commissions

III. Actions that require approval from top management
   A. Legal political contributions
   B. Payment of extortion
   C. Any action of questionable legality

IV. Compliance and enforcement
   A. Disclosure of matters set forth above
   B. Disciplinary actions
      1. Demotion
      2. Termination
      3. Legal action

EXPAND YOUR KNOWLEDGE: THE MANAGEMENT CONSULTANT'S TOOL KIT

Management consulting has boomed recently, as all kinds of organizations turn to outside specialists for help with a variety of problems and decisions. Management consultants are skilled business analysts who are hired to supplement the organization's staff for a particular project.

The assignments that management consultants handle are as varied as business itself. They may suggest ways to reduce overhead expenses, analyze new product opportunities, or diagnose profitability problems. Some specialize in one or two areas; others are generalists. Some work for large consulting firms; others operate independently or with a partner.

Regardless of their orientation, all management consultants need certain talents. They must be able to get to the root of a problem and solve it quickly—while their clients wait. They must also be articulate and versatile enough to sell their solutions to both the plant manager and the company president, without offending either. And they must be able to write well, because reports are an important part of their product.

Management consultants usually supply a potential client with a proposal outlining the work to be done, its objectives, and a target completion date. The proposal also states the fees and expenses to be charged, as well as the tasks to be performed and the critical dates in the project.

When a consultant is hired, the organization supplies a "commitment memorandum" that states why the consultant has been hired and what work will be done. Also, a "project-control memorandum" outlines the roles of the company's project team that will work with the consultant. This team supplies progress reports on the project.

At the conclusion of the project, the management consultant submits recommendations in the form of a written report. This report examines the problem and the proposed solution in depth. It may also explain how to implement the solution and monitor the results. Thus it can serve to guide management decisions long after the work of the consultant is done.

1. Why do you suppose that management consulting has boomed recently?

2. Could you be, would you like to be, a management consultant? Explain your answer.

DEVELOP YOUR WORD POWER

Spelling Challenge   Identify the misspelled word in each of the following sentences, and spell it correctly in the space provided. If all the words in a sentence are spelled correctly, write *C* in the space.

_____   1. Her poor vocabulary is a hinderance to her career.

_____   2. Those figures are not immedeately available.

_____   3. We could look for someone who is inexperienced but intelegent.

_____   4. Your service will be interrupted on September 7.

_____   5. Can you judge how well we are doing?

_____   6. He is quire knowledgible about data communications.

_____   7. We like to educate ignorant consumers.

_____   8. Since we can choose only two, some disappointment is inevitible.

_____   9. I will try not to interfear with your decisions.

_____ 10. At this point, 1980s sales figures are irrevelant.

Vocabulary Challenge   Match the words in the first column with the definitions in the second column.

_____ 11. inveterate   A. praising

_____ 12. judicious   B. chronic

_____ 13. laudable   C. clear

_____ 14. laudatory   D. praiseworthy

_____ 15. lucid   E. prudent

Circle the best definition of the highlighted word in each of the following sentences.

16. Ms. Jaskowitz refused to **intervene** in the dispute between the two employees.

    A. keep score   B. ignore   C. interfere

17. The television state was **inundated** with letters protesting one of its documentaries.

    A. flooded   B. sued   C. perversely pleased

18. The temporary loss of a liquor license **jeopardizes** the financial health of restaurants.

    A. increases   B. explains   C. imperils

19. Robin's attitude about the ideal relationship between government and business could best be described as **laissez faire**.

    A. noninterference   B. all's fair   C. let the buyer beware

20. You will receive a refund in **lieu** of tickets for Saturday's performance.

    A. payment   B. view   C. place

Select one of these words to complete each of the following sentences, and write the word in the space provided.

interval   **intrigue**   **introvert**   **inverse**   **liaison**

21. The tone will sound after a ten-second _____.

22. The _____ of on is off.

23. No _____ would eagerly volunteer to host a hospitality suite.

24. Their efforts to take over the company were characterized by much _____.

25. Phil will be the _____ between Marketing and Production.

Follow-up Word Study   Check your answers at the end of this chapter. In the spaces below, write the words that you spelled or used incorrectly. (Use a separate piece of paper if you missed more than five words.) Then look up each word in your dictionary, and carefully study its spelling, pronunciation, definition, and history (etymology). Finally, to help fix the word in your memory, write it in a sentence.

Word   Sentence

_____   _____

_____   _____

_____   _____

_____   _____

_____   _____

CHECK YOUR ANSWERS

Master Key Concepts

I. A. dislikes, needs
     B. tailored, receptive

II. verifiable
    A. plans
    B. policies, position papers
    C. regulatory
    D. proposals, solicited, unsolicited
    E. elaborate
    F. justification

Quiz Yourself

1. A business report is any written, factual account that objectively communicates information about some aspect of a business. (p. 410)

2. Six specific questions to ask yourself before you decide on the format, style, and organization of your report are:
   a. Who initiated the report?
   b. What subject does it cover?
   c. When is it being prepared?
   d. Where is it being sent?
   e. Why is it being prepared?
   f. How receptive is the reader? (pp. 410–411)

3. _Voluntary_ reports, prepared on your own initiative, require more detail and support than _authorized_ reports, which are prepared at the request of another person. (p. 410)

4. The six most common categories of business report are
   a. Monitor/control reports
   b. Reports for implementing policies and procedures
   c. Reports for complying with regulating agencies
   d. Proposals
   e. Reports for documenting client work
   f. Reports for guiding decisions (p. 411)

5. Personal activity reports are a type of monitor and control report. They are prepared by individuals to help keep managers abreast of employee activities. Typical examples include sales-call reports, conference reports, expense reports, performance reviews, and recruiting reports. (p. 415)

6. Policy/procedure reports are comprehensive, detailed documents written in paragraph form according to the direct plan and containing ample introductory and background information. The goal is to hit the right balance between the general and the specific. It is best to keep the policies broad and the procedures as simple as possible. (p. 417)

7. Here are the characteristics of most compliance reports:
   a. They are prepared for external readers (regulatory bodies) who review many similar documents; they are often recurring reports prepared on an annual basis.
   b. Most follow a standardized format dictated by the regulatory agency.
   c. They are written in a brief style that emphasizes detail as opposed to broad concepts. The language is often legalistic and impersonal.
   d. They are organized generally in direct order and specifically in the order dictated by the regulatory agency. (p. 419)

8. *Proposals* vary in length and complexity, but all are basically attempts to get products, services, or projects accepted by outside business or government clients. (p. 421)

9. Interim progress reports are relatively brief, whereas final reports are generally more elaborate and tend to be longer. Interim reports give an idea of work accomplished to date; final reports, on the contrary, focus on results rather than on progress. (p. 424)

10. Three of the most common decision-oriented reports are
    a. Research reports
    b. Justification reports
    c. Troubleshooting reports (pp. 426–427)

Develop Your Word Power

1. hindrance	6. knowledgeable	11. B	16. C	21. interval
2. immediately	7. C	12. E	17. A	22. inverse
3. intelligent	8. inevitable	13. D	18. C	23. introvert
4. C	9. interfere	14. A	19. A	24. intrigue
5. C	10. irrelevant	15. C	20. C	25. liaison

Chapter 15

Planning and Researching Reports and Proposals

The main point of Chapter 15 is that careful research is a necessary foundation of any report. As you read the chapter, think about how researching a business report differs from—and resembles—researching a report for school. When you finish reading, plan the research for a business report that you might be required to write sometime during your career.

MASTER KEY CONCEPTS

Use the following terms to fill in the blanks in the outline. All terms are used, but none is used more than once.

analytical	factoring	interpretations	suggestions
boundaries	goal	problem	trends
decimal	infinitive phrase	secondary	work plan
experiments	informational		

I. The research process begins when you define the _____ (p. 434) you plan to study in order to set the limits of your investigation.
   A. Before beginning a study, be sure that you and the person who authorized the report agree on the _____ (pp. 434–435) of the assignment: what needs to be determined, why the issue is important, who is involved in the situation, where the trouble is located, when it started, how the situation originated.
   B. The most useful way to phrase your statement of purpose is to begin with an _____ (p. 435). When you choose such a phrase, you pin down your general _____ (p. 435) in preparing the report.

II. Once you have defined the problem and established the purpose of the study, you have to develop a logical structure for investigation, identifying the questions that you will ask and answer during the course of the study.
   A. _____ (p. 436) the problem means breaking the central problem into a hierarchy of narrower and narrower questions; _____ (p. 437) reports, which offer little analysis or interpretation, are factored into specific subtopics of the main topic, whereas _____ (p. 438) reports are factored into categories based on problem-solving methods.
   B. To guide your analysis, you can represent your breakdown of the problem in outline form; to indicate levels of thought, you may use either alphanumeric format (combining roman numerals, letters, and Arabic numerals) or _____ (p. 439) format, and for each item you may use either descriptive labels or more informative headings.
   C. Any given problem may be subdivided in many different ways, as long as all the important questions are asked. You can help ensure the logic of your breakdown if you choose a significant, useful basis or guiding principle for the division, if you limit yourself to one basis at a time in subdividing a whole into its parts, if you make sure that each group is separate and distinct, and if you are careful to list all the parts of a whole.

III. Once the outline is ready, you establish a _____ (p. 441) that identifies the tasks you will perform in your research, the end products of the research, and a review of schedules and budgets.

IV. The research phase is the most important part of the investigation, because the value of the report depends on the quality of the research.
   A. Indispensable _____ (p. 443) sources of information that have already been collected include general reference works, periodicals, government documents, and internal reports and publications.
   B. Four main ways to collect primary data are to examine documents, observe people, conduct surveys, and perform _____ (p. 448).

V. As you collect information, you constantly sift and analyze what you learn in order to draw conclusions and make recommendations.
   A. When information you have collected is in numerical form, you must manipulate the numbers—calculate averages, analyze _____ (p. 450), and find correlations—to interpret their significance.
   B. Analytical reports draw conclusions, which are opinions or _____ (p. 450) based on the information you have obtained.
   C. Analytical reports may also provide recommendations, _____ (p. 452) about what should be done based on the information you have obtained.

Check your answers at the end of this chapter.

QUIZ YOURSELF

1. What do you accomplish be defining the problem to be investigated during your research?

2. Once you have defined the problem, you have to break it down into more specific areas for investigation. This process is sometimes referred to as outlining the issues, or

   _____ the problem.

3. Briefly discuss the differences in identifying key issues for investigation in informational reports versus analytical reports.

4. When wording an outline, you must choose between _____ (topical) and

   _____ (talking) headings. _____ headings label the subject

   that will be discussed, whereas _____ headings suggest more about the meaning of the issues.

5. What elements should be included in an informal work plan prepared for your own purposes? What elements would you have to add to make a formal work plan for a lengthy, formal study?

6. Business research begins with a thorough review of the available literature on the subject. This already published material is known as _____ data.

7. What is the difference between "reliability" and "validity," as used in describing surveys?

8. What eight general guidelines should you follow in developing a questionnaire?

9. Calculate the mean, median, and mode for the following annual salaries:

$16,000	$17,000	$22,000	$26,000
$16,500	$18,000	$22,500	$29,000
$16,500	$19,000	$23,000	

10. What is the difference between a conclusion and a recommendation?

Check your answers at the end of this chapter.

BUILD YOUR SKILLS: HOW WOULD YOU ATTACK THE PROBLEM?

If your hometown is like many, it offers few activities for teenagers. As a result, young people "hang out" and make their own fun. Unfortunately, what starts out as innocent fun sometimes develops into vandalism and rowdiness, which lead to tensions with the adults in the community. All too often adults react by cutting back on teenagers' legitimate opportunities to socialize.

Your assignment is to study this problem. The first step is to define it in terms that narrow the focus of your investigation and to develop a clear statement of purpose. Then you are ready to outline the issues you plan to study. Break the general problem into a hierarchy of narrower and narrower questions that have to be answered. The result should be a preliminary outline that you can use to guide your research. Finally, prepare a step-by-step work plan that summarizes your approach for attacking the problem and that provides a schedule for completing the effort.

EXPAND YOUR KNOWLEDGE: TECHNIQUES FOR PICKING AN EXPERT'S BRAIN

The key to successful research is often to interview an expert on your subject. But this may be easier said than done. Just finding an expert requires patience and persistence—and once found, such a person must be persuaded to help you.

Angela Fox Dunn, whose articles are distributed by the *Los Angeles Times* Syndicate, specializes in profiles of prominent people. Because these people have many demands on their time, she usually writes to request interviews instead of calling. What is the secret of her success? "I always prepare before I make contact. If I'm lucky, the person is listed in *Current Biography*. If not, I check the periodical indexes for listings of articles by or about the person. Nothing pleases people more than knowing that I know about their background and achievements."

With this basic legwork done, Angela is ready to request an interview. "If a prominent person has paved the way, I mention him or her in my opening sentence," Angela says. "In my opening, I also focus on the person I'm writing to. I use praise, not superlatives, and if the person is tops in the field, a known authority, I add a few words of tribute. I'm subtle, but I let people know that I'm aware of their stature.

"Above all, I don't ramble. I get to the reason I'm writing as quickly as possible. Years ago someone gave me 'four magic words' for success in communication. I have used them in letters and in person. They are 'I need your help.' If you get this idea across simply and sincerely, you'll find you are seldom refused."

Getting an expert to agree to an interview is one thing; the actual interview is quite another. Here are a few tips for making the most of your opportunity:

- *Know exactly how the expert can help you.* Do not expect a busy person to do all your work for you. Use printed sources to get a basic understanding of your subject, and then as the expert to update your facts or to give you insights into personalities, organizations, or an entire industry.
- *Make a positive first impression.* Be warm and cheerful, self-confident but not cocky.
- *Consider the person you're talking to.* You would phrase questions differently for a rock star than for an environmental specialist.
- *Be open.* State what you're after and why. Deception in explaining your needs and motives may make your source hesitant to provide information.
- *Do not overstate your knowledge of the subject.* Once you have demonstrated your basic understanding of the subject, let the expert take over. Experts do not mind your being uninformed about the specifics and may even help you more if you humbly acknowledge your ignorance.
- *Do not be too quick to accept a no.* You may have to ask a question several different ways to get an answer.
- *Ask for names of other contacts and other places to look for information.* If you get nothing else out of an interview, you may as well get a name. The next person or resource may provide what you need.
- *Be respectful and considerate.* Let experts know that you realize their time and their good name are precious.
- *Be lavish with your praise and your thanks.* A well-placed compliment about the person's expertise and insight is bound to come back to you. And a handwritten thank-you note to a particularly helpful expert may encourage cooperation in the future.

1. Identify local experts who might be able to provide information for a project you are doing in school. For example, in connection with Chapter 15 of the textbook, make a list of professional market researchers who frequently pick other people's brains. Then write a letter to one of the people on the list and request an interview.

2. If your letter to professional market researchers has produced the desired results, you will soon be interviewing your expert. To prepare yourself, follow Angela Fox Dunn's suggestions. Develop an interview guide in advance so that you will have a specific list of questions ready. To get the most out of the interview, either record the conversation or take notes. Immediately afterward, summarize the gist of the interview in writing. Then analyze the success of the interview. Did you learn all you had hoped to learn? Were you able to cover your questions in the time available? What would you do differently? Finish the project by writing a thank-you note to the person you interviewed.

DEVELOP YOUR WORD POWER

Spelling Challenge   Identify the misspelled word in each of the following sentences, and spell it correctly in the space provided. If all the words in a sentence are spelled correctly, write *C* in the space.

_____   1. Make sure that your address and phone number are legible.

_____   2. Sheila will go to almost any lenths to get a promotion.

_____ 3. Tracy is a likeable, energetic young woman.

_____ 4. What is the likelyhood of getting delivery by midweek?

_____ 5. Please send some literture on your new personal computers.

_____ 6. We don't have the luxery of waiting for third-quarter figures.

_____ 7. Gardening—what a wonderful way to spend your leesure time!

_____ 8. All our technicians are fully licenced.

_____ 9. Listen before you jump to conclusions about his limitations.

_____ 10. We have steadily been loosing market share.

Vocabulary Challenge   Match the words in the first column with the definitions in the second column.

_____ 11. malign   A. to show plainly

_____ 12. mandate   B. to keep to oneself

_____ 13. maneuver   C. to slander

_____ 14. manifest   D. to manipulate

_____ 15. monopolize   E. to authorize

Circle the best definition of the highlighted word in each of the following sentences.

16. His **Machiavellian** nature finally yielded him leadership.

   A. masculine   B. cunning   C. ambitious

17. We cannot afford to include any **mavericks** on the team for this project.

   A. cowboys   B. incompetents   C. loners

18. My **mentor** was a 50-year-old woman with a reputation for covering her iron fist with a velvet glove.

   A. boss   B. confidant   C. adviser

19. Judy has undergone a **metamorphosis** since taking the Dale Carnegie course.

   A. period of self-doubt   B. attitude adjustment   C. complete change

20. With a **modicum** of training, Andy could become a good manager.

   A. little bit   B. great deal   C. modern type

Select one of these words to complete each of the following sentences, and write the word in the space provided.

malleable   mercurial   meticulous   moot   moribund

21. The proper level of government intervention in the marketplace is a _____ point, but it seems useless to discuss it here.

22. His _____ changes, from calm to anger in moments, unsettle the staff.

23. Tom's _____ nature helps him adjust to many different situations.

24. The employee relations committee has been _____ during the strike.

25. The best accountants are _____ in handling complicated financial reports.

Follow-up Word Study   Check your answers at the end of this chapter. In the spaces below, write the words that you spelled or used incorrectly. (Use a separate piece of paper if you missed more than five words.) Then look up each word in your dictionary, and carefully study its spelling, pronunciation, definition, and history (etymology). Finally, to help fix the word in your memory, write it in a sentence.

<u>Word</u>   <u>Sentence</u>

_____   _____

_____   _____

_____   _____

_____   _____

_____   _____

CHECK YOUR ANSWERS

Master Key Concepts

I. problem
   A. boundaries
   B. infinitive phrase, goal

II. A. factoring, informational,
      analytical
   B. decimal

III. work plan

IV. A. secondary
   B. experiments

V. A. trends
   B. interpretations
   C. suggestions

Quiz Yourself

1. By defining the problem to be investigated, you narrow the focus of your investigation and establish its framework. Your definition of the problem helps you decide what information you need to complete your report. (pp. 434–435)

2. Once you have defined the problem, you have to break it down into more specific areas for investigation. This process is sometimes referred to as outlining the issues, or *factoring* the problem. (p. 436)

3. Informational reports are generally broken down into subtopics dealing with specific subjects. These subtopics might be arranged in order of importance, sequentially, chronologically, spatially, geographically, or categorically.

    Analytical reports are generally broken down into categories based on problem-solving methods. The two most common methods are hypotheses and relative merits. (pp. 437–438)

4. When wording an outline, you must choose between *descriptive* (topical) and *informative* (talking) headings. *Descriptive* headings label the subject that will be discussed, whereas *informative* headings suggest more about the meaning of the issues. (pp. 439–440)

5. A simple, informal work plan should include a list of steps that will be taken, an estimate of their sequence and timing, and a list of sources of information.
    A formal work plan should include
    a. A statement of the problem
    b. A statement of the purpose and scope of the investigation
    c. A discussion of the sequence of tasks to be accomplished, together with an indication of sources, research methods, and limitations
    d. A description of end products, such as reports, plans operating improvements, or tangible products
    e. A review of project assignments, schedules, and resource requirements (p. 441)

6. Business research begins with a thorough review of the available literature on the subject. This already published material is known as *secondary* data. (p. 441)

7. A survey is considered "reliable" when the same results would be obtained if the research were repeated at a later date. A survey is considered "valid" if it measures what it was intended to measure and gives a true reflection of the sample group's opinions on a subject. (p. 446)

8. The following guidelines should be applied when developing a questionnaire:
    a. Provide clear instructions so that respondents will know how to fill it out.
    b. Keep it short and easy to answer.
    c. Use questions that are easily tabulated.
    d. Avoid questions that lead to a particular answer.
    e. Ask only one thing at a time.
    f. Avoid questions with vague or abstract words.
    g. Pretest the questionnaire with a sample group.
    h. Include a few questions that rephrase earlier questions. (pp. 446–448)

9. The mean is $20,500; the median is $19,000; the mode is $16,500. (p. 449)

10. A conclusion is an opinion or an interpretation of what the facts mean; a recommendation suggests what ought to be done about the facts. (pp. 450–452)

Develop Your Word Power

1. *C*
2. lengths
3. likable
4. likelihood
5. literature

6. luxury
7. leisure
8. licensed
9. *C*
10. losing

11. C
12. E
13. D
14. A
15. B

16. B
17. C
18. C
19. C
20. A

21. moot
22. mercurial
23. malleable
24. moribund
25. meticulous

Chapter 16

Developing Visual Aids

The main point of Chapter 16 is that properly selected and crafted visual aids simplify and dramatize the information in a report. As you read the chapter, think about which situations are most appropriate for using the types of visual aids that are discussed. When you finish reading, look for visual aids in business reports and consumer publications and then analyze how well they communicate.

MASTER KEY CONCEPTS

Use the following terms to fill in the blanks in the outline. All terms are used, but none is used more than once.

accurate	bar	continuity	spreadsheet
attention	captions	discussion	tables
balance	charts	photographs	whole

I. It is often a good idea to prepare visual aids before writing the rest of the report.
   A. Visual aids attract and hold people's _____ (p. 458) and help them understand and remember the message.
   B. When planning visual aids, you need to decide on the message, identify points that require visual support, and maintain a _____ (p. 459) between visuals and words.

II. Designing visual aids involves understanding the art of graphic design and choosing the appropriate visual aid for the situation.
   A. To create effective visual aids, you need to observe the principle of _____ (p. 461) (making sure that the visual aids are treated consistently from one page to the next), of contrast, and of emphasis.
   B. Use _____ (p. 461) to present large quantities of detailed, specific information; line and surface _____ (p. 463) to show changes over time of the interaction of two variables; _____ (pp. 464–466) charts to compare the size of several items at one time or the composition of several items over time; pie charts to show the relative sizes of parts of a _____ (p. 467); flow charts and organization charts to illustrate physical or conceptual relationships; maps to show geographic information; and drawings, diagrams, and _____ (p. 468) to show how something looks or how it is used.

III. The cost and methods of producing visual aids have been altered greatly with the appearance of computer graphics systems.
   A. To produce good-looking graphics in printed form or as slides, transparencies, or screen images, your choices include presentation-graphics programs, drawing programs, painting programs, and _____ (p. 470) programs.
   B. To fit visual aids into your _____ (p. 471), clearly introduce them in the text, place them near the points they illustrate, and choose titles and _____ (p. 474) with a message.
   C. As a final step, visual aids should be checked to make sure they are necessary, convenient, _____ (p. 476), and honest.

Check your answers at the end of this chapter.

QUIZ YOURSELF

1. Give eight purposes for using visual aids in business reports.

2. Describe the design principles of continuity, contrast, and emphasis.

3. What type of visual aid would you use to present detailed statistical or financial data? What type would you use to dramatize key points?

4. What is a "text" table?

5. A form of line chart with a cumulative effect is a _____, in which all the lines add up to the top line.

6. What are some of the creative things you can do with bar charts?

7. Ideally, the biggest slice of a pie chart is placed at the _____ position.

8. What are three ways to make a strong connection between your discussion and your visual aids?

9. What is the difference between a descriptive title and an informative title?

10. In a graph or chart, you can transform modest results into dramatic ones by _____, but you abandon good business ethics and mislead your readers in the process.

Check your answers at the end of this chapter.

BUILD YOUR SKILLS: CHOOSE THE RIGHT VISUAL AID FOR THE SITUATION

You are preparing a report on the mail-order market for books. Which visual aid would you use to portray each of the following points?

1. You want to show that mail-order purchases accounted for 13 percent of all books purchased this year.
2. You want to show that the mail-order book market consists of two segments: book clubs and other forms of mail order. You want to show the relative size of the two segments over the past five years, as well as the size of the total book market.
3. You want to show statistics on the people who buy mail-order books. You have data on their gender, age, education, and annual income, which you want to display for both book-club purchases and other mail-order purchases.
4. You want to show that of all the books bought this year, 27 percent were purchased at a discount. You want to contrast this with the fact that 49 percent of all book-club books were purchased at a discount, whereas 40 percent of all other mail-order books were discounted.
5. You want to contrast the types of books purchased through retail outlets, book clubs, and other mail-order sources. You have compiled data on the source of purchases for various categories of fiction (mystery, romance, western, science fiction, adventure, the classics, and so on), as well as various nonfiction categories (reference, history, health/diet, religion, home and garden, cooking, finance and investment, biography, art, and so on).

EXPAND YOUR KNOWLEDGE: PICTURES THAT TELL THE WRONG STORY

Visual aids and statistics are a valuable tool to writers of reports, because they invest facts with credibility and drama. But readers beware. The following flaws could hide significant problems with the facts that the report is based on:

*   *Overwhelming facade.* Don't let dazzling photographs, charming drawings, and expensive covers and paper blind you to the content of a report. These niceties are intended to make the facts more palatable, but nothing says you have to suspend all judgment.
*   *Apples-and-oranges graphs.* A series of graphs on the same subject should use similar scales—or clearly indicate that a change has been made. Otherwise, you cannot sensibly compare the graphs' ups and downs.
*   *Chopped-off graph.* The vertical (upright) axis of a graph is supposed to start with 0 at the base. But when all the numbers being plotted are significantly above 0, some people erroneously chop off the lower part of the axis and use a higher number at the base. As a result, the plotted line appears to be much more dramatic than warranted by the facts.
*   *Souped-up graph.* One way to solve the problem of a boring, undramatic graph is to change the units of measurement. If the vertical axis is compressed by making the gradations smaller, the line seems to rise and fall much more vigorously. Unfortunately, changes over time are sometimes minor, and no amount of fiddling with the graph will affect the truth—only your perception of the truth.
*   *One-dimensional picture.* When pictures are used in a line or bar chart, beware. For instance, if a number A is represented by a house 1 inch tall, number B, which is twice number A, should not be represented by a house 2 inches tall. That's because the houses are multidimensional, and their true size is measured by multiplying their height by their width. To be fair, number A should be represented by one little house 1 inch tall, and number B should be represented by two little houses 1 inch tall.
*   *Well-chosen average.* Most so-called averages are the mean, which is derived by adding a string of numbers and dividing by the number of numbers. But the median, which is the number in the exact middle of the group, may also be presented as the average. A clever writer may select the most advantageous of these averages; the clever reader looks for information to clarify which one has been used.

- *Ever-impressive decimal.* Numbers carried out to decimal places look good, but don't let yourself be unduly impressed by them. Would a secretary, average or otherwise, type 5.3 letters a day? It would be more useful to say that a secretary types about five letters a day. At the same time, using a decimal figure is meaningless if the statistic is based on approximate numbers or people's guesses.
- *Sample with built-in bias.* When you read statistics based on a sample, you should also study the procedures used to select the sample so that you can judge for yourself whether it has been selected fairly. For example, consider the statement that a company's average profit for the past three years is $1 million. What this statistic does not say is that the company's profit three years ago was $3 million; 2 years ago, $1 million; and last year, (-) $1 million (i.e., a $1 million loss). In all likelihood, the author of the statistic was trying to beautify last year's dismal results by selecting a more favorable sample.
- *Insignificant difference.* Before choosing one option over another on the basis of a rather small statistical difference, look for a number that represents the "probable error." For example, say that 52 percent of a survey sample prefer higher quality, 48 percent prefer lower prices, and the probable error is ±3 points. That means 49 to 55 percent may prefer higher quality and 45 to 51 percent may prefer lower prices. Because these ranges of numbers overlap, it is foolhardy to choose to offer higher quality over lower prices; if anything, the results show that the sample is evenly divided.
- *Semiattached figure.* Someone with a difficult point to prove may borrow credibility from an unrelated statistic. For example, the claim that "nine out of ten track stars wear Mercury shoes" may be used to convince a small retailer of the value of stocking Mercuries. What the statistic does not say is that the typical jogger does not need shoes of the same high quality—and price—and will not be so easily fooled.
- *Unwarranted assumption.* Do not let someone confuse you about cause and effect. So what if statistics show that those who graduate with high grade-point averages are more likely to become managers than those who graduate with lower grades? The discrepancy may only show that high academic achievers tend to be channeled into management-training programs and receive more attention from supervisors who have high expectations. Some of those who graduated with lower grades may actually have more native management ability but never get the chance to prove it.

1. Develop your own powers of critical thinking by looking for examples of misleading pictures. Over the next week, collect at least five visual aids or statistical descriptions that are likely to be misinterpreted by an unwary reader. What, specifically, is wrong with each of your examples?

2. Pick a major story of national significance from the front page of a recent issues of the local newspaper. Now obtain at least four other versions of the same story from other sources, such as *USA Today, The New York Times, The Wall Street Journal, Time,* and *Newsweek.* How do the different publications handle the story? Are the same facts presented? How are the various articles illustrated? Can you honestly pick the most accurate version? How?

DEVELOP YOUR WORD POWER

Spelling Challenge   Identify the misspelled word in each of the following sentences, and spell it correctly in the space provided. If all the words in a sentence are spelled correctly, write *C* in the space.

_____ 1. Would you like a maintainance contract for your new computer?

_____ 2. A company of that size is no longer manageable.

_____ 3. Did you understand what Dave ment?

_____ 4. Drop in sometime for a look at our array of merchendise.

_____   5. My new company car gets great gas milage.

_____   6. Let's put all the miselaneous tables in an appendix at the back.

_____   7. Proofread carefully for mispelled words.

_____   8. The Operations Department will maintain all the equipment.

_____   9. Darlene is good at manageing people.

_____   10. Send now for your set of minature musical instruments!

Vocabulary Challenge   Match the words in the first column with the definitions in the second column.

_____ 11. obstinate   A. hateful

_____ 12. obtuse   B. unyielding

_____ 13. odious   C. dull

_____ 14. officious   D. suitable

_____ 15. opportune   E. meddlesome

Circle the best definition of the highlighted word in each of the following sentences.

16. Tampering with the internal mechanism **nullifies** the warranty.

    A. invalidates   B. extends   C. shortens

17. The writing style used in this memo **obscures** the meaning.

    A. clarifies   B. enhances   C. conceals

18. The motto "To the Stars We Aspire" is stamped on the **obverse** of the medallion.

    A. front   B. back   C. margin

19. An important **omission** from your proposal is a budget.

    A. concept   B. conclusion   C. exclusion

20. Her disappointment at not getting the job is **palpable**.

    A. understandable   B. unjustified   C. obvious

Select one of these words to complete each of the following sentences, and write the word in the space provided.

    multifarious   **mundane**   **nonchalant**   **noncommittal**   **nondescript**

21. Underwear was a _____ product until clothing designers started differentiating brands and styles.

22. By remaining _____, she has avoided the appearance of siding with either party in the dispute.

23. Supervisors deal with such _____ concerns as counting supplies.

24. With all his _____ activities, I don't see how he can do another project.

25. I was amazed by your _____ reaction during the massive layoffs.

Follow-up Word Study   Check your answers at the end of this chapter. In the spaces below, write the words that you spelled or used incorrectly. (Use a separate piece of paper if you missed more than five words.) Then look up each word in your dictionary, and carefully study its spelling, pronunciation, definition, and history (etymology). Finally, to help fix the word in your memory, write it in a sentence.

Word   Sentence

_____   _____

_____   _____

_____   _____

_____   _____

_____   _____

CHECK YOUR ANSWERS

Master Key Concepts

I. A. attention
    B. balance

II. A. continuity
    B. tables, charts, bar,
       whole, photographs

III. A. spreadsheet
     B. discussion,
        captions
     C. accurate

Quiz Yourself

1. Eight purposes for using visual aids in business reports are
   a. To clarify
   b. To simplify
   c. To emphasize
   d. To summarize
   e. To reinforce
   f. To attract
   g. To impress
   h. To unify (p. 459)

2. *Continuity* refers to handling all design elements in visuals in a consistent way, including color, shape, size, texture, position, scale, and typeface. *Contrast* refers to making visual distinctions that match verbal distinctions. *Emphasis* refers to giving the greatest visual emphasis to the most important points. (p. 461)

3. A numerical table would be the best choice for presenting detailed statistical or financial information; a more graphic or pictorial format would be better for highlighting key points. (pp. 461–469)

4. A "text" table is, in essence, a part of the paragraph that is typed in tabular format. It is introduced with a sentence that leads directly into the tabulated information and does not have a formal title. (p. 462)

5. A form of line chart with a cumulative effect is a *surface chart*, in which all the lines add up to the top line. (p. 464)

6. Here are some of the creative options available with bar charts:
   a. Draw the charts either vertically or horizontally.
   b. Show both positive and negative quantities.
   c. Subdivide the bars to show the composition of something.
   d. Double the bars for comparisons.
   e. String a series of bar charts together.
   f. Convert the bars into symbols (pictograms). (pp. 465–466)

7. Ideally, the biggest slice of a pie chart is placed at the *twelve o'clock* position. (p. 467)

8. To make a strong connection between the text and the visual aids
   a. Introduce each visual aid in the text.
   b. Place the visual aid as close as possible to the point you are trying to illustrate.
   c. Reinforce the connection by repeating the important textual point in the title or the caption of the visual aid. (p. 471)

9. A descriptive title identifies the topic of the visual aid; an informative title calls attention to the conclusion that ought to be drawn from the data. (pp. 474–475)

10. In a graph or chart, you can transform modest results into dramatic ones by *compressing the horizontal scale or expanding the vertical scale,* but you abandon good business ethics and mislead your readers in the process. (pp. 476–477)

Develop Your Word Power

1. maintenance	6. miscellaneous	11. B	16. A	21. nondescript
2. C	7. misspelled	12. C	17. C	22. noncommittal
3. meant	8. C	13. A	18. A	23. mundane
4. merchandise	9. managing	14. E	19. C	24. multifarious
5. mileage	10. miniature	15. D	20. C	25. nonchalant

Chapter 17

Writing Reports and Proposals

The main point of Chapter 17 is that, in general, reports are organized according to their purpose—informational or analytical. As you read the chapter, think about how the direct and indirect organizational plans mesh with the basic outlines for informational and analytical reports. When you finish reading, look at a business report and analyze the effectiveness of the organizational plan that it uses.

MASTER KEY CONCEPTS

Use the following terms to fill in the blanks in the outline. All terms are used, but none is used more than once.

chronologically	informal	present	transitions
controversial	memo	previews	understand
direct	parallel	receptive	yardstick
indirect	periodic	resistance	

I. The division of ideas that helped you do your research may be quite different from the division of ideas that will help your audience _____ (p. 484) and accept your message, particularly if your message contains _____ (p. 484) material.

   A. A report may be formatted as a preprinted form, a letter, a _____ (pp. 484–485), or a manuscript; the length depends on the subject and purpose and on your relationship with the reader.

   B. When deciding on a basic structure for your report, you must decide what to include and exclude, whether to introduce ideas in direct or _____ (p. 487) order, and how to subdivide and develop ideas.

II. The purpose of informational reports is to explain something in straightforward terms; generally, because your readers will respond unemotionally, you can present your material in the most _____ (pp. 488–489) fashion possible.

   A. _____ (p. 489) reports generally follow the same format and organization from period to period, often containing an overview of routine responsibilities, a discussion of special projects, plans for the coming period, and an analysis of problems; it should be honest about problems as well as accomplishments.

   B. Personal activity reports on nonrecurring events are usually written in memo format and are often organized _____ (p. 491), although some are organized around topics that reflect the audience's interests.

III. When writing an analytical report for people in your own organization who have asked you to study something, you're writing for your most _____ (p. 491) readers. Because they're likely to accept your conclusions, you can usually use the direct approach.

   A. When readers have reservations either about you or about your material, strong statements at the beginning of your report may intensify their _____ (p. 492).

   B. When you want your audience to concentrate on why your ideas make sense, let your logical arguments provide the structure for your report. Three types of logical arguments that can be used in this case are the 2 + 2 = 4 approach (a list of reasons that collectively add up to the main point), the scientific method (an evaluation of alternative solutions), or the _____ (p. 502) approach (a list of criteria for evaluating a situation or solution).

IV. In addition to deciding on the length, format, and organization of the report, you have to consider a number of other factors as well.
   A. For brief reports to someone you know well, you can use a relatively _____ (p. 504) tone; You can achieve a more formal tone by eliminating all references to *I* and *you.*
   B. Decide whether to write in the past or the _____ (p. 504) tense, and then use it consistently.
   C. The longer the report, the more useful are clues to the structure of the report. The opening introduces the subject, explains why it is important, and _____ (p. 505) the main ideas and the order in which they will be covered. Headings and lists help readers scan the report and recognize the relationship among ideas; they should be phrased in _____ (p. 507) form. _____ (p. 508) tie ideas together and keep readers moving along the right track. The ending ties up all the pieces, reminds readers how they fit together, and (in analytical reports) explicitly states the conclusions and recommendations.

Check your answers at the end of this chapter.

QUIZ YOURSELF

1. What are some of the things to consider when deciding on the length of a report?

2. What three issues should you consider when establishing the basic structure of a report?

3. Should informational reports be organized in direct or indirect order? Why?

4. What are the two basic ways analytical reports can be organized?

5. What is the five-step sequence of points in an analytical report based on recommendations?

6. When you want readers to concentrate on why your ideas make sense, your best bet is to let _____ provide the structure of the report.

7. Briefly describe three possible organizational plans based on logical arguments.

8. What is the difference between a formal and an informal tone, and when is each appropriate?

9. Is it better to use the past or the present tense when establishing the time perspective of a report?

10. What three things does the opening of a report accomplish?

Check your answers at the end of this chapter.

BUILD YOUR SKILLS: WHAT'S WRONG WITH THIS OUTLINE?

You have recently been hired by a bank as the administrative assistant to the Vice President of Commercial Loans. Your boss, the vice president, has asked you to prepare a 10- to 15-page report on the life insurance industry as background information for the bank's board of directors. Your report is intended to give the board members an overview of the life insurance business so that they will be better able to evaluate a loan to finance the start-up of a new insurance company.

Here is your preliminary outline for the report. Take a close look at it and make any necessary changes before showing it to your boss.

Overview of the Life Insurance Industry

I. Introduction
   A. History of the industry
      1. In Europe
      2. In the United States
      3. Role of minority-owned companies
   B. Size of the industry
      1. Assets
      2. Employees
      3. Income
      4. Number of companies

II. Structure of the industry
   A. Mutual companies dominate the industry
      1. Control 70 percent of assets
      2. Generate the bulk of premium income
   B. Stock companies outnumber mutual companies but are less influential
      1. Generate only 20 percent of premium income
      2. Account for less than half the insurance in force
   C. Some life insurance companies carry health insurance too
      1. Life insurance accounts for 71 percent of premium income
         a. Ordinary accounts for 43 percent
         b. Group accounts for 13 percent
         c. Annuities accounts for 12 percent
         d. Industrial accounts for 3 percent
      2. Health insurance accounts for 29 percent of premium income
         a. Hospital/medical accounts for 21 percent
         b. Disability accounts for 8 percent

    D. Distribution channels
       1. Ordinary agents
       2. Combination agents
       3. Independent agents
       4. Mail order (small share)
    E. High degree of government regulation
       1. Restrictions on investment portfolios
       2. Selling expenses
       3. Varies from state to state

III. Industry growth
    A. Ten-year statistics
       1. New business issued
       2. Premium income
       3. Assets
       4. Insurance in force
    B. Profit growth
    C. Future outlook is good
       1. Growth of 25- to 34-year-old age group
       2. Higher incomes

IV. Industry outlook
    A. Negative factors
       1. Price competition
       2. National health insurance
       3. Social Security benefits
       4. Decline in interest rates
       5. Increasing overhead expenses
    B. However, companies have good opportunities
       1. New products
       2. New markets
       3. New sales approaches
       4. More aggressive investing

V. Profit economics
    A. Industry has three ways to improve profits
       1. Higher premium prices
       2. Changes in mix and volume of sales
       3. Better return on investment of surplus funds.

BUILD YOUR SKILLS: YOU BE THE EDITOR

The following pages are taken from a report on the U.S. market for home health care. The report was prepared by Jack Williams, a former hospital administrator who is starting a company to provide home-health-care supplies through retail outlets. Williams prepared this report as a means of attracting potential financial backers. He has asked you to critique the report for him and to make any necessary improvements. Here is the introduction of the report, which is intended to give the reader an overview of the market and the role of Jack's proposed company.

The Market for Home Health Care

This is a report on the market for home health care, which is a large and growing market. Already, over 34 million Americans are more than 65 years old. These people tend to be big health-care consumers. In fact, people over 65 require twice as much health care as the rest of us.

The U.S. government, in its divine wisdom, has committed us to paying the medical bills of these old people. But the fact is, the country can't really afford to pay the price. Medicare and Medicaid are rapidly growing broke.

The solution to this problem is to encourage these old folks to stay out of hospitals and nursing homes and get the care they need at home. The cost of caring for a person at home is a fraction of the cost of caring for a person in a nursing home or hospital. For this reason, the government will probably pass laws that require it to reimburse people for their home-health-care expenses.

In 1988 the market was $5.2 billion, and I figure that the current market for home-health-care services is a whopping $10 billion. As more and more old folks get their health care at home, they will need equipment such as hospital beds, wheelchairs, walkers, traction devices, pads and cushions, toilet devices, and other nondisposables. Disposable supplies are another big segment, including such items as tapes, dressings, disinfectants, antiseptics, splints, restraints, curettes, adult diapers, diagnostic kits, and the like. A smaller segment of the market consists of sales of nutritional items for people who are unable to eat in the normal way. Finally, the home-health-care services market consists of services such as chemotherapy, kidney dialysis, and respiratory therapy. Each of these segments should keep this market expanding well beyond the turn of the century.

My proposed company would initially be involved in segments I and II above (durable equipment and disposable supplies). I plan to open retail stores that will sell and rent these supplies. The stores will be located in areas with a high concentration of old people, preferably next door to clinics or medical buildings.

The rest of this report explains the need for a company like mine, the strategy I would use to make my operation successful, and the way you can participate in the great home-health-care boom by investing with me.

EXPAND YOUR KNOWLEDGE: A LOOK AT ANNUAL REPORTS

One type of business report that you are most likely to see, as a member of the general public, is the corporate annual report. Each year, public corporations publish reports to inform shareholders and other interested parties of their financial performance and future plans. In addition, many private corporations and nonprofit organizations put out annual reports to enhance their image.

Although annual reports were once produced simply to supply financial data, they have evolved to become important promotional tools for corporations. As a result, most tend to be slick, professional productions resembling consumer magazines.

The great majority of annual reports include (1) an attractive cover, often featuring a photograph; (2) a financial highlights page, usually inside the front cover; (3) a table of contents; (4) a message from the chairman, usually titled something like "Report to the Shareholders," that summarizes the company's financial performance for the previous year and discusses its future outlook; (5) a financial summary; (6) information on programs, activities, and operations of the corporation over the previous year; (7) detailed financial data; (8) the auditor's report, assessing the company's financial health; and (9) a list (often with photos) of the company's directors and officers. The average report is 38 pages, although some are nearly 100 pages. The cost of producing these reports varies from 60 cents a copy to as much as $8 per copy.

Annual reports are usually put together by a team of employees, headed by the director of corporate communications. This individual, the editor of the report, meets with the chairman of the corporation and other key officers to decide on a theme or emphasis for the year's report. The editor then assigns writers and photographers to produce the creative parts of the report, works with a designer to develop the look of the report, and coordinates production (working with typesetters and printers, selecting paper stock, and so on). The editor and his or her assistants must also acquire the various other elements to be included in the report, such as financial data, the chairman's message, and the auditor's report. Most companies allot five or six months to put together an annual report.

Because the annual report is designed to promote the company's image and is seen by employees, customers, suppliers, and journalists as well as current and prospective investors, great care is usually put into preparing it. As publisher of a newsletter devoted to annual reports, Sid Cato says, "The annual report is corporate America's No. 1 communication document. If it's not easy to read, companies' messages will not be understood."

1. Obtain copies of four or five annual reports; libraries are a good source, but you can also call local corporations or write to distant ones for specific reports. Compare the reports in terms of writing style, design, and production values. If you were an investor, which company would you most likely invest in, based solely on the look and feel of the report?

2. An annual report creates an image for a company. Examine four or five annual reports and briefly state the company image presented by each.

DEVELOP YOUR WORD POWER

Spelling Challenge   Identify the misspelled word in each of the following sentences, and spell it correctly in the space provided. If all the words in a sentence are spelled correctly, write *C* in the space.

_____   1. It is hard to maintain employee moral in an uncertain economy.

_____   2. You should take all nesessary precautions against a takeover bid.

_____   3. One of your nabers has given us your name.

_____   4. Niether Tom nor Tim has ever negotiated a contract before.

_____   5. About nintey people are expected to attend the seminar.

_____   6. The mar is barely notisable, but we will still give you a discount.

_____   7. An extraordinary vista awaits you on the nineth green.

_____   8. Be sure to report on munisiple services as well.

_____   9. Dick Moore is the nineteenth 60-year-old to be laid off this year.

_____   10. I couldn't help noticeing that your performance has deteriorated.

Vocabulary Challenge   Match the words in the first column with the definitions in the second column.

_____ 11. panacea   A. model of excellence

_____ 12. paradox   B. something that lasts

_____ 13. paragon   C. something that seems self-contradictory

_____ 14. parody   D. cure-all

_____ 15. perennial   E. satirical imitation

Circle the best definition of the highlighted word in each of the following sentences.

16. In general, racism is **passé** in American society.

    A. unacceptable   B. outmoded   C. everywhere

17. How many market tests are **pending**?

    A. in progress   B. about to take place   C. in the planning stage

18. Cathryn's **penetrating** stare seems to help her elicit the truth.

    A. rude   B. liquid   C. keen

19. The **per capita** income in Hartford, Connecticut, is relatively high.

    A. per person   B. reported   C. disposable

20. Her handling of customer complaints is too **perfunctory**.

    A. perfectionistic   B. tardy   C. uninterested

Select one of these words to complete each of the following sentences, and write the word in the space provided.

perpendicular   perpetual   picayune   pithy   plausible

21. We should analyze all _____ explanations of O'Grady & Mason's decline.

22. B Street is _____ to 15th Street.

23. We had a _____ stream of accidents until we instituted the safety program.

24. Jorge's _____ comments are few but worth waiting for.

25. Try to focus on the truly important problems instead of the _____.

Follow-up Word Study   Check your answers at the end of this chapter. In the spaces below, write the words that you spelled or used incorrectly. (Use a separate piece of paper if you missed more than five words.) Then look up each word in your dictionary, and carefully study its spelling, pronunciation, definition, and history (etymology). Finally, to help fix the word in your memory, write it in a sentence.

Word   Sentence

_____   _____

_____   _____

_____   _____

_____   _____

_____   _____

CHECK YOUR ANSWERS

Master Key Concepts

I. understand, controversial
   A. memo
   B. indirect

II. direct
   A. periodic
   B. chronologically

III. receptive
   A. resistance
   B. yardstick

IV. A. informal
    B. present
    C. previews, parallel, transitions

Quiz Yourself

1. When deciding on the length of a report, such factors as the subject, purpose, and nature of the audience should be taken into account. If the audience consists of strangers, if they are skeptical or hostile, or if the material is nonroutine and controversial, then you have to explain the points in more detail; the resulting report will be relatively long. On the other hand, the report can be brief if the audience is familiar to you and receptive and the information is routine or uncomplicated. Generally, short reports are more common than long ones. (p. 485)

2. Deciding on the basic structure of a report involves three issues:
   a. Selecting information. What information should you include, and what should you exclude? Should you cover all the material you've acquired in your research, or should you leave some things out?
   b. Selecting the direct or indirect approach. Which psychological approach is better—direct or indirect order? Should main ideas be presented early, or should they be introduced later in the report, after a discussion of the evidence that supports them?
   c. Structuring the ideas. Which method of subdivision will make the material both clear and convincing? Should the main ideas be categorized according to topics, or should they be grouped as points in a logical argument? (pp. 486–489)

3. Informational reports, which are designed to explain something in straightforward terms, are generally presented in direct order. Because informational reports do not attempt to persuade readers of anything, most readers react to informational reports in an unemotional way. For this reason, you do not have to worry about introducing ideas gradually to overcome resistance. (p. 489)

4. The two basic ways or organizing analytical reports are
   a. Around conclusions and recommendations
   b. Around logical arguments (pp. 491–503)

5. An analytical report based on recommendations generally follows this five-step sequence of points:
   a. Establish the need for action in the introduction, generally by briefly describing the problem or opportunity.
   b. Introduce the benefit that can be achieved, without providing any details.
   c. List the steps (recommendations) required to achieve the benefit, using action verbs for emphasis.
   d. Explain each step more fully, giving details on procedures, costs, and benefits.
   e. Summarize the recommendations. (p. 494)

6. When you want readers to concentrate on why your ideas make sense, your best bet is to let *logical arguments* provide the structure of the report. (p. 495)

7. Here are three possible organizational plans based on logical arguments:
   a. The 2 + 2 = 4 approach depends on the accumulation of evidence to persuade readers. The report is organized around a list of reasons that collectively support the main point you are trying to prove. The approach is useful when you have a variety of reasons for your conclusions or recommendations but no single reason that is particularly strong by itself.
   b. The scientific method evaluates alternative hypotheses to help readers work through the problem and understand the reasons for a solution. This structure runs through all the alternatives—good and bad.
   c. The yardstick approach uses stated criteria to evaluate a situation or a proposed program. It is useful when you want to demonstrate the need for action or the soundness of a proposal or when you want to compare alternatives. Its success depends on the readers' acceptance of the criteria. (pp. 496–503)

8. An informal tone presumes a closer relationship with the reader than a formal tone does. Reports with an informal tone use personal pronouns (*I* and *you*) and employ conversational language; reports written in a formal tone avoid the use of personal pronouns and of colorful language. They attempt to establish a businesslike, unemotional, objective relationship between the writer and the reader.

   An informal tone is generally appropriate for brief, internal documents. A formal tone is often adopted for longer reports dealing with controversial or complex information, particularly if the audience consists of outsiders. (p. 504)

9. It is acceptable to use either the past or the present tense, as long as you do not switch back and forth between the two. (pp. 504–505)

10. The opening of a report accomplishes these three things:
    a. Introducing the subject of the report
    b. Indicating why the subject is important
    c. Giving the reader a preview of the main ideas and their sequence (p. 505)

Develop Your Word Power

1. morale	6. noticeable	11. D	16. B	21. plausible
2. necessary	7. ninth	12. C	17. B	22. perpendicular
3. neighbors	8. municipal	13. A	18. C	23. perpetual
4. neither	9. *C*	14. E	19. A	24. pithy
5. ninety	10. noticing	15. B	20. C	25. picayune

Chapter 18

Completing Formal Reports and Proposals

The main point of Chapter 18 is that producing the final polished version of a formal report or proposal requires following an accepted format and sequence of parts. As you read the chapter, think about how the parts correspond to the parts for reports you have written for school. When you finish reading, check the guidelines in this chapter against a few formal business reports.

MASTER KEY CONCEPTS

Use the following terms to fill in the blanks in the outline. All terms are used, but none is used more than once.

acceptance	formal	prefatory	scope
appendixes	information	recommendations	synopsis
costs	organization	RFP	time

I. The production of a final version of a report may involve the interaction of a number of people and may make use of sophisticated computer equipment; whatever method is used, set aside enough _____ (p. 520) for a thorough job.

II. The more _____ (p. 521) a report, the more components you'll include.
   A. The _____ (p. 521) parts, which precede the text of the report, consist of a cover, an optional title fly, a title page, possibly a letter of authorization and a letter _____ (p. 521), a letter of transmittal, a table of contents, a list of illustrations (if needed), and a _____ (p. 521) or executive summary.
   B. The text of the report consists of three basic parts: the introduction, which establishes the purpose, _____ (p. 525), background, and organization of the report; the body, which presents the detailed _____ (p. 526) obtained during the study; and the final section, which contains the summary, conclusions, and any _____ (p. 526), plus source notes.
   C. The supplementary parts at the end of the report may include _____ (p. 547) containing additional related material, a bibliography, and an index.

III. Formal proposals contain many of the same components as formal reports.
   A. In addition to the cover, title fly, title page, contents, and list of illustrations, the prefatory section of a proposal usually contains a copy of the _____ (p. 548) issued by the client and a letter of transmittal; a synopsis or executive summary is not usually needed.
   B. The text of a proposal follows a prescribed format: The introduction usually includes subheadings for background or statement of the problem, overview of approach, scope, and _____ (p. 549); the body usually includes the proposed approach, the work plan, a statement of qualifications, and a breakdown of _____ (p. 549); there may be a brief summary, but there are rarely supplemental materials.

Check your answers at the end of this chapter.

QUIZ YOURSELF

1. How much time should you allow for typing a report? For editing a report?

2. What are the three basic divisions of a formal report?

3. List all the elements that might be included in the prefatory section of a formal report.

4. What differentiates a letter of authorization, a letter of acceptance, and a letter of transmittal?

5. What is the difference between an informative synopsis and a descriptive synopsis?

6. How does an executive summary differ from a synopsis?

7. What eight topics might you cover in the introduction of a long formal report?

8. How do summaries, conclusions, and recommendations vary in purpose?

9. What types of information might be included in an appendix?

10. What main element is found in the prefatory section of a proposal that is not found in the prefatory section of a formal report?

Check your answers at the end of this chapter.

BUILD YOUR SKILLS: ORGANIZE THESE REPORT ELEMENTS

You are leader of a team that, over the past eight months, has been researching opportunities in the airline industry. Now it's time to put together your report.

David Howley gives you a stack of papers that include
    A six-page section about government regulation of the airline industry
    A ten-page table that lists every major piece of government legislation affecting the airlines, along with a description of each law
    The conclusions section of the report

Jim Scofield gives you
    A two-page overview of the airline industry
    A ten-page section on the economic characteristics of airlines
    A five-page section on labor relations in the airline industry
    A seven-page computer printout that provides statistics on all current airlines, both national and commuter
    The bibliography for the report

Gail Bedrosian gives you
    A nine-page section describing the marketing aspects of the airline industry
    A six-page section that forecasts future trends in the airline industry

Joe Piper gives you
    A twelve-page section on types of aircraft being used
    A ten-page section on schedules for aircraft maintenance
    Sample aircraft maintenance schedules from United and American Airlines

Dorothy Howard gives you
    A nine-page section on methods of financing in the aircraft industry
    A seven-page section on flight scheduling and airport availability

You have in your files
    The letter of authorization for the research
    The letter of acceptance

You need to prepare
    The other prefatory parts of the report
    The introduction
    The recommendations

To simplify the task of putting all these elements together, prepare an outline that includes all the prefatory and supplementary parts for the report, as well as a final outline for the text of the report. Indicate where each existing element has come from and which elements still need to be prepared.

EXPAND YOUR KNOWLEDGE: IN BRIEF

The synopsis at the beginning of a report is a small but significant element. Some readers are interested only in the synopsis (and perhaps the conclusions and recommendations), because they have little time to read a long report or little interest in all the details that contribute to your findings. Even those readers who are willing to read the whole report tend to read the synopsis first. If it is poorly written, they may read no further or read with skepticism. However, a well-written synopsis gets readers thinking about the subject as you perceive it and helps them understand why it is important. Here are some guidelines to help you write a synopsis that does the job:

- *Include enough specific information about your investigation and/or analysis to satisfy the needs of a busy manager.* Do not assume that the manager will remember all the details of the assignment. Briefly recall the problem that led to the assignment and the limits that were set. Then cover the basics in the same general order that they are presented in the report.
- *Make the synopsis a self-contained unit, a complete report-in-miniature.* Write so that someone who does not have time to read the whole report can get the most important details from reading just the summary, or so that the summary can stand alone if it is circulated independently. If possible, eliminate references to parts of the report and to the report itself (such phrases as "this report contains").
- *Keep your synopsis short.* Synopses vary in length, depending on the length of the entire report, the ease with which the contents can be summarized, and the amount of detail that must be included in the synopsis. Some executives expect a synopsis to be a page long or a paragraph long or some other specific length corresponding to their needs or attention span; you may want to check existing reports or company style manuals for guidelines on this point. Usually, however, a synopsis should be no more than a tenth the length of the entire report—much shorter for a very long report. Aim to make your synopsis as short as possible while still covering all the important details.
- *Write your synopsis in fluent, easy-to-read prose.* Assume that readers are not familiar with jargon or are not experts in the subject of the report. Apply all the principles of writing clear, concise sentences and paragraphs to the synopsis, just as you would in writing any other letter, memo, or report.
- *Keep the tone and emphasis of the synopsis consistent with the tone and emphasis of the report.* Do not put any information or analysis into the synopsis that is not in the report. Make sure that your conclusions and recommendations are presented in the same way, with the same qualifications, in both places.

Although you will usually write the synopsis of your report last, take care to write it well. Schedule plenty of time for a first-class writing job and an objective review. The payoff may be that readers pay more attention to the whole report.

1. Can you boil things down to the bare essentials? Spend the next three minutes looking at your surroundings. Then summarize what you have seen in one paragraph, so that a complete stranger will get a reasonable idea of your environment.

2. With practice, you can improve your ability to synopsize. Each day for the next week, read a different article from a recent issue of a business magazine like *Fortune* or *Business Week.* Select articles of roughly the same length—three to five pages. After reading each article, write a 250-word synopsis. Keep track of how long it takes you to write these synopses.

DEVELOP YOUR WORD POWER

Spelling Challenge   Identify the misspelled word in each of the following sentences, and spell it correctly in the space provided. If all the words in a sentence are spelled correctly, write *C* in the space.

_____   1. We carry greeting cards for any ocassion.

_____   2. When did the accident ocurr?

_____   3. FastFood, Inc., is the offcal caterer to the U.S. team.

_____   4. How offen will I be required to travel out of town?

_____   5. The enclosed pamplet will tell you more about our line of shoes.

_____ 6. Please send at least partial payment for the items you ordered.

_____ 7. She has made numrous mistakes during her first week.

_____ 8. Has it ever occurred to you that you might have hurt his feelings?

_____ 9. The section on personal telephone calls has been ommitted from the new edition of the employee manual.

_____ 10. He had an oppertunity to apply for the position, but he didn't.

Vocabulary Challenge   Match the words in the first column with the definitions in the second column.

_____ 11. precaution   A. bias

_____ 12. precedent   B. harbinger

_____ 13. precursor   C. safeguard

_____ 14. predecessor   D. forerunner

_____ 15. predilection   E. model

Circle the best definition of the highlighted word in each of the following sentences.

16.   Give me a week to **ponder** your proposal.

   A. research   B. criticize   C. consider

17.   Their good sales figures for the past quarter should **precipitate** a major acquisition.

   A. dampen   B. hasten   C. precede

18.   Accounting experience does not **preclude** management experience as well.

   A. come before   B. make impossible   C. coincide with

19.   Bonnie works for the most **prestigious** law firm in the city.

   A. esteemed   B. tricky   C. wealthy

20.   Alan has a **prodigious** capacity for work.

   A. professional   B. modest   C. immense

Select one of these words to complete each of the following sentences, and write the word in the space provided.

    portfolio   **premise**   **proficiency**   **profusion**   **prognosis**

21. Past and present customers have supplied a _____ of suggestions, and we are working overtime to evaluate them all.

22. Larry's _____ in computing is what got him the job.

23. What is your _____ for the outcome of the new advertising campaign?

24. Mary's conclusion seemed reasonable, even though it was based on a faulty _____.

25. Ask all those interviewing for the graphic design position to bring a _____ containing samples of their most recent work.

Follow-up Word Study   Check your answers at the end of this chapter. In the spaces below, write the words that you spelled or used incorrectly. (Use a separate piece of paper if you missed more than five words.) Then look up each word in your dictionary, and carefully study its spelling, pronunciation, definition, and history (etymology). Finally, to help fix the word in your memory, write it in a sentence.

<u>Word</u>   <u>Sentence</u>

_____   _____

_____   _____

_____   _____

_____   _____

_____   _____

CHECK YOUR ANSWERS

Master Key Concepts

    I. time

    II. formal
        A. prefatory, acceptance, synopsis
        B. scope, information, recommendations
        C. appendixes

    III. A. RFP
          B. organization, costs

Quiz Yourself

1. You should allow at least an hour for every eight pages for typing, and 10 to 15 minutes a page for editing. (p. 520)

2. The three basic divisions of a formal report are the prefatory parts, the text, and the supplementary parts. (p. 521)

3. The prefatory section of a formal report may include these parts:
   a. Cover
   b. Title fly
   c. Title page
   d. Letter of authorization
   e. Letter of acceptance
   f. Letter of transmittal
   g. Table of contents
   h. List of illustrations
   i. Synopsis or executive summary (p. 521)

4. A letter of authorization is written by the person who requests the report. It generally discusses the problem, scope, time and money limitations, special instructions, and due date for the report. A letter of acceptance is a reply to the letter authorization, written by the person who is in charge of doing the study. It confirms the arrangements for doing the work. A letter of transmittal conveys the report from the writer to the reader. This letter is often merely a brief statement that effectively says, "Here is the report you asked for." However, in some situations, the letter of transmittal might be used to make certain comments "off the record" to some, but not all, of the audience. Or it might call attention to important points, make comments on side issues, suggest follow-up work, or convey helpful information about the background of the report. If the report does not have a synopsis, the transmittal letter might summarize the major findings, conclusions, and recommendations. (pp. 522–523)

5. An informative synopsis presents the main points of the report in the order in which they appear in the text. A descriptive synopsis states what the report is about and leaves out the actual findings of the report. (p. 523)

6. An executive summary is more comprehensive than a synopsis. It may contain headings, well-developed transitions, and visual aids, and it is generally about 10 percent as long as the overall document. (p. 524)

7. The introduction of a long formal report might cover these eight topics:
   a. Authorization: who asked for the report and who prepared it
   b. Problem/purpose: what the report is supposed to accomplish
   c. Scope: what is and is not covered in the report
   d. Backgrounds: conditions leading up to the report
   e. Sources and methods: how the research was conducted
   f. Definitions: explanations of unfamiliar terms
   g. Limitations: factors affecting the quality of the report
   h. Report organization: sequence of topics to be covered (p. 525)

8. The purpose of a summary is to present the key findings of a report. The purpose of the conclusions section is to analyze the meaning of the findings. The purpose of the recommendations section is to outline a course of action that should be taken based on the conclusions. (p. 527)

9. An appendix contains material that is related to the report but is too lengthy or bulky to include in the report or is not of direct or vital interest to the reader. Some typical items that might be placed in an appendix are sample questionnaires and cover letters, sample forms, computer printouts, statistical formulas, and a glossary of terms. (p. 547)

10. The main element found in the prefatory material for a proposal that is not found in a formal report is the RFP (request for proposal). (p. 547)

Develop Your Word Power

1. occasion	6. *C*	11. C	16. C	21. profusion
2. occur	7. numerous	12. E	17. B	22. proficiency
3. official	8. *C*	13. B	18. B	23. prognosis
4. often	9. omitted	14. D	19. A	24. premise
5. pamphlet	10. opportunity	15. A	20. C	25. portfolio

PART SIX
ORAL COMMUNICATION

Chapter 19

Listening, Interviewing, and Conducting Meetings

The main point of Chapter 19 is that the success of interviews and meetings relies greatly on the participants' listening and planning skills. As you read the chapter, think about how the "you" attitude and self-confidence might also help someone participate successfully in interviews and meetings. When you finish reading, categorize the problems that came up in an interview or meeting in which you participated, and speculate on the actions or attitudes that could have solved those problems.

MASTER KEY CONCEPTS

Use the following terms to fill in the blanks in the outline. All terms are used, but none is used more than once.

agenda	evaluation	interpersonal	negotiations
conversation	feedback	listening	nonverbal
disciplinary	group dynamics	minutes	open-ended

I. Oral communication—speaking and listening—saves time, provides opportunities for _____ (p. 568) and social interaction, and conveys nonverbal information, but it also limits the ability to edit one's thoughts, requires close attention, and is influenced by the speaker's appearance and delivery style.

   A. In business, you need to think before you speak, to adjust your speaking style to fit the situation, to be sure that your _____ (p. 569) signals are consistent with your words, and to use the "you" attitude.

   B. _____ (p. 570) is a process of five related activities: sensing, interpreting, evaluating, remembering, and responding; there are three types of listening, which differ in their purpose and in the amount of feedback that occurs: content listening, critical listening, and active or empathic listening.

   C. Considerable skill is required to cope with difficult situations that arise in business settings: _____ (p. 572) conflicts, resistance to your ideas, and _____ (p. 572).

II. A business interview is a planned _____ (p. 575) with a predetermined purpose that involve asking and answering questions.

   A. Interviews can be categorized as job interviews, information interviews, persuasive interviews, exit interviews, _____ (pp. 575–576) interviews, counseling interviews, conflict-resolution interviews, _____ (p. 576) interviews, and termination interviews.

B. When planning an interview, you need to think about the kinds of questions you will ask and the structure of the interview. The four basic types of interview questions are _____ (pp. 577–578) questions that invite the interviewee to offer an opinion, direct open-ended questions, closed-ended questions, and restatement questions; the sequence of questions depends on the purpose of the interview, but the interview should always have an opening, a body, and a close.

III. Meetings are called to solve problems or share information.
A. A meeting's success depends in great part on the interactions and processes that take place—the _____ (p. 580); members take on various roles, are governed by unwritten norms, and make decisions in a predictable pattern.
B. The key to productive meetings is careful planning of purpose, participants, _____ (pp. 583–584), and location.
C. The meeting leader's duties include pacing the meeting, appointing a note taker, following the agenda, stimulating participation and discussion, summarizing the debate, reviewing recommendations, and circulating copies of the _____ (p. 585).

Check your answers at the end of this chapter.

QUIZ YOURSELF

1. Describe the process you should use for effective oral communication.

2. List and briefly describe the five stages of the listening process.

3. List three forms of listening, and indicate the goals of each.

4. What are seven measures a manager might take to help resolve a conflict to the satisfaction of both parties?

5. What are three main measures you can take to overcome resistance and defuse explosive situations?

6. Define the term "business interview."

7. What is a persuasive interview?

8. Briefly describe four basic types of interview questions.

9. What are the four phases of the group decision-making process?

10. List four main steps that meeting leaders can take during the planning stage to ensure that meetings will be productive.

Check your answers at the end of this chapter.

BUILD YOUR SKILLS: PLAN YOUR HIGH-STAKES INTERVIEW

To develop your ability to handle challenging interviews, try your hand at planning your strategy for asking for a raise. Use a current or past job as a frame of reference, or invent a job. Write down your plan for conducting the conversation with your boss. Include a list of questions you should ask, points you want to make, and responses you can give to your boss's possible objections.

EXPAND YOUR KNOWLEDGE: HOW TO NEGOTIATE LIKE A PRO

The point of many business interviews and meetings is to negotiate something: a job offer, a raise in pay, a new office or assignment, a contract for work, a purchase. What all these situations have in common is that they bring together two or more parties with competing needs and interests who nevertheless must come to some agreement. The process by which that agreement is reached is called negotiating.

A lot of people are afraid of negotiating. True, some "hard-ball" types don't consider a negotiation successful unless they win and the other party loses. This sort of negotiation is understandably somewhat intimidating. Most people, however, approach a negotiation with much the same feeling: a simple desire to get what they need. They do not have any particular desire to win at the other party's expense.

How can you negotiate successfully? The following list refines the general advice offered in the text, breaking it into specific tasks:

- *Know what you need and what you would like.* The minimum acceptable outcome—what you need—is the ammunition you keep in reserve. But aim for the ideal solution; you just might get it. The secret is to have confidence that your needs are legitimate and that your desires are justified.
- *Accentuate the positive.* Always negotiate for something positive, never against something negative. A positive attitude is easier for the other party to accept—and therefore is more effective. Also remember that negotiation is a compromise; you will get some of what you want, and the other party will get some of what it wants. Assume that both parties can find some common ground, and plan on doing your best to reach it.
- *Prepare, prepare, prepare.* Learn all you can in advance about the other party's strengths, weaknesses, goals, and motives. Don't assume that the other party's goals are the same as yours. If hard data about the other party aren't available, develop some reasonable hunches. Then get all the facts so that you can explain why your position is a good deal for everyone. The more facts you have, the more convincing you will be. Finally, rehearse the negotiation with a colleague who can play the role of the other party.

- *Be ethical.* Don't risk losing your credibility by being tricky or deceitful. The other party is probably just as worried as you are about taken advantage of. But if you demonstrate that you can be trusted, you probably will be.
- *Negotiate from physical as well as moral strength.* You need to be rested and alert to do your best in a situation like this. A comfortable environment is important too, so do what you can to find suitable seating and to regulate the temperature and lighting to your liking.
- *Use the "you" attitude to encourage the other party's cooperation.* Avoid being judgmental; adopt a helpful, cooperative stance; look for the real meaning behind the other party's words. Then, when it's time to present your proposal, try to put it in terms of benefits to the other party. If you can, let the other party seem to come up with the best ideas and to get the better deal.
- *Present yourself as a human being.* You are an individual with your own style, just as the other party is. Be yourself. Don't be afraid to let the other party know that you have a life beyond the negotiating table.
- *Stay flexible.* Examine the issue from every possible angle. You may come up with a compromise that is fairer to both parties than your original solution. Remember, too, that money isn't everything. Focusing too much on the financial aspects of the issue may cause you to neglect other, more important points.
- *Remain cool, calm, and collected.* Don't let yourself be rushed; set your own pace. If the other party tries to push for a quick agreement or bully you into accepting a solution you won't be happy with, stand your ground. And if you are faced with someone who seems determined to provoke you, don't overreact. Remain the capable professional that you are, and keep on negotiating.
- *Be a gracious winner.* If you gloat over your victory, you can win the battle but lose the war; that is, you can get what you want but destroy any future relationship with the other party. Remember that the other party not only has needs for a certain outcome of negotiations but also has the human need to save face. Exercise your tact.
- *Get any agreement in writing.* In the process of writing out the agreement, issues are often clarified. And signing on the dotted line cements the negotiated agreement.

The ability to negotiate successfully enhances your job satisfaction and may increase your financial rewards, to give it your best effort.

1. Everyday life is full of situations that involve negotiation—although few people are conscious of "bargaining" with friends or relatives. But the next time you are in a situation that involves two opposing views—yours and someone else's—try to negotiate like a pro. The issue may be which movie to attend, where to go for dinner, who cleans what, or any of a host of other routine decisions. Do you find that behaving like a professional negotiator gives you an edge in convincing the other person to agree with you?

2. Identify a time in your life when you have been involved in an important negotiation—perhaps buying a car, convincing your parents to let you do something, or making housing arrangements with friends. Was the outcome totally satisfactory? Did you consciously or unconsciously apply any of the principles of negotiation listed here? If you have it to do over again, what would you do differently?

DEVELOP YOUR WORD POWER

Spelling Challenge   Identify the misspelled word in each of the following sentences, and spell it correctly in the space provided. If all the words in a sentence are spelled correctly, write *C* in the space.

_____ 1. Do you preceive any differences between this loaf and that one?

_____ 2. Julie is persistant and should eventually find a job she wants.

_____   3. Try to persuade Mr. Mitchell to send full payment tomorrow.

_____   4. Do you have any phisical problems that may affect your work?

_____   5. Greg's preferrence is the oak finish.

_____   6. The urge to avoid all taxes is quite prevalent.

_____   7. I would have preferred to discuss this matter in private.

_____   8. In about a week, we will install the permenent awning.

_____   9. Your visit Monday was a pleasent surprise.

_____   10. Having some of the new models is preferrable to having none.

Vocabulary Challenge   Match the words in the first column with the definitions in the second column.

_____   11. prohibitive   A. exciting

_____   12. provisional   B. repetitive

_____   13. provocative   C. forbidding

_____   14. redundant   D. negligent

_____   15. remiss   E. temporary

Circle the best definition of the highlighted word in each of the following sentences.

16. Dr. Jepson has been a **prolific** writer.

    A. productive   B. antiabortion   C. wordy

17. The new lobby will **protrude** into the courtyard.

    A. meld   B. project   C. flow

18. What does the letter from their attorney **purport**?

    A. say   B. recommend   C. signify

19. Jeff's career has been his **raison d'être**.

    A. constant problem   B. means of support   C. reason for being

20. Remember to **recapitulate** at the end of your presentation.

    A. summarize   B. surrender   C. retrench

Select one of these words to complete each of the following sentences, and write the word in the space provided.

| **propensity** | **protégé** | **proxy** | **rendezvous** | **repertoire** |

21. Sylvia has a _____ for accepting more work than she can handle.

22. What other skills do you have in your _____?

23. You will be my _____ during my absence.

24. Miss Blackmer's _____ is being groomed to take over when she retires.

25. They have scheduled a _____ for discussing the details face to face.

Follow-up Word Study   Check your answers at the end of this chapter. In the spaces below, write the words that you spelled or used incorrectly. (Use a separate piece of paper if you missed more than five words.) Then look up each word in your dictionary, and carefully study its spelling, pronunciation, definition, and history (etymology). Finally, to help fix the word in your memory, write it in a sentence.

Word   Sentence

_____   _____

_____   _____

_____   _____

_____   _____

_____   _____

CHECK YOUR ANSWERS

Master Key Concepts

I. feedback
    A. nonverbal
    B. listening
    C. interpersonal, negotiations

II. conversation
     A. evaluation, disciplinary
     B. open-ended

III. A. group
        dynamics
     B. agenda
     C. minutes

Quiz Yourself

1. To communicate effectively, you should apply the same process to oral communication as you use in written communication. Before you speak, think about your purpose, your main idea, and your audience. Organize your thoughts in a logical way; decide on a style that suits the occasion; then

edit your remarks mentally. Revise your message if it does not appear to be having the desired effect on your listeners. (p. 569)

2. The five stages of the listening process are
    a. Sensing—physically hearing the message and taking note of it
    b. Interpreting—decoding and absorbing the message
    c. Evaluating—forming an opinion about the message
    d. Remembering—storing a message for future reference
    e. Responding—acknowledging the message by reacting to the speaker in some fashion (p. 570)

3. Three forms of listening are
    a. Content listening, in which the goal is to understand and retain information imparted by a speaker
    b. Critical listening, in which the goal is to evaluate the message
    c. Active or empathic listening, in which the goal is to understand the speaker's feelings, needs, and wants in order to solve a problem (pp. 570–571)

4. Seven measures a manager might use to help resolve a conflict are
    a. Deal with a minor conflict promptly, before it becomes major.
    b. Get those most directly involved to participate in solving the conflict.
    c. Get feelings out in the open before dealing with the main issues.
    d. Seek reasons for the problem before seeking solutions.
    e. Don't let either party become "locked into" one position.
    f. Don't let either party hide behind the rules to avoid a fair solution.
    g. Try to get parties to fight together against an outside force. (p. 573)

5. To overcome resistance and defuse an explosive situation,
    a. Express understanding; show sympathy for the other person's situation so that he or she will relax and talk about his or her anxiety.
    b. Make the person aware of the resistance; point out how the person is displaying resistance, but do not do so in an accusing way.
    c. Evaluate objections fairly; find out the basis for the other person's resistance. (pp. 573–574)

6. A business interview is a planned conversation with a predetermined purpose that involve asking and answering questions. (p. 575)

7. A persuasive interview is one in which you try to convince the other person of something. Persuasive interviews are often associated with selling. You discuss the other person's needs and show how your produce or concept is able to fulfill those needs. (p. 575)

8. The four basic types of interview questions are
    a. Open-ended questions, which invite the interviewee to offer an opinion as opposed to a yes-or-no or one-word answer
    b. Direct open-ended questions, which suggest a specific response
    c. Closed-ended questions, which require a yes-or-no or one-word answer
    d. Restatement questions, which restate an interviewee's answer in order to invite a more detailed response (pp. 577–578)

9. The four stages in group decision making are
    a. Orientation phase
    b. Conflict phase
    c. Emergency phase
    d. Reinforcement phase (p. 582)

10. Meeting planners need to
    a. Determine the purpose—is the meeting really needed?
    b. Select the participants, inviting only those whose presence is essential.
    c. Set the agenda and distribute it so participants will be prepared.
    d. Prepare the location, recognizing that setting and facilities can have a significant impact on the meeting. (pp. 583–584)

Develop Your Word Power

1. perceive	6. *C*	11. C	16. A	21. propensity
2. persistent	7. *C*	12. E	17. B	22. repertoire
3. *C*	8. permanent	13. A	18. C	23. proxy
4. physical	9. pleasant	14. B	19. C	24. protégé
5. preference	10. preferable	15. D	20. A	25. rendezvous

Chapter 20

Giving Speeches and Oral Presentations

The main point of Chapter 20 is that speeches and oral presentations require just as much preparation and skillful execution as a formal report does. As you read the chapter, think about the parallels between these "oral reports" and their written cousins. When you finish reading, analyze the strengths and weaknesses of someone else's speech or oral presentation; then list ways that the weaknesses could have been overcome.

MASTER KEY CONCEPTS

Use the following terms to fill in the blanks in the outline. All terms are used, but none is used more than once.

audience	location	presentations	summarizing
handouts	notes	purpose	transitions
idea	positive	stage fright	visual aids
interest			

I. Although they resemble any other message, speeches and _____ (p. 592) are delivered orally under relatively public circumstances, so they require a few special communication techniques.
   A. The first step in preparing for a speech or presentation is to define the _____ (pp. 592–593), which helps determine content, style, and amount of audience interaction.
   B. The second step in preparing to speak is to analyze the _____ (p. 593), including its size, composition, and attitude.
   C. The third step in preparing to speak is to plan your strategy: developing the main _____ (p. 594), developing an outline, estimating length, and deciding on the style.

II. When preparing a speech or oral presentation, you must use special techniques to develop the various elements: the introduction, the body, the close, the questions-and-answer period, and the _____ (p. 601).
   A. In the introduction of your speech you need to arouse the audience's _____ (p. 601), build credibility, and preview the topics to be covered.
   B. In the body of your speech, you can help the audience understand by emphasizing structure, that is, by _____ (p. 603) your remarks as you go along and by providing _____ (p. 603) from one idea to the next; you also need to make a special effort to keep the audience's attention.
   C. In your final summary you should restate the main points, outline any specific actions that should be taken, and end on a _____ (pp. 604–605) note.
   D. Give people an opportunity to ask questions either during or after the talk.
   E. When preparing visual aids for your talk, make sure they are necessary and useful; among media to choose from are _____ (pp. 607–608) for members of the audience, chalkboards, flip charts, overheads, and slides.

III. You have a variety of methods to choose from when delivering your talk, including memorizing the speech, reading it, speaking from _____ (p. 609), and impromptu speaking.
   A. Before you speak, you should practice your presentation and try to check out the _____ (p. 609) in advance.
   B. When delivering the speech, you can use a number of techniques to overcome _____ (p. 611) and to keep the attention and interest of the audience.
   C. Prepare in advance for questions that may arise during the question-and-answer period; give short, direct, unemotional answers to questions.

Check your answers at the end of this chapter.

QUIZ YOURSELF

1. Briefly describe three main purposes for presentations, and explain how each affects the amount of audience interaction.

2. What are the main things you should learn about your audience when preparing for a speech or presentation?

3. How should a short (ten minutes or less) speech be organized? How should a longer speech be organized?

4. What is involved in estimating the length of a speech or presentation?

5. In general, when would you use a casual, informal style in a presentation, and when would you use a more formal approach?

6. What are the three main tasks to be accomplished in the introduction to a speech or presentation?

7. List three things you can do to hold audience attention during a speech.

8. Briefly describe some of the most commonly used visual aids for speeches and oral presentations.

9. Briefly describe the four speech delivery modes. When might you use each approach?

10. List at least five things you could do to overcome stage fright.

Check your answers at the end of this chapter.

BUILD YOUR SKILLS: PLAN YOUR FIVE-MINUTE SPEECH

You have been asked to prepare a five-minute speech about your school to present to a group of high school seniors who are deciding which college to attend. You don't know any of the students, but you have been told that they are 25 high achievers from Des Moines, Iowa, who are visiting your campus and others. Write out a plan for this speech.

EXPAND YOUR KNOWLEDGE: A MASTER'S VOICE

When an audience cannot hear the speaker or is lulled into inattention by the qualify of the speaker's voice, the communication process is impeded. An authoritative and compelling voice is not easy to develop, but you can improve the way you sound by diligent practice.

Producing Words

Most people have trouble concentrating on the content of a speech when the speaker has problems with pronunciation (correctness) or articulation (distinctness). To improve your pronunciation, make sure you know the correct way to say every word that is likely to be used in your speech. If in doubt, consult the pronunciation key in a dictionary.

You can begin attacking any articulation problems you may have by trying these exercises:

- Sit about 15 feet away from a friend in an unoccupied room. Then converse in a whisper. Your friend will not be able to understand what you are saying unless you articulate carefully.
- Say these sounds rapidly while exaggerating your lip movements: *oo, ee, oo, ah, oo, ee, oo, ah.* Then, exaggerating your lip and tongue movements, say these sounds: *pppppp pah, pppppp pay, pppppp pee, bbbbbb bah, bbbbbb bay, bbbbbb bee, ttttt tah, ttttt tay, ttttt tee, dddddd, dah, dddddd day, dddddd dee.*
- Make a list of the sounds that you have trouble articulating. While you say words that contain these sounds, record your voice and look in a mirror. Watch how your lips, jaw, and tongue move as you articulate the words correctly and incorrectly; close your eyes and feel the differences too. Finally, listen critically to the tape.
- Make a list of the common words that you tend to articulate carelessly, such as *jist* and *git.* Every week, select one or two of these words and make a point of articulating them correctly in your everyday conversations.

Your accent may cause problems too, but only if it differs considerably from what your audience is used to. People with unusually heavy accents—foreign or domestic—may find it worthwhile to consult a speech therapist for help in developing a general American accent.

Producing Tones

The first step in developing your ability to produce tones that can reach and excite an audience is to record your voice. Try some general conversation, an extemporaneous speech, and prose and poetry reading. When you play back the tape, take notes about the loudness of your voice, the variety in your voice's rate and pitch, and its tone of pleasantness.

If the loudness of your voice seems to be a problem, try some of these exercises:

- Practice speaking louder or softer (as necessary) in your everyday conversations.
- Speak from the front of an unused classroom with a friend sitting two feet away, then in one of the front rows, then in the middle of the room, then in the back row. Your friend can use hand signals to tell you when your voice is too soft or too loud. Remember that when speaking to an audience, your goal is to project your voice to the back row.
- While talking normally, observe in a mirror the amount of space between your upper and lower teeth. Observe the jaw movements and the space between your teeth that produce the appropriate voice volume.

Here are some exercises for developing vocal variety:

- To learn how to vary your speaking rate, count or recite the alphabet at different speeds.
- Read aloud several literary passages. Speak slowly when reading the serious passages; speak more quickly when reading the lighter passages.
- Draw slash lines to indicate appropriate pauses between groups of words in a literary passage. Then read the passage, pausing at each slash line. When you finish, draw a different set of slash lines and read again; notice how the meaning seems to change.
- Practice using volume for variety. Read a passage, count, or recite the alphabet in several different ways: starting out with a soft voice that gradually becomes louder, starting loudly and ending softly, and then emphasizing selected words of phrases by speaking either more loudly or more softly than the normal volume.
- Limber up the pitch you use by counting in different tones; start with the lowest note your voice can comfortably reach, and progress to the highest note—as if you were doing vocal scales. Then start counting from the highest note and progress to the lowest note. Finally, experiment with pitch as you read a literary passage.

If you need to improve the tone of pleasantness in your voice, try these:

- Pretend that you are different sorts of people as you count or recite the alphabet: a conceited snob; someone sincere and genuine; a bitter, malicious person; a caring friend; a listless, lifeless person; a healthy, vigorous, enthusiastic person; someone who is insensitive and intolerant; a sensitive, obliging, helpful person.
- To come across as an interesting speaker, you must be an interesting person. As you conduct your life, try to become more aware of the things you see, hear, smell, taste, and touch. Become more sensitive to ideas, feelings, and beauty. Your discoveries will help you put more meaning into your words.

1. The quality of your voice depends to a great extent on how well you breathe. To test your breath control, take a deep, deep breath, and then gradually exhale, letting the air hiss out through slightly pursed lips. Time yourself. How long does it take you to exhale?

2. How articulate are you: Test yourself on these tongue twisters:

> Betty Botta bought some butter.
> "But," she said, "this butter's bitter.
> If I put it in my batter,
> It will make by batter bitter.
> But a bit of better butter
> Will make my bitter batter better."

So she bought a bit of butter—
Better than the bitter butter—
And it made her bitter batter better.
So 'twas better Betty Botta
Bought a bit of better butter.

Theophilus Thistle, the successful thistle sifter, in sifting a sieve full of unsifted thistles, thrust three thousand thistles through the thick of his thumb. Now if Theophilus Thistle, the successful thistle sifter, in sifting a sieve full of unsifted thistles, thrust three thousand thistles through the thick of his thumb, see that thou, in sifting a sieve full of unsifted thistles, thrust not three thousand thistles through the thick of thy thumb. Success to the successful thistle sifter.

Luke Luck likes lakes.
Luck's duck likes lakes.
Luke Luck licks lakes.
Luke's duck licks lakes.
Duck takes licks
In lakes Luke Luck likes.
Luke Luck takes licks
In lakes Luck's duck likes.

DEVELOP YOUR WORD POWER

Spelling Challenge   Identify the misspelled word in each of the following sentences, and spell it correctly in the space provided. If all the words in a sentence are spelled correctly, write *C* in the space.

_____ 1. We should establish a prosedure for handling returns.

_____ 2. Dr. Stein is a promenent psychologist.

_____ 3. At the next meeting, let's persue the idea of reorganizing.

_____ 4. Your losses in the second quarter may be bigger than you realise.

_____ 5. How many responses did we receive?

_____ 6. Try to avoid a recurence of that unfortunate episode.

_____ 7. All moving parts are replicible within 30 days of purchase.

_____ 8. It is my priviledge to recommend Samuel Sharpe for the award.

_____ 9. The questionnaire has 50 items on two pages.

_____ 10. I didn't reconnize any of the names on the list.

Vocabulary Challenge   Match the words in the first column with the definitions in the second column.

_____ 11. repugnant   A. firm

_____ 12. resilient   B. severe

_____ 13. rigorous   C. doubtful

_____ 14. skeptical   D. offensive

_____ 15. steadfast   E. buoyant

Circle the best definition of the highlighted word in each of the following sentences.

16. We recommend **retention** of all register receipts for at least five years.

   A. analysis   B. keeping   C. memorization

17. A new vacation policy is **retroactive** to January 1.

   A. effective to a past date   B. scheduled for review   C. effective to a future date

18. In **retrospect**, we can be proud of our modest gains during that period.

   A. looking back   B. all due modesty   C. conclusion

19. He has **reverted** to his old habit of smoking.

   A. referred   B. returned   C. become hostile

20. Her **savoir faire** is an asset in dealing with clients.

   A. nice appearance   B. bubbly personality   C. diplomacy and tact

Select one of these words to complete each of the following sentences, and write the word in the space provided.

   reprimand   reproach   respite   stalemate   stigma

21. Christmas Day is only a brief _____ in the hectic Christmas shopping season.

22. With time, you will overcome the _____ of bankruptcy.

23. Until we resolve this _____, we cannot negotiate further.

24. Robert's handling of the situation is beyond _____.

25. A formal _____ should make our extreme displeasure clear.

Follow-up Word Study   Check your answers at the end of this chapter. In the spaces below, write the words that you spelled or used incorrectly. (Use a separate piece of paper if you missed more than five words.) Then look up each word in your dictionary, and carefully study its spelling, pronunciation, definition, and history (etymology). Finally, to help fix the word in your memory, write it in a sentence.

Word   Sentence

_____   _____

_____   _____

_____   _____

_____   _____

_____   _____

_____

CHECK YOUR ANSWERS

_____

Master Key Concepts

I. presentations
   A. purpose
   B. audience
   C. idea

II. visual aids
   A. interest
   B. summarizing, transitions
   C. positive
   E. handouts

III. notes
   A. location
   B. stage fright

Quiz Yourself

1. The three main purposes of speeches and oral presentations are
   a. To motivate or entertain, in which case the audience plays essentially a passive role
   b. To inform or analyze, in which case the speaker and audience interact somewhat
   c. To persuade or collaborate, in which case the speaker and audience interact considerably (p. 592)

2. When analyzing the audience for a speech or presentation, you should find out its size, its composition, people's likely reaction to what you have to say, their level of understanding, and their relationship with you. (p. 593)

3. A short speech should be organized like a letter or brief memo, using the direct approach if the subject involves routine information or good news and using the indirect approach if the subject involves bad news or persuasion.

   A longer speech should be organized like a formal report, using a direct approach if the purpose is to entertain, motivate, or inform, and using conclusions/recommendations or a logical argument if the purpose is to analyze, persuade, or collaborate. (p. 595)

4. When estimating the length of a speech or presentation, you should keep in mind that the average speaker talks at the rate 125 to 150 words a minute, which is approximately one paragraph. You need to allot a reasonable amount of time for your introduction, your conclusion, and the question-and-answer session. If you deduct this time from the overall time allotted, you will know the number of minutes remaining for the body of your speech. (p. 599)

5. You would use a casual, informal style for a relatively small group, especially if you want audience participation. You would use a formal tone if you are addressing a large audience or if it is an important occasion. (p. 600)

6. The three main tasks to be accomplished in the introduction of a talk are arousing audience interest, building credibility, and previewing the presentation. (p. 601)

7. Ways to hold audience attention during a speech include
   a. Relating your subject to the audience's needs.
   b. Using clear, vivid language.
   c. Explaining the relationship between your subject and familiar ideas. (p. 604)

8. The most commonly used visual aids are
   a. Handouts: papers that the audience can refer to after the presentation to remind themselves of important ideas. Handouts may be given to the audience before or after the presentation.
   b. Chalkboards and whiteboards: useful in illustrating points during a presentation.
   c. Flip charts: large sheets of paper, attached at the top like a tablet and propped against an easel. The speaker can either prepare the charts in advance or create them on the spot as the presentation progresses.
   d. Overheads: transparent sheets of film, with information written or drawn on them, that can be projected on a screen in full daylight, or images of any regular typed or printed material that can be cast on a screen with the use of a special projector.
   e. Slides: mounted pieces of film showing either text or visual material that are projected on a screen in a darkened room. Slides must be prepared in advance; showing slides tends to limit audience interaction.
   f. Computers: when attached to special projectors, this technology allows you to create and modify your visual aids as the presentation unfolds. (pp. 607–608)

9. The four delivery modes and their characteristics are as follows:
   a. Memorizing: committing all or part of the speech to memory, word for word. This is not generally a good way to deliver an entire speech or presentation, but it is often an effective technique for the introduction, the conclusion, or special quotations or stories.
   b. Reading: delivering a prepared script by reading it verbatim. Reading is an appropriate approach when precise wording is necessary and is often used for delivering policy statements and technical papers. Reading has the disadvantage of limiting eye contact and interaction with the audience.
   c. Speaking from notes: speaking in a conversational way with the help of notes, transparencies, or an outline. This method permits eye contact and audience interaction and gives the speaker flexibility to deviate from the planned material. Notes are used for most decision-making presentations and for many brief speeches.
   d. Impromptu speaking: delivering remarks spontaneously, without any advance preparation. Impromptu speaking is not recommended for long, formal presentations, but it is appropriate for responding to questions during a meeting. (p. 609)

10. Things you can do to overcome stage fright include
    a. Prepare more material than necessary.
    b. Think positively about your audience, yourself, and what you have to say.
    c. Be realistic about stage fright.
    d. Before going on tell yourself that you're ready.
    e. Have your first sentence memorized.
    f. If your throat is dry, drink some water.
    g. Don't panic.
    h. Use visual aids to maintain audience interest.
    i. Keep going.
    j. Concentrate on your message and audience, not on yourself. (p. 611)

Develop Your Word Power

1. procedure	6. recurrence	11. D	16. B	21. respite
2. prominent	7. replaceable	12. E	17. A	22. stigma
3. pursue	8. privilege	13. B	18. A	23. stalemate
4. realize	9. *C*	14. C	19. B	24. reproach
5. *C*	10. recognize	15. A	20. C	25. reprimand

PART SEVEN

SPECIAL TOPICS IN BUSINESS COMMUNICATION

Component Chapter A

Format and Layout of Business Documents

The main point of Component Chapter A is that conscientious attention to format and layout makes business documents more effective by helping them get to the right person, makes an impression of professionalism, and tells the recipient who wrote them and when. As you read the chapter, think about how the various elements of format and layout contribute to these goals. When you finish reading, study some business documents that you have received for real-life variations on the patterns recommended in this chapter.

MASTER KEY CONCEPTS

Use the following terms to fill in the blanks in the outline. All terms are used, but none is used more than once.

agendas	complimentary	mailing	reference
attention	correspondence	memo-letters	salutation
block	internationally	minutes	simplified
centered	letterhead	paper	thirds

I. Readers unconsciously judge business _____ (p. 618) on the basis of appearance: neatness, professionalism, and reading ease.
   A. High-quality _____ (p. 618) of a standard size and color is especially important in letters and other correspondence directed to outsiders.
   B. Letters to outsiders are commonly written on _____ (p. 619) stationery, which has the company name and address and other information printed at the top; internal documents, such as memos and standardized reports, are often typed on printed forms designed to highlight the required information in minimal space.
   C. To make the best impression, letters are _____ (p. 619) on the page with good-size margins all around; the proper spacing should be used after all punctuation; and the typing should appear clean, dark, and neat.

II. Regardless of their content, letters have certain standard parts and optional additional parts and are generally arranged in one of three basic letter styles.
   A. Business letters typically have seven standard parts: (1) heading, usually in the form of a letterhead; (2) date; (3) inside address identifying the recipient of the letter; (4) _____ (p. 622), a greeting to the recipient; (5) body, or main message; (6) _____ (p. 623) close, a word or two of courtesy to conclude the letter; and (7) a signature block.
   B. Depending on the requirements of the letter, any combination of these additional letter parts may also be used: addressee notations indicating special handling required for delivering the letter; _____ (p. 623) line identifying the recipient when the inside address

does not include the name of a specific person; subject line telling the recipient what the letter is about; second-page heading for long letters; company name in the signature block if it does not appear in the letterhead; _____ (p. 625) initials indicating who typed and who composed the letter; enclosure notation indicating the inclusion of additional materials; copy notation indicating the names of those who are receiving copies of the letter, preferably in order of rank or in alphabetical order; _____ (p. 626) notation indicating special mailing procedures; and postscript, which is an afterthought or a message requiring special emphasis.

C. The three most common formats for business letters are the _____ (p. 626) format, in which each part of the letter begins at the left margin; the modified block format, in which all items begin at the left except for the date, complimentary close, and typewritten name, which start in the center of the page; and the _____ (p. 626) format, in which the salutation and complimentary close are eliminated.

III. Envelopes should match the company letterhead and are sized to accommodate the stationery.
A. Envelopes contain two blocks of copy—the sender's name and address and the recipient's name and address—both of which should conform to U.S. Postal Service standards.
B. An 8-1/2-by-11-inch piece of paper can be folded in _____ (p. 631) lengthwise to fit in a standard No. 10 envelope; if it must be sent in a smaller envelope, it should first be folded in half and then in thirds.

IV. When sending mail _____ (p. 631), remember that postal service differs from country to country.

V. Clarity, careful arrangement, and neatness are important in internal memos, whether they are typed on preprinted forms or on plain paper; the heading identifies the date, writer, recipient, and subject; the complimentary close is eliminated.

VI. Special time-saving message formats reduce the amount of time spent typing and writing messages: _____ (p. 634) are printed like memos but provide space for an inside address so the message can be folded and sent in a window envelope; short-note replies are responses written at the bottom of original documents instead of on a new piece of paper; letterhead postcards bear the organization's name and address and may also be preprinted with a list of responses that the "writer" can check off.

VII. When laying out reports, special attention should be paid to margins, headings, spacing, indents, and page numbers.

VIII. Two types of documents are used in connection with meetings: _____ (p. 636) are outlines of the topics that will be covered in a meeting, and _____ (p. 636) are the official notes of what has occurred during the meeting.

Check your answers at the end of this chapter.

QUIZ YOURSELF

1. What items of information are frequently provided in a company's letterhead? Why might a company decide to limit the number of items included in the letterhead?

2. What are the seven standard parts of a letter?

3. Give two examples of an acceptable complimentary close.

4. Letters that have a restricted readership or that must be handled in a special way should include

    such _____ as "Personal," "Confidential," or "Please Forward."

5. What do these notations mean?

    a. cc

    b. pc

    c. c

    d. bc

    e. bcc

    f. bpc

6. Letters may be classified according to the style of punctuation they use. _____,
    or mixed, punctuation uses a colon after the salutation (a comma if the letter is social or personal)

    and a comma after the complimentary close. _____ punctuation uses no colon
    or comma after the salutation or the complimentary close.

7. What format is used for typing an envelope?

8. What order should be used for the names on a memo's distribution list?

9. Organizations that often deal with individuals by mail frequently have _____
    preprinted with a list of responses; the "writer" merely checks the appropriate response.

10. What are the items that typically appear on an agenda?

Check your answers at the end of this chapter.

BUILD YOUR SKILLS: FIX THE FORMAT

Your secretary is on vacation, and a student is filling in. You assumed that everyone knows how to format a business letter, but you were wrong. The student presented the following letter for your signature. Using arrows to show where things should be moved and little boxes to show where blank lines should be left (one for each line), mark the letter for retyping.

ECO-CARE DISPOSAL SERVICES, INC.
2572 North Pine
Davenport, Iowa 52804
319/287-3892

June 21, 1995

Miss Marybeth Cosentino

Subject: Dumpsters for new apartment buildings

Hagedorn Property Services, Inc.

2809 Fair Avenue, Suite 101

Davenport, Iowa 52803

Dear Ms. Cosentino:

Congratulations on finishing the new Davenport Gardens complex. We look forward to helping you keep it clean and tidy.

Your dumpsters have been ordered from the factory and should arrive sometime next week. As soon as the dumpsters arrive, I will call you to set up delivery to Davenport Gardens.

Keep us in mind as you put the finishing touches on the complex. We'd be pleased to send over one of our experienced clean-up crews if you find the scheduled completion date approaching too quickly.

gw

Sincerely,

Lou Shafer, Manager

Residential Services

PS: After only a little negotiation, the factory agreed to use the custom paint color you asked for. The plant manager liked it so much that he supposedly has repainted his office Davenport Beige!

pc: Dana Evans, Traffic Department

EXPAND YOUR KNOWLEDGE: HOW TO CREATE A WINNING IMPRESSION

"When clients come to us for letterhead, what they really want is a corporate-image program," says Tom Michael, head of Graphic Designers, Inc. "They want a trademark or logo—a symbol, word, or mark—that they can use to identify their company and to distinguish it from others." Michael's firm has designed corporate-image programs for such clients as Honda, Johnson & Johnson, Bristol-Meyers, Warner Brothers, and the Bank of America. Some clients want Michael's company to design only the bare essentials, such as letterhead and envelopes. Others want him to go a step further and show them how their trademark can be used in ads and on signs, T-shirts, shopping bags, trucks, uniforms, and other items.

"Letterhead is often the only introduction that an outsider has to a company," Michael observes. "It represents the company—and tells a lot about it." The key factors, according to Michael, are color, continuity, and white space. "Color has real psychological impact. Warm colors, for example, tend to stimulate and excite an active response." Continuity refers to the harmony of the design elements—for example, how the logo design and the type style used for the company's name hold together. White space can be used to focus attention on a given design element. "If you surround a block of type with white space," Michael points out, "the type appears to be in a spotlight."

Placement of the heading must also be considered, because many companies have preferences for setting up a typewritten page. Some want more space at the top or prefer to have the address at the bottom. "The trend in letterhead design today is toward simplicity and clarity. Most companies prefer a clean, uncluttered look. Most companies also print their letterhead on two grades of paper, using the premium-quality letterhead only when appropriate."

And how does Michael go about designing a logo for letterhead stationery and other items? "I start by finding out what the client is currently using for its symbol," he explains. "That symbol tells me how the public now perceives the company and what the client may once have liked as a logo." Michael then asks the client what image the company wants to convey. Does it want to seem traditional? High tech? Does it want to inspire confidence, build trust? Says Michael: "A logo is a very personal statement about a company—one that it can't afford to change frequently."

Michael also feels that it is important to consider the end uses of the company logo. Will it be read quickly? Must it be highly visible? What type style would suit it best? "The type I'd use for a cosmetics company," he notes, "would be quite different from what I'd use for a motorcycle manufacturer."

After discussing these matters with the client, Michael does some independent research. He examines the logos that the client's competitors are using and learns something about the industry. All this information influences the type of image that he creates for the company. Then Michael starts sketching. When he comes up with a solution that seems to work, he shows it to the client. If the client approves, Michael produces the finished artwork.

Michael has this final bit of advice for those who balk at the expense of hiring a professional designer: "If your company wants to look like a winner, it's usually worth paying the price for quality design and printing. It may make a real difference in the level of response you get."

1. Go to a stationery store and ask to look through the catalogs of personalized and letterhead stationery. Pick something appropriate for the following businesses:
   a.   An advertising agency
   b.   A Wall Street law firm
   c.   A pet store
   d.   An interior decorating store

   What qualities of each design make it appropriate for the business?

2. Leaf through an issue of *Fortune* or some other business magazine and study the logos in the ads. Which of them appeal to you? What are the common denominators of your favorites?

DEVELOP YOUR WORD POWER

Use the spelling and vocabulary words from previous chapters to complete the crossword puzzle.

Across

1. administration
5. something outdated
11. breakable
14. to invalidate
16. being
17. person under the care of someone influential
22. discontented
23. pause
24. predicament
26. to spend
31. directing
33. brings about
35. dull
37. beat
40. obvious
41. skillful
42. place
43. trite saying
44. right away
45. to deal in broad concepts

Down

1. to promise
2. wavering
3. in position number 9
4. effectiveness
5. to prevent
6. to publicize
7. obstacle
8. unconcerned
9. diplomacy and tact
10. one or the other
12. keen insight
13. primary
15. debatable
17. outmoded
18. social blunder
19. contact person
20. succinct
21. 4 times 10
25. intended
27. trifling
28. uninformed guess
29. supposition
30. faultfinding
32. proper to be recommended
34. cure-all
36. shortage
38. pertaining to everyday concerns
39. representative

CHECK YOUR ANSWERS

Master Key Concepts

I. correspondence
    A. paper
    B. letterhead
    C. centered

II. A. salutation, complimentary
     B. attention, reference, mailing
     C. block, simplified

III. B. thirds

IV. internationally

VI. memo-letters

VIII. agendas, minutes

Quiz Yourself

1. Letterhead is typically printed with the name and address of the company. It may also contain the company's telephone number, cable address, product lines, date of establishment, officers and directors, slogan, and symbol (logo). A company might decide to limit the amount of information printed on the letterhead in order to avoid a cluttered appearance, save space, and prevent the stationery from becoming outdated. (p. 619)

2. The seven standard parts of a letter are
    a. Heading
    b. Date
    c. Inside address
    d. Salutation
    e. Body
    f. Complimentary close
    g. Signature block (pp. 620–623)

3. The complimentary close should reflect the relationship between the writer and the reader. Currently, the trend seems to be toward using one-word closes, such as *Sincerely* or *Cordially*. (p. 623)

4. Letters that have a restricted readership or that must be handled in a special way should include such *addressee notations* as "Personal," "confidential," or "Please Forward." (p. 623)

5. These notations have the following meanings:
    a. cc—carbon copy
    b. pc—photocopy
    c. c—copy
    d. bc—blind copy
    e. bcc—blind carbon copy
    f. bpc—blind photocopy (p. 626)

6. Letters may be classified according to the style of punctuation they use. *Standard*, or mixed, punctuation uses a colon after the salutation (a comma if the letter is social or personal) and a comma after the complimentary close. *Open* punctuation uses no colon or comma after the salutation or the complimentary close. (p. 627)

7. Envelopes are typed in block form and single-spaced. If a No. 10 envelope is used, the block identifying the recipient should begin 4 inches from the left side and 2-1/2 inches from the top; if a No. 6-3/4 envelope is used, the recipient's address should begin 2-1/2 inches from the left edge and 2 inches from the top. (pp. 628–630)

8. The names on a memo's distribution list should generally be listed in alphabetical order; however, some organizations prefer to list people in order of their tank in the organization. (p. 633)

9. Organizations that often deal with individuals by mail frequently have *letterhead postcards* preprinted with a list of responses; the "writer" merely checks the appropriate response. (p. 635)

10. Most agendas follow this order:
    a. Call to order
    b. Roll call
    c. Approval of agenda
    d. Approval of minutes
    e. Chairperson's report
    f. Subcommittee reports
    g. Unfinished business
    h. New business
    i. Announcements
    j Adjournment (p. 637)

Develop Your Word Power

Component Chapter B

Documentation of Report Sources

The main point of Component Chapter B is that documenting your work gives it credibility, gives readers the means for checking your findings and pursuing the subject further, and is the accepted way to give credit to the people whose ideas you have drawn on. As you read the chapter, think about how the recommended formats and practices would help someone trying to look up references for further information. When you finish reading, practice documenting several types of reference works.

MASTER KEY CONCEPTS

Use the following terms to fill in the blanks in the outline. All terms are used, but none is used more than once.

author-date	copyright	MLA	secondary
bibliography	fair use	note card	source
consecutively	key-number	publication	title
content			

I. To consult _____ (pp. 638–640) sources you need to make use of libraries, computerized data banks, and note cards.
   A. Libraries can be used to consult basic references, books, articles, abstracts, and government documents.
   B. Large masses of data are stored in computerized data banks; many companies have such data bases, in addition to providing access to commercial databases.
   C. When recording information from documents onto a _____ (p. 640), be sure to include all relevant data about the source.

II. Under the _____ (pp. 640–641) laws, you must acknowledge the source of direct quotations and paraphrased passages but need not cite the source of general knowledge; the _____ (p. 641) doctrine requires you to obtain written permission from the copyright holder if, generally speaking, your use of the material would prevent the author from selling it.

III. _____ (p. 642) notes documenting quotations and paraphrased passages generally appear at the end of a document; _____ (p. 642) notes elaborating on the text are usually presented at the bottom of the page they refer to.
   A. Notes are referenced and typed according to several stylistic conventions: the placement of a note is indicated with a superscript, the superscripts are numbered _____ (p. 642) throughout a document, direct quotes over three lines long are set off as extracts, and notes are single-spaced and separated by a double space.
   B. Regardless of their precise form, all source notes include the author's name, the _____ (p. 643) of the work, and such _____ (p. 643) information as the publisher's name and location, the publication date, and the page reference; to save time, later references to the same source may use a shortened format.
   C. Source notes referring to books, periodicals, newspapers, unpublished material, and other material differ in detail.

IV. A _____ (p. 645), arranged in alphabetical order by author's last name, serves as a reading list for those who want to do further research; it should include all the sources referenced in notes as well as additional references that may be useful to readers.

   A. A single bibliography may be placed at the end of the report, or separate bibliographies may be prepared for each chapter; a bibliography may be subdivided according to subject matter or type of reference.

   B. Notes and bibliography entries have several differences, especially in punctuation; bibliography entries for books, periodicals, newspapers, and unpublished and other material all vary to a certain extent.

V. Several methods of reference citations have been developed for handling notes and bibliographies; the _____ (p. 647) system provides an end-of-report list of references and refers to them in the text by author's last name and publication date; the _____ (p. 647) system identifies items in the reference list by Arabic numeral and then uses this number in parentheses with a colon and the page number; the _____ (p. 647) simplified style identifies items by author and page number.

VI. For additional details on preparing bibliographies and notes, consult one of the style books available in the reference sections of libraries or in bookstores.

Check your answers at the end of this chapter.

QUIZ YOURSELF

1. What information should be put on note cards?

2. Discuss the fair use doctrine.

3. _____ notes are used to document quotations and paraphrased passes.

   _____ notes are used to supplement the text with asides about a particular issue or event or to direct the reader to another section of the report or to a related source.

4. If a book has four or more authors, how do you handle the authors' names in a source note?

5. What punctuation is used to set off publication information in a source note referring to a book?

6. In general, what is the difference between the formal and the informal style in shortened note references?

7. What information should be included in a reference to a letter, a speech, or an interview?

8. An _____ bibliography comments on the subject matter and viewpoint of the source, as well as on its usefulness to readers.

9. Describe three basic methods for handling reference citations.

10. List five style books that provide additional information on the format for notes and bibliographies.

Check your answers at the end of this chapter.

BUILD YOUR SKILLS: COMPILE A BIBLIOGRAPHY

To hone your ability to prepare a bibliography, compile one on the subject of marketing products in underdeveloped countries. Use a mix of reference types, including books, business journals, popular magazines, academic papers, and newspapers. Include at least 20 entries, presented in acceptable format and arranged in the proper order.

EXPAND YOUR KNOWLEDGE: HOW TO TAKE BETTER NOTES FASTER

Unless you have adequate resources at your fingertips, research usually means taking notes while you conduct an interview or scan books at the library. This time-consuming procedure becomes a lot quicker if you know one of the many shorthand systems, such as Gregg, Speedwriting, or Century 21. But if you don't, you can still save time by using some of the following shortcuts:

- Use such common abbreviations as 1, 2, 3, 1st, 2nd, 3rd, &, %, #, *dept., co.,* and *acct.*
- Use such "natural" abbreviations as *bus (business), dif (difference),* and *pic (pictures).*
- Write what you hear, such as *hi* instead of *high.*
- Leave out vowels whenever possible, as in *Lv t vls wnvr posbl.*
- Abbreviate suffixes: attribu*n* (attribu*tion*), commemor*v* (commemor*ative*), rad*l* (rad*ical*), monu*mt* (monu*ment*).
- Use letters for common short words, such as *b (be, been, but, buy, by), c (can), d (would), e (ever, every), f (for, from), h (had, he, him), l (well, will), n (in, not), o (on, own), p (please, up), r (are, our), t (to, too), u (under), v (of, have, very), w (with), x (extra), y (why), z (was, as).*
- Use a standard abbreviation for common phrases, such as *lb (will be)* and *db (would be), nvrls (nevertheless)* and *nnls (nonetheless), tb (to be)* and *tk (to come), vb (have been)* and *vn (have not), zlz (as well as)* and *zz (as soon as).*
- Underscore the last letter to add *ing* or *thing* as a word ending, as in *smil̲* (smil*ing*).
- Form the past tense of a regular verb by placing a hyphen at the end, as in *stay-* (stay*ed*).
- Use an apostrophe at the end of any word ending in *ness,* as in *kind'* (kind*ness*).

Once you have practiced these techniques a few times, your note taking will go much faster. Remember, however, that putting notes on paper is only half the battle. The other half, which is equally critical, is to translate them when the need arises. You can save yourself the trouble of going back to the source by reading over your notes as soon as you get back to your office. While your memory is fresh, write out words that you think you might not recognize in a couple of days or weeks. To be really safe, you might even want to type out all your notes for future reference.

1. Analyze your own class lecture notes. How useful are they? Are you able to decipher them later? Have you included too much? Not enough? Is the relationship among ideas clear? What can you do to improve in the future?

2. Try to come up with your own "shorthand" techniques to augment those listed here. For example, during any given research effort, certain concepts are mentioned repeatedly. Can you abbreviate these common terms in some way?

DEVELOP YOUR WORD POWER

Use the spelling and vocabulary words from previous chapters to complete the crossword puzzle.

Across

1. hateful
5. genuine
8. well known
9. polite
11. directly
14. frequently
15. pertinent
16. agility
19. to leave out
20. severe
25. beneficial
26. indirect criticism
29. social blunder
30. something given stress
31. implied
34. being
35. facts behind a conclusion
38. to authorize
39. conspicuous
41. take advantage of
42. admits
43. person under the care of someone influential
44. aware

Down

1. event
2. flooded
3. skepticism
4. concise
5. pamphlet
6. to struggle
7. heterogeneity
10. severity
12. dash
13. case for samples
17. analysis
18. something outdated
21. to prevent
22. possessing understanding
23. group formed for a purpose
24. direct opposite
27. in position number 19
28. opinionated
32. in position number 9
33. pertaining to everyday concerns
36. to slander
37. pleasant
40. uninvolved

CHECK YOUR ANSWERS

Master Key Concepts

I. secondary
   C. note card

II. copyright, fair use

III. source, content
   A. consecutively
   B. title, publication

IV. bibliography

V. author-date, key-number, MLA

Quiz Yourself

1. A separate note card should be made for each fact, quotation, or general concept you want to record. In addition to this information, include the author's name, the book or article title, and other information necessary for your bibliography. (p. 640)

2. The fair use doctrine says that you cannot use other people's work without written permission if your use might unfairly prevent the author from benefiting in some way—say, by selling a copy of the work or by receiving a royalty payment for it. In such cases, even if you credit the source in your report, you must obtain written permission from the copyright holder to reprint the material. You should probably get permission to use
   a. More than 250 words from a book
   b. Any piece of artwork
   c. Any dialogue from a play or line from a poem or song
   d. Any portion of consumable materials, such as workbooks
   e. Multiple copies of copyrighted work (p. 641)

3. *Source* notes are used to document quotations and paraphrased passages. *Content* notes are used to supplement the text with asides about a particular issue or event or to direct the reader to another section of the report or to a related source. (p. 642)

4. If a book has four or more authors, the first author's name is spelled out in full (with the first name first). This is followed by the Latin *et al.* or the more informal *and others*, with no preceding comma. (p. 643)

5. In a source note, publication information for books is set off in parentheses. The first item following the opening parenthesis is the name of the city in which the publisher is located. A colon follows the name of the city, after which the name of the publisher appears (often in shortened form). A comma separates the publisher's name from the publication date. The closing parenthesis follows the date. (p. 643)

6. The formal style for shortened references uses the Latin abbreviations *ibid., op. cit.,* and *loc. cit.* to indicate previously cited sources. The informal style uses the author's last name, a short form of the title, and the page number where the information can be found. (pp. 643–644)

7. When referencing a letter, a speech, or an interview, begin with the name, title, and affiliation of the "author"; then describe the nature of the communication, the date, possibly the place, and (if appropriate) the location of any files containing the reference. (p. 645)

8. An *annotated* bibliography comments on the subject matter and viewpoint of the source, as well as on its usefulness to readers. (p. 645)

9. Ways to handle reference citations include
   a. The author-date system uses regular bibliography style for the list of references. In the text, reference to a given work is documented by noting the author, date of publication, and page number, set off in parentheses within the text.
   b. The key-number system also uses regular bibliography style for the list of references but numbers each reference in sequence in Arabic numerals, followed by a period. (Sometimes the "bibliography" is arranged in order of the appearance of each source in the text, rather than in alphabetical order.) In the text, references are documented with two numbers separated by a colon; the first is the number assigned to the source, the second is the page number.
   c. The MLA simplified style uses an author-page number system instead of author, date. (p. 647)

10. These references provide additional information on preparing notes and bibliographies:
    a. *The MLA Handbook for Writers of Research Papers*, by Joseph Gibaldi and Walter S. Achtert
    b. *Publication Manual of the American Psychological Association*
    c. *Form and Style: Theses, Reports, Term Papers*, by William Giles Campbell and Stephen Vaughan Ballou
    d. *The Chicago Manual of Style*, by The University of Chicago Press
    e. *Where Credit Is Due*, by Nancy E. Shields and Mary E. Uhle
    f. *A Manual for Writers of Term Papers, Theses, and Dissertations*, by Kate L. Turabian
    g. *U.S. Government Printing Office Style Manual* (p. 648)

Develop Your Word Power

APPENDIX I

Fundamentals of Grammar and Usage

The main point of Appendix I is that the misuse of language can impede communication. As you read the chapter, think about the ways that errors in grammar, punctuation, mechanics, and vocabulary may contribute to misunderstandings. When you finish reading and doing the exercises, analyze your weak points and work to overcome them.

MASTER KEY CONCEPTS

Use the following terms to fill in the blanks in the outline. All terms are used, but none is used more than once.

abbreviations	dashes	mechanics	proper
antecedents	ellipsis	mood	punctuation
capitals	grammar	possessive	semicolons
clauses	hyphens	prepositions	

I. _____ (p. 649) is the way that words are combined into sentences; sentences are composed of parts of speech, the most basic of which are nouns, pronouns, verbs, adjectives, and adverbs.

   A. Nouns name a person, a place, a thing, or an idea; to use nouns correctly, learn the difference between _____ (p. 650) nouns and common nouns, the method of making a noun plural, and the method of making a noun possessive.

   B. Pronouns are words that stand for nouns; to use pronouns correctly, learn how to deal with multiple _____ (p. 651), how to avoid unclear antecedents, how to select gender-neutral pronouns, how to select the correct case for pronouns, and when to use possessive pronouns.

   C. Verbs describe an action or a state of being; to use verbs correctly, learn about verb tenses, irregular verbs, transitive and intransitive verbs, the voice of verbs, and the _____ (p. 654) of verbs.

   D. Adjectives modify (tell something about) nouns and pronouns. .

   E. Adverbs modify verbs, adjectives, and other adverbs.

   F. Nouns, pronouns, verbs, adjectives, and adverbs are linked together in sentences by four other parts of speech: _____ (p. 655), conjunctions, articles, and interjections.

   G. Whole sentences contain, at minimum, a subject and a predicate; to be able to construct whole sentences, learn about commands, the difference between phrases and _____ (p. 656) in longer sentences, sentence fragments, fused sentences, sentences with linking verbs, and misplaced modifiers.

II. When used properly to mark different sorts of sentences and sentence elements, _____ (p. 659) keeps readers from losing track of your meaning.

   A. Periods are used at the end of sentences that are not questions, after some _____ (p. 609), and in money expressions.

   B. Question marks are used after any direct question that requires an answer.

   C. Exclamation points are used after highly emotional sentences.

D. _____ (pp. 659–660) are used to separate closely related independent clauses, items in a series that already contain commas, and independent clauses when the second one begins with a transitional word or phrase.

E. Colons are used after salutations in a letter and at the end of a sentence or phrase introducing a list, a quotation, or an idea.

F. Commas separate the items in a series, separate an opening phrase or dependent clause from an independent clause, follow an introductory statement, surround parenthetical phrases or words, separate adjectives modifying the same noun, separate some abbreviations (such as *Inc.* and *Jr.*) from the words they identify, separate days from years in dates, separate quotations from the rest of the sentence, and separate words and phrases whenever needed to prevent confusion or an unintended meaning.

G. _____ (pp. 660–661) are used around parenthetical comments that represent a sudden turn in thought, around parenthetical comments that require emphasis, and around parenthetical phrases that contain commas.

H. _____ (p. 661) are used to separate the parts of compound words, to separate the parts of compound adjectives that come before the noun (but not after the noun), and to divide words at the ends of lines.

I. Apostrophes are used in the _____ (p. 661) form of nouns and in contractions.

J. Quotation marks surround words that are repeated exactly as they were said or written, set off the titles of newspaper and magazine articles, and indicate special treatment for words and phrases.

K. Parentheses surround comments that are entirely incidental and surround dollar amounts in legal documents.

L. _____ (p. 662) points are used to indicate that material has been left out of a direct quotation.

M. Underscores and italics provide emphasis and indicate the titles of books, magazines, and the like.

III. A number of small details known as _____ (p. 662) demonstrate a writer's polish and reflect on the organization's professionalism.

A. _____ (p. 662) are used at the beginning of sentences, as the first letter of proper nouns and adjectives, for official titles, and as the first letter of salutations and complimentary closes.

B. Abbreviations are used mainly in tables, graphs, lists, and forms.

C. Numbers from one to ten are generally spelled out, and numbers over ten are generally indicated with Arabic numerals; for handling numbers in other situations, many other rules exist.

D. Dividing words at the ends of lines should be done at syllables or existing hyphens.

IV. Using the right word in the right place is a crucial element in business communication.

A. Frequently confused words are sets of words that sound similar but are spelled differently; be careful not to mistake one for another.

B. Frequently misused words tend to be misused for reasons other than sound.

C. Frequently misspelled words are commonly used words that are difficult to spell for a variety of reasons.

D. Transitional words and phrases are useful for showing the relationship between two sentences or clauses.

Check your answers at the end of this chapter.

QUIZ YOURSELF

1. _____ is nothing more than the way words are combined into sentences, and

   _____ is the way language is used by a network of people.

2. In general, which nouns are capitalized, and which are not?

3. Explain what an antecedent is, in grammatical terms, and name two types of antecedents that cause confusion.

4. List the six verb tenses, and briefly describe how they are regularly formed.

5. Name the two voices of verbs, and explain when each should be used.

6. What are the five most important parts of speech, and what are the four other parts of speech that link them together in sentences?

7. Because it does not have both a subject and a predicate, the group of words known as a

   _____ can never be written as a sentence; a group of words that does contain

   both a subject and a predicate, known as a _____, can be written as a sentence if it is an independent thought.

8. Explain what sentence fragments and fused sentences are and why both are unacceptable.

9. How can you text the appropriateness of inserting a comma between adjectives modifying the same noun?

10. In the absence of a different company style, generally spell out all numbers from

   _____ to _____ and use Arabic numerals for the rest.

Check your answers at the end of this chapter.

BUILD YOUR SKILLS: CAN YOU CORRECT THE ERRORS IN THIS MEMO?

The following memo contains errors in grammar, punctuation, mechanics, and spelling. Find them and correct them.

TO: All employees

FROM: Martin Smores, V.P. Administration

SUBJECT: Educational Refund Plans

It is the policy of this company to encourage employees to continue there education in fields which are related to their current work, or deemed in the companies best interests in the soul judgement of the Company.

To be eligible for the program, full-time employment is required.

Only course work taken at accredited schools and colleges by a nationally recognized accrediting agency are eligible for refunds under the plan.

An employee wishing to participate in the refund plan will obtain written approval from their supervisor prior to enrollment in courses.

All initial costs associated with taking courses will be born by the employee.

Upon completion of courses, evidence of course completion such as grades received and receipts for bills paid must be submitted to the company.

When the requirements of the refund plan having been met, costs will be reimbursed as follows:

Tuition costs and labratory fees—100%
Required textbooks—50%

EXPAND YOUR KNOWLEDGE: WRITING WITH STYLE

Writing involves two kinds of style. One is a set of guidelines for handling certain grammatical elements—as in "house style" and "style manual." The other is an individualized pattern of word choice, sentence construction, and paragraph organization—a sort of personalized "signature"—that each writer develops. In most business writing, you are expected to suppress this individual style; you are, after all, representing your organization and not yourself. You can never totally eliminate your outlook from your writing, however. You can only learn to make the most of it.

Word Choice

- *Use the best word you can think of.* The word that most accurately says what you mean is probably harder for you to identify and use correctly than for a reader to recognize in context. So develop your vocabulary, and eschew only pompous words and unnecessary jargon.
- *Use figures of speech appropriately.* In one sense, your ability to come up with a clever metaphor or simile is a mark of style. This sort of style, however, is to be avoided in business writing. The same goes for slang and the breezier idioms. You can exercise plenty of creativity by selecting solid, objective words and putting them together for maximum impact.
- *Use contractions knowledgeably.* In formal writing, contractions should be avoided. But in informal writing that includes contractions, you can gain impact by sometimes using a complete phrase instead—for example, *will not* instead of *won't.*

Sentence Construction

- *Repeat words, phrases, and constructions for emphasis.* Awkward repetition is a sign of ignorance. Deft repetition is a sign of sophistication.
- *Place modifiers as close as possible to the words they modify.* In long, complicated sentences, it is easy to get lost. Help your readers by telling them the how and the why as soon as you tell them who or what. If you end up with verbal spaghetti, you probably need to rewrite—perhaps making more than one sentence out of the mess.
- *Use a variety of sentence structures.* Some sentences should be simple and short. When your ideas are a bit more complicated, you can use complex sentences. Other thoughts naturally go together, and you can use compound sentences to show that they are related.
- *Begin sentences in different ways.* Most sentences begin with the main clause, consisting of a subject and a predicate and a few modifiers. For variety, however, and to show how your ideas are related, occasionally begin sentences with more complicated modifying words, phrases, and clauses. Just don't overdo any one device.
- *Make sure that every sentence has its own logic.* If you're talking about a series of things or ideas, put them in logical order. In compound and complex sentences, give the main idea the stronger position; in other words, do not subordinate the main idea. Also, make sure that the ideas in a compound sentence are truly related.

Paragraph Organization

- *Vary the placement of your topic sentences.* Every paragraph must somewhere state exactly what its point is, but that statement does not always have to come first.
- *Use sentence structure to build a rhythm in your paragraphs.* Short, punchy sentences have impact. But they tend to become boring if used exclusively, so you should build paragraphs with sentences that are long and short, simple and complex and compound.
- *Vary the length of your paragraphs.* Paragraphs that are all about the same length also become monotonous. You can make some paragraphs short, with only three or four sentences, and add a couple of sentences to the paragraphs that require more development. Remember that although longer paragraphs may sometimes be necessary, long paragraphs tend to bore readers.

The more you write, the more you will be able to refine these and other techniques. You will eventually notice, however, that they all have one purpose: to make your ideas clear and interesting to readers.

1. Style is a mix of elements, involving choices between passive and active, formal and informal, bland and colorful language. In the following situations, what mix of elements would be appropriate?
   a. You are a newly hired researcher, with a relatively low position in the organization. You are writing your first memo to your boss.
   b. You are the vice president of a large corporation and must announce to the employees that, because of disappointing financial performance, your company will not be offering generous raises this year.
   c. You have been asked to take charge of the company picnic. You are writing a memo for general distribution announcing the time, place, and program for the event.

2. One good way to learn how to control your style is to study other writers who have a clear "voice." Analyze the writing style of these writers:
   a. Ernest Hemingway (twentieth-century American novelist)
   b. Samuel Johnson (eighteenth-century English essayist)
   c. An unknown reporter for *The New York Times*

DEVELOP YOUR WORD POWER

Use the spelling and vocabulary words from previous chapters to complete the crossword puzzle.

Across

1. noninterference
4. insolent
7. intended
8. trifling
10. verbal attack
11. to examine
13. adviser
14. friendly
16. to cause
18. skillful
19. option
20. opinionated
21. bodily
23. on guard
24. unending
25. yearly
27. discord
31. death
33. representative
34. frequently
35. book of words in a language
37. sincerely
38. frivolously amusing
39. shortage
40. person under the care of someone influential
41. up and down
42. not committing oneself

Down

1. praiseworthy
2. right away
3. clothing
4. indirect criticism
5. advantageous
6. to try to equal or excel
9. very
12. capable of being put on credit
13. mixed
15. plotting
17. between seventh and ninth
22. outmoded
26. arousing longing
28. discreet
29. debatable
30. equivalent
32. workable
34. event
36. habitual

CHECK YOUR ANSWERS

Master Key Concepts

I. grammar
   A. proper
   B. antecedents
   C. mood
   F. prepositions
   G. clauses

II. punctuation
   A. abbreviations
   D. semicolons
   G. dashes
   H. hyphens
   I. possessive
   L. ellipsis

III. mechanics
   A. capitals

Quiz Yourself

1. *Grammar* is nothing more than the way words are combined into sentences, and *usage* is the way language is used by a network of people. (p. 649)

2. Common nouns, which refer to general classes of things, are not capitalized; proper nouns, which refer to particular persons, places, and things, are capitalized. (p. 650)

3. An antecedent is a noun in the beginning of a sentence that corresponds to a pronoun later in the sentence. Both multiple antecedents and unclear antecedents cause confusion if not handled knowledgeably. (p. 651)

4. These are the six verb tenses and how they are regularly formed:
   a. Present: the basic form
   b. Past: the basic form with an *ed* ending
   c. Future: *will* or *shall* followed by the basic form
   d. Present perfect: *have* or *has* followed by the past tense of the main verb
   e. Past perfect: *had* followed by the past tense of the main verb
   f. Future perfect: *will have* followed by the past tense of the main verb (pp. 652–653)

5. Verbs have two voices, active and passive. The active voice is preferable in most sentences, because it allows fewer words to be used and is more direct. But when the writer doesn't know (or doesn't want to say) who performed the action, the passive voice becomes necessary. (p. 654)

6. These are the five most important parts of speech:
   a. Nouns
   b. Pronouns
   c. Verbs
   d. Adjectives
   e. Adverbs (p. 655)

   The following four parts of speech link them together in sentences:
   f. Prepositions
   g. Conjunctions
   h. Articles
   i. Interjections (p. 655)

7. Because it does not have both a subject and a predicate, the group of words known as a *phrase* can never be written as a sentence; a group of words that does contain both a subject and a predicate, known as a *clause*, can be written as a sentence if it is an independent thought. (p. 656)

8. A sentence fragment is an incomplete sentence (a phrase or dependent clause) written as though it were a complete sentence. A fused sentence combines two independent thoughts without showing any point of separation. Because sentence fragments and fused sentences do not clearly express a single thought, they are easily misinterpreted by the reader. (p. 657)

9. To test the appropriateness of inserting a comma between adjectives modifying the same noun, try reversing the order of the adjectives. If the order cannot be reversed, leave out the comma. A comma is also left out when one of the adjectives is part of the noun. (p. 660)

10. In the absence of a different company style, generally spell out all numbers from *one* to *ten* and use Arabic numerals for the rest. (p. 663)

Develop Your Word Power

Lesson 1

Sentences

What is a sentence? Saying that it is a word or group of words that starts with a capital letter and ends with a period is only partly right. Sentences also require a subject (someone or something) and a predicate (doing or being):

Rosemarie conducts the meeting.

In this sentence, *Rosemarie* is the subject, the someone or something; *conducts the meeting* is the predicate that explains what Rosemarie does.

Subjects are usually nouns or pronouns, and predicates always include at least one verb. However, subjects and predicates may take many different forms. In the following sentences, the subject is underlined once and the predicate verb is underlined twice:

He quit.
She was ready to start legal proceedings.
Deborah and Stephen worked together on the BNA account.
The typing pool copied and collated the report.
They are working on a new business plan.
Has he had any trouble with the audit?
Give us your analysis.

In the last sentence in this list, the subject, *you* is understood; therefore, only the predicate is present. Some sentences with an understood subject—for example, *Stop!*—contain only one word.

Some sentences use a certain type of predicate verb—usually a form of *is*—to link the subject with a word that further describes it:

The man is happy.

Occasionally this order is inverted, especially in questions:

Happy is the man.
Is the man happy?

Regardless of the order of the words, these statements are sentences—because they have both a subject and a predicate.

The most basic sentences consist of a subject and a predicate verb in a simple one-two pattern: *They paid.* But sentences are usually more complicated. Many sentences also have modifiers that further describe the subject or predicate verb; they often have an object as well, someone or something that is acted on by the subject of the sentence. For example:

In most cases, new customers promptly pay bills.

191

In this sentence, *bills* is the object. Customers pay what? They pay bills. In addition, *new* modifies the subject, and *promptly* and *in most cases* modify the predicate verb. If you took away all these extra words and were left with only *Customers pay*, you would still have a sentence.

In the following exercises, underline subjects once and predicate verbs twice:

1. He found a tactful way to tell her.

2. While adding the column, she noticed a couple of errors.

3. The letter gave him a clue to their thinking.

4. Her favorite activity in her new job was analysis of letters from customers.

5. Were his methods fair?

6. Tracy and Susanne were awarded the top positions.

7. Take one.

8. We are sending the replacement postpaid.

9. Under the desk was a wastebasket.

10. Were his supplies all in order?

Some sentences contain more than one subject-predicate set:

Ben discovered the faulty typewriter, and he was the one who took it to be fixed.

Notice the comma separating the two subject-predicate sets. You could split the one long sentence into two shorter sentences at this comma, and each of the new sentences would have a subject and a predicate. But be careful. Not every sentence containing a comma can be broken in two:

Looking around for a replacement, we found Judy.

Only the latter part of this statement has a subject and a predicate verb and could therefore stand alone as a sentence. The same is true of the following statement:

Because she had the experience, she got the job.

Although the first part of this statement has a subject and a predicate verb (*she had*), it could not stand alone; *because she had the experience* actually modifies the predicate and tells why she got the job.

In the following exercises, circle all the complete sentences.

11. Show me how to do it.

12. Writing and speaking to perfection.

13. Michael, Betty, and Tom, without whom we would not have succeeded.

14. In an emergency, use it to signal passing motorists.

15. Spending enough to make it worthwhile.

16. With everyone else on vacation, she became responsible for completing the report.

17. Since he became a supervisor.

18. Punctuate correctly, and then retype.

19. When our company first got into the ice cream business, profits were spectacular, and soon we became too confident.

20. Expenses down, profits up.

Including too much in one sentence is just as serious a problem as leaving out a subject or predicate. The following sentence pastes together too many ideas:

> When she was offered the job, she immediately wrote a letter accepting it and then sat down to list the things she had to do to start work the following Monday, including buying a new dress and shoes, and then she decided to take a break so she could call some of her friends to tell them about her good fortune.

This account is easier to understand when broken into shorter sentences. For example:

> When she was offered the job, she immediately wrote a letter accepting it. Then she sat down to list the things she had to do to start work the following Monday, including buying a new dress and shoes. Then she decided to take a break so she could call some of her friends to tell them about her good fortune.

Although a sentence may contain more than one subject-predicate set, you must be careful not to use a comma to combine what should be two separate sentences:

> He <u>sat</u> down at his desk to prepare a reply, meanwhile his <u>supervisor</u> <u>talked</u> to the customer on the phone.

A solitary comma is not strong enough to link these two subject-predicate sets. A comma teamed with a linking words such as *and, but, for, nor, or, so,* or *yet* would solve the problem. But if you did not want to add any words, you could use stronger punctuation:

> He <u>sat</u> down at his desk to prepare a reply. Meanwhile, his <u>supervisor</u> <u>talked</u> to the customer on the phone.
> He <u>sat</u> down at his desk to prepare a reply; meanwhile, his <u>supervisor</u> <u>talked</u> to the customer on the phone.

If you were willing to add, take out, or rearrange words, you could find many other solutions to the problem.

Correct the sentences in the following exercises by crossing out extra words and inserting only periods and capital letters—not by adding any words or other punctuation:

21. The best part of the day had gone she decided to try something less demanding.

22. Thank you for your prompt payment whenever you need cleaning services for your offices, give us a call.

23. After I thought about your performance, I decided to let you take over while I am gone. I hope everything goes well in my absence.

24. Give him the report, he will know what to do with it.

25. Jackie and Bob reported exceptional sales this past month, and they surely deserve some reward, and I know they would like a cash bonus.

If you have had trouble with the exercises in this section, you may want to consult a grammar book on the following subjects:

clauses	complex sentences	phrases	sentence fragments
comma splices	compound sentences	run-on sentences	simple sentences

You might also wish to consult Section 1.7, "Sentences," in Appendix I, "Fundamentals of Grammar and Usage," in *Business Communication Today*, Fourth Edition.

Lesson 2

Parts of Speech: Nouns

Words that stand for a person, a place, an idea, or a thing are called nouns. Here are some examples of common nouns:

industry	assistant	compiler	administration
markup	lunch	fitness	downtown

A word preceded by *a, an,* or *the* in a sentence is usually a noun; so is a word that ends in *ation, ism, ity, ment,* or *ness.*

Nouns may be used in sentences as subjects or objects. That is, the person, place, idea, or thing that is being or doing (subject) is represented by a noun. So is the person, place, idea, or thing that is being acted on (object). In the following sentence, the nouns are underlined:

The secretary typed the report.

The secretary (subject) is acting in a way that affects the report (object).

In this more complicated sentence, *installer* is used as a subject, and *carpeting* and *customer* are used as objects:

The installer delivered the carpeting to the customer.

Notice that *carpeting* is the object of the main part of the sentence (is acted on by the installer), whereas *customer* is the object of the phrase *to the customer.* Nevertheless, both *carpeting* and *customer* are objects.

In the following exercises, underline the subjects and circle the objects:

1. The technician has already repaired the machine for the client.

2. An attorney will talk to the group about incorporation.

3. After her vacation, the buyer prepared a third-quarter budget.

4. The new typewriters are serving our department very well.

5. Accuracy overrides speed in importance.

Some nouns are actually composed of two or more words. *Work load,* for example, is considered a single noun; in fact, you may see it spelled as one word in some places. Here are a few of the many other nouns that combine two or more words:

vice president	attorney general
coffee maker	administrative assistant
profit-and-loss statement	hanger-on

The way to tell whether word groups like these should be considered single nouns is to try separating the parts. Can the parts be used alone, or do you need both parts to talk about the same thing? Is the word group used as a single unit to mean something distinct? For example, a coffee maker is never called just a maker, not can it correctly be called a coffee pot.

So far, all the examples have been common nouns—that is, they refer to general classes of things. In business, however, you will often need to refer to specific examples of buildings, companies, people, and so on. Thus you will often need to use proper nouns, which are always capitalized:

Crandall Corporation   Wyandotte Building
Eleanor Kramer   President Abraham Lincoln
Tuesday   Crest (toothpaste)

Underline the common and proper nouns in the following exercises:

6. Perhaps the client will provide more time.

7. Has the messenger delivered a package without a label?

8. Give the balance sheet to Melissa.

9. The climate for investment might improve.

10. With a wink and a nod, the assistant ushered the visitor into the office.

11. The clerks gave up their break so they could discuss the new policies with the manager.

12. We'd like to order more satchels for Craigmont Stores.

13. Tarnower Corporation donates a portion of its profits to charity every year.

14. Which aluminum bolts are packaged?

15. Please send a dozen of the following: stopwatches, canteens, headbands, wristbands, and white shoelaces.

When you refer to more than one person, place, idea, or thing of a certain class, you must use the plural form of the noun. Most plurals are formed by adding s to the end of the singular form, as in *pencils* and *special offers*. Many nouns, however, are irregular and therefore form the plural in a different way. For example, when a word gains an extra syllable by being made plural, you should add an *es* instead of just an *s*:

boss/bosses   batch/batches   Harris/Harrises

Words ending in *ay, ey, oy,* or *uy* form the plural by adding *s*, but words ending in a consonant and a *y* form the plural by changing the *y* to *i* and adding *es*—except when the word is a proper name:

day/days   party/parties   Henry/Henrys

Similarly, nouns that end in *ao, eo, io, oo,* and *uo* form the plural by adding *s*:

video/vidoes   duo/duos   tattoo/tattoos

Some nouns that end in a consonant and *o* form the plural by adding *s*, others by adding *es*:

veto/vetoes   tomato/tomatoes   memo/memos

But some words ending in a consonant and *o* may form the plural by adding either *s* or *es*, like *zeros* and *zeroes*. Because of all this variation, you should consult a dictionary whenever you are in doubt about forming the plural of any word that ends in a consonant and an *o*.

Most words that end in a single *f* form the plural by changing the *f* to a *v* and adding *es*:

shelf/shelves   loaf/loaves   wharf/wharves

Then there are the words that form the plural by changing radically:

man/men   foot/feet   salesperson/salespeople

Some words derived from Greek and Latin roots form the plural by changing an *is* ending to *es*:

analysis/analyses   crisis/crises   diagnosis/diagnoses

But other frequently used foreign plurals are treated more like English words in business writing. For example, instead of using *appendices* or *maxima*, you may use *appendixes* or *maximums*.

Finally, some words are the same in both singular and plural form:

trousers   scissors   deer   headquarters

The only way to tell whether these words are singular or plural is to study the rest of the sentence.

When trying to make a plural out of a noun that is actually a combination of words, you must figure out which word in the group is most important. Then you can make a plural out of that word and leave the other in its singular form:

editors-in-chief   vice presidents   attorneys general

These are just a few examples. You can save yourself the embarrassment of using the wrong plural form by consulting a dictionary whenever you have any doubts. If it says nothing about the plural of the word, just add an s. Otherwise, use the form specified in the dictionary.

Supply the plural form of each of the nouns in the following exercises:

16. copy _____

17. bonus _____

18. son-in-law _____

19. folio _____

20. Amy _____

21. sheaf _____

22. child _____

23. parenthesis _____

24. supply _____

25. mess _____

If you need more help with nouns, consult a grammar book on the following subjects:

collective nouns	objects	proper nouns
common nouns	plural nouns	subjects
compound nouns		

You might also check Section 1.1, "Nouns," in Appendix I, "Fundamentals of Grammar and Usage," in *Business Communication Today*, Fourth Edition.

Lesson 3

Parts of Speech: Pronouns

These are the pronouns that substitute for nouns referring to specific people or things:

	Subject	Object	Possessive
Singular	I	me	my, mine
	he, she, it	him, her, it	his, her, hers, its
Plural	we	us	our, ours
	they	them	their, theirs
Singular and Plural	you	you	your, yours,
	who	whom	whose

Your choice of a pronoun from this list depends on whether the person or thing represented by the pronoun is acting, is being acted on, or possesses something. If acting, the pronoun is standing in for the subject of a sentence or phrase; if being acted on, the pronoun is standing in for the object of a sentence or phrase; if possessing something, the pronoun is showing the ownership. (Notice that none of the possessive pronouns, not even *its*, has an apostrophe.)

Study the pronouns in these sentences, noting whether they are subjects (S), objects (O), or possessives (P):

Who (S) gave the receipts to her (O)?
She (S) looked at my (P) resume.
They (S) returned the defective parts to us (O).
Our (P) major concern is your (P) satisfaction.
He (S) sent me (O) a check for $239.28.
To whom (O) will you (S) give the assignment?
I (S) will sell them (O) to you (O) at a discount.

If a noun is singular, the pronoun that stands in for it is also singular. If a noun is plural, the pronoun that stands in for it is also plural:

The ledger sat on the desk.
It sat on the desk.
The desks were delivered Tuesday.
They were delivered Tuesday.

A plural pronoun may also be used to stand in for two or more singular nouns:

Put the typewriter and adding machine into the empty office.
Put them into the empty office.

Complete the following exercises by replacing the underlined nouns with the correct pronouns:

1. To <u>which retailer</u> will you send <u>your merchandise</u>?

2. Have you given <u>John and Nancy</u> a list of parts?

3. <u>The main office</u> sent the invoice to <u>Mr. and Mrs. Litvak</u> on December 5.

4. The company settled <u>the company's</u> accounts before the end of the year.

5. <u>Which person's</u> umbrella is this?

6. <u>Peter</u> gave <u>Martin</u> a great pep talk.

7. I saw Bill at the conference, and <u>Bill</u> gave me a directory for the <u>conference</u>.

8. Where did Mr. Schiller get <u>Mr. Schiller's</u> new car?

9. Tell the Randolphs about <u>the Randolphs's</u> obligations.

10. When do you want Meg and Robert to take <u>Meg's and Robert's</u> break?

Replacing nouns with pronouns streamlines a sentence:

Roy gave <u>Roy's</u> pencil to Terri so <u>Terri</u> should add the figures.
Roy gave his pencil to Terri so she should add the figures.

In some sentences, however, you must sometimes reuse a noun for clarity, even though you could substitute a pronoun. For example:

Tom told Richard that <u>he</u> would be going to the meeting.

Who will be going to the meeting, Tom or Richard? Readers will be less confused if you use the appropriate noun again:

Tom told Richard that Richard would be going to the meeting.

(This problem may also be solved by rewriting the sentence.)

In the following exercises, cross out nouns and write pronouns above them wherever appropriate:

11. Customers always receive what customers expect from Blomberg's.

12. Janet and Anne are preparing a report for Janet and Anne's boss that tells the boss about Janet and Anne's results for the first quarter of the year.

13. Bob broke the chair, and so now Bob has to fix the chair.

14. When Mara spoke at the last gathering of the company's sales representatives, Mara gave the sales representatives a complete picture of the company's operations.

15. Tell Edward to turn in Edward's expense account before the expense account is overdue.

What pronoun should you use when referring to a group? Use a singular pronoun if the focus is on the group as a single unit, a plural pronoun if the focus is on individuals within the group:

The <u>staff</u> completed <u>its</u> report on time.
The <u>staff</u> turned in <u>their</u> reports at various times.

In the first sentence, the staff is working together on a report and is therefore seen as a unit, requiring a singular pronoun. In the second sentence, staff members are preparing individual reports, and thus a plural pronoun is required.

In most cases, companies are considered as units. Therefore, a singular pronoun is usually used to stand in for the name of a company:

<u>Starbright Enterprises</u> has lower prices than <u>its</u> competitors.
<u>Flyway Airlines</u> has just had <u>its</u> best year ever.

Another problem area for business communicators is indefinite pronouns. Words like *everyone, neither,* and *each* are singular, referring to one person or thing, and so require a singular pronoun:

<u>Neither</u> Elizabeth nor Connie has reached <u>her</u> potential yet.
<u>Each</u> display area has <u>its</u> limitations.

Words like *many* and several, however, take plural pronouns:

<u>Many</u> have requested <u>their</u> holidays already.

Still other indefinite pronouns—such as *all, any, most,* and *some*—may be either singular or plural, depending on the context:

<u>Some</u> is still left in <u>its</u> container.
<u>Some</u> are already asking for <u>their</u> bonuses.

Write the correct pronouns in the following exercises:

16. The typing pool is preparing guidelines for _____ clients.

17. Few of the sales representatives turn in _____ reports on time.

18. The board of directors has chosen _____ officers.

19. Several of the account executives have told _____ clients about the new program.

20. Mondo Taco, Inc., plans to expand _____ operations dramatically over the next two years.

21. Has everyone supplied _____ Social Security number yet?

22. Give the staff _____ raises early this year.

23. All can voice _____ opinions here.

24. City Securities has just announced _____ year-end dividends.

25. Either of the new products would readily find _____ niche in the marketplace.

You can learn more about pronouns by looking in a grammar book under the following headings:

agreement with antecedents	indefinite pronouns	possessive pronouns
case of pronouns	interrogative pronouns	reciprocal pronouns
demonstrative pronouns	numeral pronouns	reflexive pronouns
gender-neutral pronouns	personal pronouns	relative pronouns

You may also want to refer to Section 1.2, "Pronouns," in Appendix I, "Fundamentals of Grammar and Usage," in *Business Communication Today*, Fourth Edition.

Lesson 4

Parts of Speech: Verbs

Verbs are a sentence's "action" or "being" words; that is, they tell what happens or what is. Verbs may consist of one or several words—*wrote* and *would have written*, for example—and the form of a verb may change to indicate subtle meaning and to complement other words in the sentence.

Among the many action verbs used in business are *send, pay,* and *produce*. The words underlined in the following sentences are action verbs as well:

> They <u>bought</u> a $15 million company and <u>turned</u> it into an even bigger company.
> I <u>have seen</u> the proposal, but I <u>cannot remember</u> some of its specific points.
> <u>Will</u> you <u>stock</u> item 6-2993 next quarter?
> Don <u>is eating</u> lunch in the cafeteria.

Notice that some of these verbs consist of a helping verb (such as *have*) and a main verb (such as *seen*).

Among being verbs, the most common is, logically enough, *be*:

	Present	Past	Other Tenses
I	am	was	will be (future), have
you	are	were	been (present perfect),
he, she, it	is	was	had been (past per-
we	are	were	fect), will have been
they	are	were	(future perfect)

But other verbs—such as *feel, seem,* and *sound*—serve the same purpose and can substitute for *be*. All being verbs link the subject of a sentence with other qualities, like an equal sign; they indicate that the word on one side is linked with the word on the other side. But they do not demonstrate any action. For example, all of the following verbs describe a state of being:

> Darla <u>was</u> happy about her promotion.
> The figures <u>seem</u> accurate.
> Your estimate <u>sounded</u> right.
> I <u>will feel</u> better tomorrow.

In the following exercises, underline all being verbs:

1. Andy feels ready to demonstrate the product.

2. Chicago Fabricating sent holiday greetings to all its major customers.

3. This procedure lasts only five minutes.

4. We were reluctant to give a refund in this case.

5. Will you be using my desk while I'm out of the office?

203

Verb tenses allow you to talk about things happening or existing in different time periods. For regular verbs, the present tense adds a final *s* to the main verb, but only when used with *he, she,* or *it*; the past tense adds *ed* to the main verb; and the future tense uses the main verb with the helping verb *will.* For example:

Present: He <u>mails</u> the letters on Tuesday.
Past: He <u>mailed</u> the letters on Tuesday.
Future: He <u>will mail</u> the letters on Tuesday.

Although these are the three tenses most frequently used, you will also have occasion to use three "perfect" tenses, which use the helping verb *have* and usually the past tense of the main verb:

Present perfect: He <u>has mailed</u> the letters on Tuesday.
Past perfect: He <u>had mailed</u> the letters on Tuesday.
Future perfect: He <u>will have mailed</u> the letters on Tuesday.

Write the verb tense called for in each of the following exercises:

6. repair (future perfect) _____

7. hire (past) _____

8. move (past perfect) _____

9. motivate (present perfect) _____

10. train (future) _____

Not all verbs are as regular as these; indeed, they are called irregular verbs because in one or more of the tenses they do not follow this pattern. The most irregular of the verbs is *be,* but many other common verbs are to some extent irregular. Here is a sample:

PRESENT PERFECT	<u>go</u>	<u>begin</u>	<u>drink</u>	<u>take</u>
PAST	went	began	drank	took
FUTURE	will go	will begin	will drink	will take
PRESENT PERFECT	have/has gone	have/has begun	have/has drunk	have/has taken
PAST PERFECT	had gone	had begun	had drunk	had taken
FUTURE PER~ ~~~.	will have gone	will have begun	will have drunk	will have taken

Provide the irregular verb form called for in the following exercises:

11. I (present perfect, *became*) _____ the resident expert on repairing the copy machine.

12. She (past, *know*) _____ how to perform an audit when she came to work for us.

13. By the time you finish the analysis, he (future perfect, *take*) _____ his vacation.

14. Next week, call John to tell him what you (future, *do*) _____ for next month's sales meeting.

15. When Susan returned to our company, she (past perfect, *rise*) _____ in rank to analyst.

Another way to distinguish among verbs is to label them either transitive or intransitive. Transitive verbs—such as *give, lay, set,* and *raise*—transfer the action from the subject to the object. For example:

> He <u>gave</u> a refund to Nissa Nelson.

In this sentence, the verb *gave* is what he (subject) did to or with the refund (object).
On the other hand, intransitive verbs—such as *feel, lie, sit,* and *rise*—do not transfer any action:

> Profits <u>rose</u> in the first quarter.

The verb *rose* is what profits (subject) did, but profits did not act directly on anything in this sentence.
Some verbs may be transitive or intransitive. Consider the following:

> He <u>feels</u> uncomfortable with the proposition.
> She <u>feels</u> the texture of the cloth before deciding to buy.

In the first sentence, *he* (subject) *feels* (predicate), but nothing in the sentence receives the direct impact of his feeling. In the second sentence, however, *she* (subject) *feels* (predicate) *texture* (object); in other words, she performs an action that has a direct impact on something.

In the exercises below, underline the intransitive verbs and circle the transitive verbs:

16. Ms. Detweiler sent him a reminder.

17. What is the purpose of this memo?

18. When you have heard her story, call me about it.

19. They mentioned a name yesterday.

20. He sat next to my desk and described the whole thing.

The way you use verbs can have a great deal to do with the tone of your writing. For example, verbs may be either passive or active. An active sentence uses direct, subject-verb-object order:

> We <u>will refund</u> your money.

Notice how much more indirect this passive sentence is:

> Your money <u>will be refunded</u>.

It is not clear who is doing the refunding in this sentence.
Active sentences are more forceful than passive sentences, which is usually desirable. However, in business communication you may sometimes want to soften a statement or to avoid assigning responsibility for an action. Then you will find passive sentences useful.
Rewrite the sentences in the following exercises so that they use active verbs instead of passive verbs:

21. The report will be written by Leslie Cartwright. _____

_____

22. The failure to record the transaction was mine. _____

_____

23. Have you been notified by the claims department of your rights? _____

_____

24. We are dependent on their services for our operation. _____

_____

25. The damaged toaster had been returned by the customer. _____

_____

If you want to learn more about verbs, look in a grammar book for information on these topics:

auxiliary verbs	mood of verbs	verb tenses
irregular verbs	subjunctive mood	voice of verbs
linking verbs	transitive and intransitive verbs	

You may also wish to consult Sections 1.3, "Verbs," and 1.7.5, "Sentences with Linking Verbs," in Appendix I, "Fundamentals of Grammar and Usage," in *Business Communication Today*, Fourth Edition.

Lesson 5

Parts of Speech: Verb Agreement

To use verbs correctly you must make decisions about verb forms based on the number represented by the subject. Take, for example, the present tense of the verb *vote*:

<u>Singular:</u>   I vote   <u>Plural:</u>   we vote
                   you vote   you vote
                   he/she/it votes   they vote

In the present tense, a regular verb like *vote* takes a final *s* or *es* to agree with the singular pronouns *he*, *she*, and *it* or with any singular noun.

Other verbs are not so easy to deal with. Consider the present tense of these irregular verbs:

<u>be:</u>   I am, we are   <u>have:</u>   I have, we have
               you are   you have
               he/she/it is, they are   he/she/it has, they have

<u>apply:</u>   I apply, we apply   <u>can:</u>   I can, we can
               you apply   you can
               he/she/it applies, they apply   he/she/it can, they can

In the following exercises, write in the present tense of each verb:

1. You (*be*) _____ eligible for a promotion already.

2. Dave (*have*) _____ another telephone line.

3. How (*be*) _____ I supposed to know when we've reached that point?

4. She (*do*) _____ her work quickly and accurately.

5. They (*be*) _____ sometimes difficult to deal with.

Getting the verb to agree with the subject in sentences like these is relatively simple. But problems arise when the sentence is complicated.

Each sentence is made up of at least one clause, a group of words with both a subject and a predicate. Sentences may also contain phrases, which do not have a subject-predicate set. Notice the difference here:

Clause: <u>he</u> <u>sent</u> an invoice
Clause: because <u>he</u> <u>sent</u> an invoice

Phrase: with an invoice
Phrase: after sending an invoice

The clauses have subjects and predicates; the phrases do not have subjects and predicates.

A simple sentence has only one clause like the first clause above, but many sentences combine clauses and phrases, like this:

He <u>sent</u> an invoice, and then <u>he</u> <u>entered</u> the amount in the books.
Because <u>he</u> <u>sent</u> an invoice, <u>he</u> <u>decided</u> not to call T&T Sales.

<u>He</u> <u>presented</u> the client with an invoice.
After sending an invoice, <u>he</u> <u>began</u> another project.

Notice that all the verbs in these examples are in the past tense; in other words, they agree. Only if there were a good reason for the verbs to be in different tenses would they not agree. For example:

Yesterday she <u>prepared</u> a sales report, today she <u>is listing</u> all her potential clients, and tomorrow she <u>will call</u> them.

In some sentences with two or more verbs, the helping verbs or the main verbs are sometimes identical. In that case, the duplicated word or words can be dropped:

Consumers <u>have been saving</u> and (*have been*) <u>spending</u>.

But do not drop any part of a verb that is not an exact duplicate. For example, this sentence is wrong:

They <u>have not</u> and <u>will not be attending</u> the workshops.

It becomes correct when part of the helping verb is restored:

They <u>have not been</u> and <u>will not be attending</u> the workshops.

Here is another type of agreement problem:

The building <u>is</u> attractive, economical, and <u>has</u> beautiful surroundings.

Because *is* and *has* are different and no verb is included with *economical*, this sentence is wrong. It can be fixed by adding another verb:

The building <u>is</u> attractive, <u>is</u> economical, and <u>has</u> beautiful surroundings.

It can also be fixed by changing one of the items in the series so that it is the same type of word as the other two:

The building <u>is</u> attractive, economical, and beautifully situated.

In the following exercises, fill in the correct verb form:

6. They identified the source of the problem, and then they (*look*) _____ for ways to solve it.

7. When success (*seem*) _____ imminent, he panics.

8. Jason Beaudry never has gone to Europe and probably never (*go*) _____.

9. Why (*do*) _____ she ignore John when he talks?

10. We (*take*) _____ that point into consideration before we decided what to do.

Another problem of verb agreement relates to the subject (noun or pronoun) of a sentence. The verb should be in the plural form when the subject is plural. Otherwise, the verb should be singular. When a phrase separates the subject and the verb, the task of deciding whether to use a singular or plural verb becomes more complicated. Look at this example:

The <u>analysis</u> of existing documents <u>takes</u> a full week.

Although *documents* is plural, the verb is in the singular form. That's because the subject of the sentence is *analysis*, a singular noun. The phrase of *existing documents* can be disregarded. Here is another example:

Their <u>answers</u> to the questions <u>are</u> in the minutes.

Take away the phrase *to the question*, and you are left with the plural subject *answers*. Therefore the verb takes the plural form.

Circle the correct verb form in the following exercises:

11. Each of the managers turn/turns in a monthly report.

12. The receptionist, not the clerks, take/takes all the calls.

13. Everyone upstairs receive/receives mail before we do.

14. The reasons for her decision sound/sounds logical.

15. All the products sell/sells well.

Verb agreement is also complicated when the subject is not a specific noun or pronoun and when the subject may be considered either singular or plural. In these cases, you have to analyze the surrounding sentence to determine which verb form to use. Observe carefully which of the following sentences contain *are* (plural form of *be*) and which contain *is* (singular form). The noun that controls the verb form is underlined in each sentence:

The <u>staff</u> is quartered in the warehouse.
The <u>staff</u> are at their desks in the warehouse.
The <u>computers</u> and the <u>staff</u> are in the warehouse.
Neither the staff nor the <u>computers</u> are in the warehouse.
<u>Every</u> computer is in the warehouse.
<u>Many a</u> computer is in the warehouse.

Did you notice that words like *every* use the singular verb form? In addition, when a *neither-nor* phrase combines singular and plural nouns, the verb takes the form that matches the noun closest to it.

Circle the correct form of the verb in the following exercises:

16.   Brenda and Bill has/have responsibility for the project.

17.   Neither the main office nor the branch offices is/are blameless.

18.   Each programmer and analyst report/reports to Jennifer.

19.   Your whole family enjoy/enjoys credit privileges at Mo's.

20.   Either the secretaries or the office manager take/takes care of all inquiries about employee benefits.

In the business world, some types of subject require extra attention. Company names, for example, are considered singular and therefore take a singular verb in most cases—even if they contain plural words.

But quantities are sometimes considered singular and sometimes plural. If a quantity refers to a total amount, it takes a singular verb; if a quantity refers to individual, countable units, it takes a plural verb. For example:

> <u>Three hours</u> is a long time.
> The <u>eight dollars</u> we collected for the fund are tacked on the bulletin board.

Fractions may also be singular or plural, depending on the noun that accompanies them:

> One-third of the <u>warehouse</u> is devoted to this product line.
> One-third of the <u>products</u> are defective.

Circle the correct verb form in the following exercises:

21.   C & B Sales is/are listed in the directory.

22.   When measuring shelves, 7 inches is/are significant.

23.   About 90 percent of the employees plan/plans to come to the company picnic.

24.   Carnegie Industries make/makes book-binding equipment.

25.   Two weeks is/are all we need to complete our analysis.

To learn more about verb agreement, consult a grammar book on these topics:

agreement with *there* and *here*	compound subjects	verb agreement
collective nouns	indefinite pronouns	*who* clauses
complements	intervening elements	

You may wish to refer to Sections 1.3.2, "Irregular Verbs," and 1.7.2, "Longer Sentences," in Appendix I, "Fundamentals of Grammar and Usage," in *Business Communication Today*, Fourth Edition.

Lesson 6

Parts of Speech: Adjectives and Articles

Adjectives modify (describe, explain, tell something about) nouns and pronouns. The adjectives in the following sentences do this job whether they come before or after the words they modify and whether they are truly adjectives or are nouns working as adjectives:

> The <u>Seattle</u> office has received <u>another</u> payment from <u>that</u> customer.
> A <u>more attractive</u> desk is earmarked for Ms. Brophy's <u>fourth-floor</u> office.
> We are <u>proud</u> of your <u>outstanding</u> performance in <u>many</u> competitions.

These sentences would be much less descriptive without adjectives telling which, what kind of, and what. (Although possessive pronouns, such as *your*, seem to function as adjectives, they are classified as pronouns.)

Observe that the adjectives in these sentences fall into three categories: purely descriptive (such as *outstanding* and *more attractive*), limiting (such as *many*), and pointing (such as *that*). Descriptive adjectives are probably the easiest to identify in any sentence; they are words like *cold, impatient, useful, good.* Limiting adjectives are a little more difficult to pick out, but numbers and such words as *most, several,* and *no* are often used to specify quantity or amount. The pointing adjectives are *this, that, these,* and *those.* The sentences also contain articles: *a, an,* and *the.*

In the following exercises, underline all the adjectives and articles:

1. A pleasant surprise awaits you for taking advantage of our fantastic offer.

2. The newest accountant on our headquarters staff is a 1991 graduate of the most prestigious university in a neighboring state.

3. She slowly rose to speak to the assembled delegates.

4. Their approach is best described as a useful combination of grand design and careful execution.

5. The color photographs in that brochure were expensive.

Adjectives change form when they are used to compare items:

One Item	Two Items	Three or More Items
large	larger	largest
easy	easier	easiest
far	farther	farthest
good	better	best
bad	worse	worst
little	less	least
some	more	most
beautiful	more beautiful	most beautiful

As you can see from this list, simple adjectives like *large* add the ending *er* when comparing two items and *est* when comparing three or more items. This is the normal pattern. Other words, such as *good*, are irregular. And words with three or more syllables use *more* and *most*, instead of the word endings, to make comparisons.

Some adjectives cannot be used to make comparisons because they themselves indicate the extreme. For example, if something is perfect, nothing can be more perfect. If something is unique or ultimate, nothing can be more unique or more ultimate.

In the following exercises, fill in the appropriate form of the adjectives that are supplied for you:

6. Of the two products, this one has the (*great*) _____ potential.

7. The (*perfect*) _____ solution is d.

8. Here is the (*interesting*) _____ of all the ideas I have heard so far.

9. Our service is (*good*) _____ than theirs.

10. The (*hard*) _____ part of my job is firing people.

Many adjectives used in the business world are actually combinations of words: *up-to-date* report, *last-minute* effort, *fifth-floor* suite, *well-built* engine. As you can see, they are hyphenated when they come before the noun they modify. However, when they come after the noun they modify, they are not hyphenated: the report is *up to date*, an effort made at the *last minute*, a suite on the *fifth floor*, an engine that is *well built*.

Hyphens are not used when part of the combination is a word ending in *ly* (because the word ending in *ly* is usually not an adjective): a rapidly *shrinking* reserve, a highly *motivated* employee.

A hyphen is also omitted from combinations of words that are used frequently: *credit card* account, *data processing* department.

In the following exercises, insert hyphens wherever required:

11. A highly placed source revealed Dotson's last ditch efforts to cover up the mistake.

12. Please send a replacement that is large enough for me.

13. A top secret document was taken from the president's office last night.

14. A 30 year old person should know better.

15. If I write a large scale report, I want to know that it will be read by upper level management.

Adjectives often pile up in front of a noun, like this:

The <u>superficial</u>, <u>obvious</u> answer was the one she gave.
The most valuable animal on the ranch is a <u>small black</u> horse.

The question is whether a comma should be used to separate the adjectives. The answer? Use a comma when the two adjectives independently modify the noun; do not use a comma when one of the adjectives is closely identified with the noun. In the first example above, the answer was both superficial and obvious. But in the second example, the black horse is small.

Another way for you to think about this problem is to use the word *and* as a replacement for the comma.

Here is another example for you to study:

We recommend a diet of <u>leafy green</u> vegetables.
We recommend a diet of <u>green</u>, <u>leafy</u> vegetables.

Because some green vegetables are not leafy (cucumbers and zucchini, for example), it is correct to leave out the comma in the first example so that you know which kind of green vegetables are being discussed. But because all leafy vegetables are also green (green and leafy), the comma must be included in the second example. Again:

He is an <u>angry young</u> man.
He is an <u>angry</u>, <u>dangerous</u> man.

There is a difference between a young man who is angry and a man who is angry and dangerous.

Another device for deciding whether to use a comma is to try switching the adjectives. If the order of the adjectives can be reversed without changing the meaning of the phrase, you should use a comma. If the order cannot be reversed, you should not use a comma. For example:

Here's our <u>simplified credit</u> application.
Here's our <u>simplified</u>, <u>easy-to-complete</u> application.
Here's our <u>easy-to-complete</u>, <u>simplified</u> application.

A credit application may be simple or complex; at any rate, you cannot talk about a *credit, simplified application*. The application in the second and third examples, however, is both simplified and easy to complete, however you arrange the words.

In the following exercises, insert required commas between adjectives:

16. The two companies are engaged in an all-out no-holds-barred struggle for dominance.

17. A tiny metal shaving is responsible for the problem.

18. She came to the office with a bruised swollen knee.

19. A chipped cracked sheet of glass is useless to us.

20. You'll receive our usual cheerful prompt service.

In these last exercises, insert both hyphens and commas as necessary:

21. It was one of the first land grant colleges in the country.

22. Joan is the stern mother hen of a busy tightly run office.

23. Energy wasting unnecessary trips must be eliminated.

24. The new past due notices will go out with today's mail.

25. If a broken down unproductive guy like Carl can get a raise why can't a take charge guy like me get one?

If you want to learn more about adjectives and articles, consult a grammar book on the following topics:

absolute adjectives	coordinate adjectives	limiting adjectives
comparative adjectives	descriptive adjectives	pointing adjectives
compound adjectives	independent adjectives	proper adjectives

You may also wish to consult Sections 1.4, "Adjectives," and 1.6.2, "Conjunctions, Articles, and Interjections," in Appendix I, "Fundamentals of Grammar and Usage," in *Business Communication Today*, Fourth Edition.

Lesson 7

Parts of Speech: Adverbs

Adverbs modify (describe, qualify, limit) verbs, adjectives, and other adverbs:

Verb:	He sent the specifications <u>promptly</u>. (How were they sent? Promptly.)
Adjective:	Their <u>grievously</u> late report will not be accepted. (How late was the report? Grievously late.)
Adverb:	He typed <u>very</u> quickly. (How quickly did he type? Very quickly.)

Most adverbs are formed simply by adding *ly* to the end of an adjective (with the last letter of the adjective sometimes dropped or changed): *highly, quickly, truly, nicely, poorly,* and so on. But some familiar adverbs—such as *quite, too, very, almost, often, soon, so,* and *many*—do not end in *ly.*

In the following exercises, underline the adverbs:

1. An unstable person is an obviously poor choice for this difficult job.

2. They are quite certain that the spaces will fill soon.

3. She often stays late to finish her rapidly accumulating paperwork.

4. Curly hair is yours with our newly developed perms.

5. A nicely organized report is soon read.

6. Too many of our customers have complained vigorously about her surly manner.

7. Trapped in a slowly shrinking market, the company is certainly doomed to fail eventually.

8. The market for anatomically correct dolls is too small.

9. Give the letter a quick review before you blithely send it.

10. A correctly operating bottom-of-the line model is much better than a malfunctioning top-of-the-line model.

Some adverbs are difficult to distinguish from adjectives. For example, in the following sentences is the underlined word an adverb or an adjective?

They worked <u>well</u>.
The baby is <u>well</u>.

In the first sentence, *well* is an adverb modifying the verb worked. In the second sentence, *well* is an adjective modifying the noun *baby.*

The secret to choosing correctly between adverbs and adjectives in this situation is to be able to identify such being verbs as *appear, be, become, feel, look, seem, smell, sound,* and *taste.* Being verbs link a noun to an adjective describing the noun. In contrast, an adverb is used if the verb that separates it from the noun is an action verb. Here is another example:

Adjective: This balance sheet looks <u>strange</u>. (The balance sheet does not itself use eyes to look; this sentence means that the balance sheet *is* strange.)

Adverb: She looks at us <u>strangely</u>. (Here *looks* is an action verb, and *strangely* tells how she performs that action.)

If you can tell the difference between an adjective and an adverb in situations like these, you should have no trouble deciding when to use *good, real,* and *slow* (adjectives modifying nouns) as opposed to *well, really,* and *slowly* (adverbs modifying verbs, adjectives, and adverbs). For example:

Adjective	Adverb
He is a <u>good</u> worker. (What kind of worker is he?)	He works <u>well</u>. (How does he work?)
It is a <u>real</u> computer. (What kind of computer is it?)	It <u>really</u> is a computer. (To what extent is it one?)
The traffic is <u>slow</u>. (What quality does the traffic have?	The traffic moves <u>slowly</u>. (How does the traffic move?)

In the following exercises, circle the correct choice:

11. Their performance has been good/well.

12. I sure/surely do not know how to help you.

13. He feels sick/sickly again today.

14. Customs dogs are chosen because they smell good/well.

15. The redecorated offices look good/well.

Like adjectives, adverbs can be used to compare items. Generally, the basic adverb is combined with *more* or *most,* just as long adjectives are—although some adverbs have one-word comparative forms:

One Item	Two Items	Three Items
quickly	more quickly	most quickly
sincerely	less sincerely	least sincerely
fast	faster	fastest
well	better	best

In these exercises, provide the correct form of the adverbs that are provided:

16. Which of the two programs computes (*fast*) _____ ?

17. Kate has 13 years of experience to draw on, but she was (*recently*) _____

employed by Graphicon.

18. Could they be (*happily*) _____ employed than they are now?

19. This is the (*well*) _____ designed model of the two we have in stock.

20. You are to be praised for presenting the (*logically*) _____ reasoned argument I have ever heard.

Negative adverbs—such as *neither, no, not, scarcely,* and *seldom*—are powerful words and therefore do not need any help in conveying a negative thought. In fact, using double negatives gives a strong impression of illiteracy, so you would be well advised to avoid sentences like these:

I <u>don't</u> want <u>no</u> mistakes. (Correct: I don't want any mistakes. I want no mistakes.)
They <u>scarcely</u> noticed <u>neither</u> one. (Correct: They scarcely noticed either one. They noticed neither one.)

In the following exercises, correct the double negatives by crossing out unnecessary letters and words and writing in necessary letters and words:

21. He doesn't seem to have none.

22. That machine is scarcely never used.

23. They can't get no replacement parts until Thursday.

24. It wasn't no different from the first event we promoted.

25. We've looked for it, and it doesn't seem to be no where.

If you would like to learn more about adverbs, consult a grammar book on the following topics:

adverbs versus adjectives   double negatives
comparative adverbs   redundant adverbs

You may also wish to refer to Section 1.5, "Adverbs," in Appendix I, "Fundamentals of Grammar and Usage," in *Business Communication Today*, Fourth Edition.

Lesson 8

Parts of Speech: Verbals

Some forms of verbs take a special role in sentences. Verbals are verbs that are used as nouns, adjectives, and adverbs instead of as predicate verbs. There are three basic types of verbals.

The first type of verbal, called a gerund, is formed by adding *ing* to the end of a verb and is used as a noun:

<u>Selling</u> is an acquired skill.

Selling (a gerund) is the subject of this sentence, and *is* is the predicate verb.

Be careful not to mistake gerunds for predicate verbs that use an *ing* ending. Compare these sentences:

Predicate verb: He <u>is merchandising</u> a new product.
Gerund: He has a knack for <u>merchandising</u>.

In the second sentence, *has* is the predicate verb, and *merchandising* is the object of a phrase.

The major problem that arises with gerunds is the use of a possessive noun or pronoun with them. The following sentence is incorrect:

We appreciate <u>you</u> calling about this matter.

Because *calling* takes the place of a noun in this sentence, *you* must be changed to a possessive pronoun, like this:

We appreciate <u>your</u> calling about this matter.

Only the second sentence below is correct:

Incorrect: <u>Deborah</u> delaying will jeopardize the whole program.
Correct: <u>Deborah's</u> delaying will jeopardize the whole program.

You can decide whether to use a possessive noun or pronoun with a gerund by replacing it with another noun. For example, if you replace the word *delaying* with the word *temper*, you will find that you must use a possessive noun in order to make sense:

<u>Deborah's</u> temper will jeopardize the whole program.

In the following exercises, circle the sentences that use gerunds correctly:

1. Waiting for anything makes me impatient.

2. His handling of the irate customer was admirable.

3. You saw the result of George training.

4. Take the results to manufacturing.

5. You could attribute the difference to them cheating.

The second kind of verbal is the participle, which serves in sentences as an adjective. In the following sentences, observe how the participles formed from the verb *finish* are used to modify nouns:

The typist put the <u>finishing</u> touches on the letter.
The <u>finished</u> assignment is in Ms. Boromisa's office.

In both of these sentences, a form of the verb *finish* is used to provide additional information about nouns: *touches* and *assignment*. Other verbs—*put* and *is*—work in these sentences as predicate verbs.
In the following exercises, underline the participles:

6. The established procedures are rarely followed.

7. Use a roasting bag to avoid an overdone turkey.

8. Twice-audited Hodgkins & Company has become more careful with its record keeping.

9. The closed factory will be reopening in May.

10. During the editing process, most written reports are strengthened.

The third form of verbal is the infinitive, which you have probably heard of (as in "splitting infinitives"). An infinitive, such as *to be*, may function as a noun, an adjective, or an adverb. For example, in this sentence the infinitive works as a noun—in fact, as the subject of the sentence:

<u>To err</u> is human. (What is human?)

Here it is a noun too, but this time it's the object of the sentence:

We hope <u>to grow</u> this year. (We hope what?)

In the following sentence, the infinitive works as an adjective:

Their plan <u>to grow</u> was hampered by a weak economy. (What kind of plan?)

And here the infinitive works as an adverb:

It eventually grew <u>to be</u> a very large company. (How did it grow?)

Now, about splitting infinitives: In general, you should avoid putting any word or phrase between *to* and the rest of the infinitive. But sometimes you must split an infinitive to protect your sentence's clarity or smoothness. For example, splitting the infinitive in this sentence is acceptable:

The best policy is <u>to</u> regularly <u>inspect</u> and <u>service</u> all the equipment.

But this one becomes awkward when the infinitive is split:

> <u>To</u> predictably, promptly, and reliably <u>call</u> on customers is part of your job.

It would be better like this:

> <u>To call</u> on customers predictably, promptly, and reliably is part of your job.

In the following exercises, circle the words that split an infinitive and draw an arrow to show where they would fit in more smoothly and logically:

11. Our goal is to, with your help, track down the error.

12. Did you tell her to promptly call me?

13. To cheerfully service these accounts, you need patience.

14. We have been trying to desperately avoid bankruptcy.

15. Ms. McMichaels tends to, with her great sense of timing, know just when she should sell.

In the next set of exercises, draw circles around the verbals and draw lines to the words they modify (if they indeed modify anything):

16. Handling explosives is our main business.

17. Your plan to analyze these trends is sound.

18. The trading experts recommend patience.

19. We planned to finish by Wednesday.

20. Streamlined DiTex has more flexibility than some of its competitors.

A glaring sign of carelessness in writing is the use of different types of verbals in situations that call for parallel structure. For instance, the following sentence is a mess:

> Your responsibilities include <u>gathering</u> sales figures, <u>analysis</u> of those figures, and <u>to report</u> them to management.

You could solve the problem by putting all the underlined verbals in the same form:

> gathering, analyzing, and reporting
> collection of, analysis of, and reporting of
> to gather, to analyze, and to report

Many other sentences can be improved by introducing parallelism:

Nonparallel: He was an expert in <u>writing</u> and had learned well how <u>to speak</u>.
Parallel: He was an expert in <u>writing</u> and <u>speaking</u>.
Parallel: He had learned well how <u>to write</u> and <u>to speak</u>.

In the following exercises, cross out and add words to give the sentences a parallel structure:

21. These were my goals: finding suitable markets and to outline a plan for penetrating them.

22. Standing firm is more difficult than to allow an exception.

23. She has demonstrated an ability to plan and skill at organizing.

24. This remarkable new product will help you to keep your time organized and with writing your correspondence.

25. Retraining people already on the payroll is better than to hire new people.

If you would like to know more about verbals, consult a grammar book on these topics:

dangling modifiers	misplaced modifiers	verbal nouns
gerunds	parallelism	verbal phrases
infinitives	participles	

You may also wish to refer to Section 1.7.6, "Misplaced Modifiers," in Appendix I, "Fundamentals of Grammar and Usage," in *Business Communication Today*, Fourth Edition.

Lesson 9

Parts of Speech: Prepositions

Prepositions are little words that can add a lot of meaning to sentences. These are some of the most frequently used prepositions:

about	before	for	out
after	between	in	through
among	by	into	to
at	during	of	with

Some prepositions consist of more than one word—like these:

because of	in addition to
except for	out of

And some prepositions are closely linked with a verb. When using phrases like *look up* and *wipe out*, keep the phrase intact and do not insert anything between the verb and the preposition.

Other prepositions do not stand alone either; they signal prepositional phrases that have a noun as an object:

<u>of</u> the company	<u>in</u> other words
<u>by</u> taking part	<u>into</u> a bank

Prepositional phrases always modify another part of a sentence:

Subject (*she*):	<u>Of all our technicians</u>, she is the best trained.
Object(*merit*):	They couldn't see the merit <u>in my proposal</u>.
Predicate verb (*left*):	Someone left a folder on <u>my desk</u>.

To prevent misreading, prepositional phrases should be placed near the element they modify. For example, in the first example here, the prepositional phrase modifies *she* and is therefore placed right next to it.

In the following exercises, underline the prepositional phrases:

1. The knob on your radio broke after the expiration date.

2. A truckload of replacements has been sent to Dayton.

3. With her luck, she will soon be named head of the department.

4. He worked for our company about two years ago.

5. You will not be included in our benefits program during our training period.

When a pronoun is part of a prepositional phrase, it should always be in the object form—*me, you, him/her/it, us, them, whom*:

>Give the documents <u>to them</u>.
>They will choose <u>between Harry and me</u>.

In the following exercises, underline the correct pronoun:

6. Send the memo to Sandra and he/him.

7. The red sports car belongs to who/whom?

8. I hope they award the contract to us/we.

9. This information is just between you and I/me.

10. They asked for help from Don and her/she.

It was once considered totally unacceptable to put a preposition at the end of a sentence. Now you may:

>I couldn't tell what they were interested <u>in</u>. (*better than I couldn't tell in what they were interested.*)
>What did she attribute it <u>to</u>? (*better than To what did she attribute it?*)

Be careful, however, not to use the wrong form of a pronoun in sentences that end in a preposition. For example, is *who* or *whom* correct in this sentence?

>(Who/Whom) did you speak <u>to</u>?

You can figure out the answer by moving the preposition and the pronoun back together:

><u>To whom</u> did you speak?

Be sure to use only the prepositions that are necessary. In the following sentences, the prepositions in parentheses should be omitted:

>All (of) the staff members were present.
>I almost fell off (of) my chair with surprise.
>Where was Mr. Steuben going (to)?
>They couldn't help (from) wondering.

The opposite problem is not including a preposition when you should. Consider the two sentences that follow:

>Sales were over $100,000 <u>for</u> Linda and Bill.
>Sales were over $100,000 <u>for</u> Linda and <u>for</u> Bill.

The first sentence indicates that Linda and Bill had combined sales over $100,000; the second, that Linda and Bill each had sales over $100,000, for a combined total in excess of $200,000. The preposition *for* is crucial here.

Prepositions are also required in sentences like this one:

Which type <u>of</u> personal computer do you prefer?

Certain prepositions are used with certain words. When the same preposition can be used for two or more words in a sentence without affecting the meaning, only the last preposition is required:

We are familiar (<u>with</u>) and satisfied <u>with</u> your company's products.

But when different prepositions are normally used with the words, all the prepositions must be included:

We are familiar <u>with</u> and interested <u>in</u> your company's products.

In the following exercises, cross out unnecessary words and prepositions that are in the wrong place and insert prepositions where they are required:

11.   Where was your argument leading to?

12.   I wish he would get off of the phone.

13.   This is a project into which you can sink your teeth.

14.   U.S. Mercantile must become aware and sensitive to its customers' concerns.

15.   We are responsible for aircraft safety in the air, the hangars, and the runways.

Here is an incomplete list of prepositions that are used in a particular way with particular words:

among/between: *among* is used to refer to three or more (*Circulate the memo among the office staff*); *between* is used to refer to two (*Put the copy machine between Judy and Dan*)

as if/like: *as if* is used before a clause (*It seems as if we should be doing something*); *like* is used before a noun or pronoun along (*He seems like a nice guy*)

have/of: *have*, a verb, is used in verb phrases (*They should have checked first*); of, a preposition, is never used in such cases

in/into: *in* is used to refer to a static position (*The file is in the cabinet*); *into* is used to refer to movement toward a position (*Put the file into the cabinet*)

And here is an incomplete list of some prepositions that have come to be used with certain words:

according to	get from (receive)	responsible for
agree to (a proposal)	get off (dismount)	similar to
agree with (a person)	in accordance with	talk to (without
buy from	in search of	interaction)
capable of	independent of	talk with (with
comply with	inferior to	interaction)
conform to	plan to	wait for (person or
differ from (things)	prefer to	thing)
differ with (person)	prior to	wait on (like a waiter)
different from	reason with	

If in doubt about the preposition to use with a word, look up the word in the dictionary. In the following exercises, insert the correct words:

16. Dr. Namaguchi will be talking _____ the marketing class on Tuesday, but she won't have time to answer students' questions.

17. Matters like this are decided after thorough discussion _____ all seven department managers.

18. Do you agree _____ this proposal?

19. We can't wait _____ their decision much longer.

20. CanCorp would _____ been in a good position if it had not diversified so soon.

21. Someone should try to reason _____ him.

22. Who is responsible _____ ordering sporting goods?

23. Their computer is similar _____ ours.

24. This model is different _____ the one we ordered.

25. She got her chair _____ the person who quit.

If you want to know more about prepositions, consult a grammar book on these topics:

idioms   *like/as if*   prepositional phrases

You may also wish to refer to Section 1.6.1, "Prepositions," in Appendix I, "Fundamentals of Grammar and Usage," in *Business Communication Today*, Fourth Edition.

Lesson 10

Parts of Speech: Conjunctions

Conjunctions connect the parts of a sentence: words, phrases, and clauses. You are probably most familiar with the following conjunctions:

and	for	or	yet
but	nor	so	

In these sentences, the conjunctions are underlined:

That model is old <u>and</u> unpopular, <u>but</u> it should not be scrapped.
<u>Either</u> you <u>or</u> Gretchen should go.
<u>Because</u> she is out of town, she can't attend the meeting.
The report was late; <u>therefore</u>, we haven't made a decision yet.

Notice in the following examples that conjunctions may be used to connect clauses (which have both a subject and a predicate) with other clauses, to connect clauses with phrases (which do not have both a subject and a predicate), and to connect words with words:

Words with words: We sell designer clothing <u>and</u> linens.
Clauses with phrases: Their products are expensive <u>but</u> still appeal to value-conscious consumers.
Clauses with clauses: I will call her on the phone today, <u>or</u> I will visit her office tomorrow.

In the following exercises, underline the conjunctions and write in each blank a code for the type of grammatical elements they join (*W-W* for word to word, *P-C* for phrase to clause, or *C-C* for clause to clause):

1. _____ She was not pleased, nor was she easy to reassure.

2. _____ The new model is sporty yet economical.

3. _____ We are proud of your accomplishments and of your reputation in the community.

4. _____ You promised but apparently forgot to send me the documents.

5. _____ We would cancel the order, for we have not yet sold the items already in stock.

Some conjunctions are used in pairs:

both . . . and	neither . . . nor	whether . . . or
either . . . or	not only . . . but also	

In the following sentences, take special note of both the underlined conjunctions and the italicized words:

226

They <u>not only</u> *are* out of racquets <u>but also</u> *are* out of balls.
They *are* <u>not only</u> out of racquets <u>but also</u> out of balls.
They are *out of* <u>not only</u> racquets <u>but also</u> balls.

With paired conjunctions, you must be careful to construct each phrase in the same way. In other words, if you write *not only are out of racquets*, you cannot write *but also out of balls*; you must include the verb *are* after *but also*. But if you write *are not only out of racquets*, with the verb before the conjunction, you should not include the verb *are* after *but also*. The same need for parallelism exists when using conjunctions to join the other parts of speech, as in these sentences:

He is listed in <u>either</u> *your* roster <u>or</u> *my* roster.
He is listed <u>neither</u> *in* your roster <u>nor</u> *on* the master list.
They <u>both</u> *gave* <u>and</u> *received* notice.

In the following exercises, cross out and insert words to make parallel the pairs of conjunctions and the other parts of speech that go with them:

6.   She is active in not only a civic group but also in an athletic organization.

7.   That is either a mistake or was an intentional omission.

8.   The question is whether to set up a booth at the convention or be hosting a hospitality suite.

9.   In both overall sales and in profits, we are doing better.

10.   She had neither the preferred educational background, nor did she have suitable experience.

In all the previous examples of using conjunctions to join clauses, the clauses have been essentially equal. A different type of conjunction is used to join clauses that are unequal—that is, to join a main clause to one that is subordinate to or dependent on it. Here is a partial list of conjunctions used to introduce dependent clauses:

although	before	once	unless
as soon as	even though	so that	until
because	if	that	when

The dependent clause in each of the following examples is italicized, and the conjunction that links each one to the main clause is underlined:

Send your check now <u>so that</u> *you will not miss this offer.*
<u>Until</u> we have seen the new personnel guidelines, *we cannot offer any raises.*
We have stopped shipping that item, <u>because</u> we have discovered problems with its safety
   mechanism.

Can you see that the italicized part of each of these sentences is indeed subordinate to or dependent on the part that is not italicized?
   Some of the conjunctions used to introduce dependent clauses, such as *before*, may also be used as prepositions. If a phrase follows such a word, the word is working in the sentence as a preposition; but if a clause follows it, the word is working in the sentence as a conjunction:

Preposition (phrase):   <u>Before</u> giving up, she tried calculating an acid-test ratio.
Conjunction (clause):   <u>Before</u> she gave up, she tried calculating an acid-test ratio.

In the following exercises, circle the conjunctions and underline the main clauses:

11.   After making this phone call, I intend to leave.

12.   He has already asked for a promotion, even though he started working here only a month ago.

13.   Be sure to sign this document before you send it back.

14.   If I show you how to use the spreadsheet program, will you show me how to use the word-processing program?

15.   She'll jump at this once-in-a-lifetime opportunity when she finds out about it.

Some conjunctions function as adverbs. Here are some of them (and related transitional phrases):

also	in fact	on the other hand
as a result	indeed	otherwise
consequently	instead	still
even so	meanwhile	that is
furthermore	nevertheless	therefore
however	next	thus

These words and phrases link clauses—and sometimes sentences—that are essentially equal. However, unlike other kinds of conjunctions, they may fall either at the beginning of a clause or somewhere within it. Observe the relationship of the conjunctions (underlined) to the verbs they modify in the following sentences:

They are, <u>in fact</u>, here today. (modifies *are*)
<u>Therefore</u>, we will send a replacement. (modifies *will send*)
The deadline has passed; <u>however</u>, we will accept your application. (modifies *will accept*)

Circle the conjunctions working as adverbs in the following exercises, and underline the verbs they modify:

16.   The factory was shut down for two weeks; consequently, our stocks of Part C-118 are low.

17.   It is indeed a fine example of cooperation.

18.   Her experience is limited; on the other hand her technical skills are excellent.

19.   Ask him if he wants it; otherwise give it to me.

20.   Meanwhile they will be preparing the proposal.

In the final exercises for this lesson, underline all words working as conjunctions:

21. After your half-day presentation to management, you were undoubtedly tired but happy to have survived.

22. Send us a lightweight motor, two pulleys, and a winch.

23. Although you could perhaps find a substitute, you would have a hard time finding one.

24. We ask our credit customers to provide either a spotless credit record or substantial collateral.

25. The company nevertheless plans to distribute dividends equal to last year's.

You can learn more about conjunctions by looking up the following topics in a grammar book:

adverbial conjunctions
conjunctive adverbs
coordinating conjunctions
correlative conjunctions

dependent clauses
independent clauses
subordinating conjunctions

You may also wish to refer to Sections 1.6.2, "Conjunctions, Articles, and Interjections," 1.7.2, "Longer Sentences," 1.7.3, "Sentence Fragments," 1.7.4, "Fused Sentences and Comma Splices," and 4.4, "Transitional Words and Phrases," in Appendix I, "Fundamentals of Grammar and Usage," in *Business Communication Today*, Fourth Edition.

Lesson 11

Parts of Speech: Modifying Elements

You have already learned that adjectives and adverbs work in sentences as modifiers. Phrases and clauses may also work as modifiers. Often, however, they are misplaced or misused. To keep meaning clear, you should place these modifying elements (underlined in the following examples) as close as possible to the word or phrase that they modify (italicized):

The *engineer* <u>with the microchip</u> said nothing was wrong.
The engineer said nothing was *wrong* <u>with the microchip</u>.

The *secretary* <u>who quit</u> left a note for the staff accountant.
The secretary left a note for the staff *accountant* <u>who quit</u>.

<u>During the meeting</u>, they *learned* of the disturbance.
They learned of the *disturbance* <u>during the meeting</u>.

Some phrases and clauses modify, in effect, nothing. Therefore, they are called dangling modifiers:

<u>Instead of introducing a new service</u>, existing services were improved.

The modifying phrase in this sentence does not refer to anything; nothing in the sentence is capable of introducing a new service. Therefore, the sentence must be changed so that the modifier clearly refers to something that makes sense (italicized in the following sentence):

<u>Instead of introducing a new service</u>, *they* improve existing services.

In the revised sentence, *they* are capable of introducing a new service.
   Here is another example that makes no sense:

<u>Although a superb speaker</u>, the organization did not invite her to make a presentation.

An organization cannot be a superb speaker. After a simple change, however, the sentence makes sense:

<u>Although she was a superb speaker</u>, the organization did not invite her to make a presentation.

   In the following exercises, underline the modifying elements that are not in the right place and do **not** make sense:

1. Hampered by a slow economy, dropping the weakest product line seemed reasonable.

2. The typing went quickly, pausing only to get a cup of tea.

3. Because I was unable to make the figures add up, the senior accountant helped me complete the balance sheet.

4. Completely depleted, we must restock the warehouse.

5. While writing the proposal for them, my clients gave me all the information I needed.

6. Obviously a good worker, we should give him a raise.

7. The industry, pressured by imports, suffered losses.

8. Having multiple product lines, poor sales of one won't hurt them.

9. Joel wrote the report in two weeks overwhelmed with other work.

10. With a new batch of products in the warehouse, all orders can be filled next week.

11. Grasping the tab firmly, pull it toward you.

12. Without a single hat in the store, you cannot buy one.

13. Customers get priority service who have maintenance contracts.

14. Exhausted after a long day, sleep seemed the only cure.

15. Despite careful preparation, the proposal was not accepted.

Another sign of careful English is the proper use of *that* and *which*. To use them properly, you must understand the difference between restrictive and nonrestrictive modifiers. A restrictive modifier is essential to the sentence and cannot be omitted without changing its meaning; a nonrestrictive modifier, on the other hand, can be omitted without changing the sentence's essential meaning. Notice the difference:

Restrictive: The proposal <u>that they submitted</u> will be accepted.
Nonrestrictive: The proposal, <u>which they submitted far in advance</u>, will be accepted.

In the first sentence, the restrictive clause tells us an important fact about the proposal being discussed; without it, we would not know which proposal is meant. But in the second sentence, the essential meaning (*The proposal will be accepted*) is not affected by the nonrestrictive clause—only modified by it.

As you can see, *that* is used to introduce restrictive modifiers, with no commas separating such a modifier from the rest of the sentence. *Which* is used to introduce nonrestrictive modifiers, which are set off from the rest of the sentence with commas.

The difference between restrictive and nonrestrictive modifiers also applies to sentences that do not use *that* or *which*:

Restrictive: The programmer <u>who designed the subroutine</u> will get a promotion. (identifies one of several programmers)
Nonrestrictive: The programmer, <u>who designed the subroutine</u>, will get a promotion. (gives additional information about the only programmer)

In the following exercises, insert and delete words and commas so that restrictive and nonrestrictive modifiers are used correctly:

16. The one audit which I was working on is for Sparks, Ltd.

17. Anyone, who wants to advance, should develop job skills.

18. DeLora Johnson the director of planning is out of town.

19. Send your resume to the following address that is the address of our personnel office.

20. The carpeting, which you ordered, is not in stock.

21. We will offer the job to John Gates who has the most experience in our industry.

22. My desk that sits under the air conditioner needs to be moved.

23. Nobody wants to use the desk which sits under the air conditioner.

24. All employees, who carpool regularly, are entitled to half a day of paid vacation per year.

25. Tammy gathering her materials from the lectern added a few last words on third-quarter profits.

If you want to learn more about modifying elements, consult a grammar book on these topics:

appositives	nonrestrictive modifiers	relative pronouns
dangling modifiers	parallelism	restrictive modifiers
misplaced modifiers		

You may also wish to consult Section 1.7.6, "Misplaced Modifiers," in Appendix I, "Fundamentals of Grammar and Usage," in *Business Communication Today*, Fourth Edition.

Lesson 12

Punctuation: The End of the Sentence

Sentences end with one of only three marks of punctuation: a period, a question mark, or an exclamation point. These marks can sometimes be used, however, in other parts of the sentence.

Most frequently, sentences end with periods. All of the following types of sentences use them:

Statement: Their services are in great demand among wealthy retired people.
Expression that stands for a complete sentence: Perhaps. Perhaps not.
Command: Make three copies of this document for tomorrow's meeting.
Polite request: Please make three copies of this document for tomorrow's meeting.
Indirect question: He wanted to know what we plan to do about upgrading our office computers.
Polite request worded like question: Could you please return this copy with your corrections by November 1.

One way to tell whether to use a period or a question mark at the end of a polite request worded like a question is to determine the type of answer you expect. If you expect action to be taken, use a period; if you expect a verbal response, use a question mark.

When a complete sentence is enclosed in parentheses, the period should fall within the closing mark. But if the parenthetical statement is merely a part of a sentence, the period should not be inside the closing mark. For example:

(Consult me later about the third-quarter sales figures.)
We should probably consult later (to talk about the third-quarter sales figures).

With quotations, you should always place the final period inside the closing marks—even if the quotation is not a complete sentence:

She said, "Employees work better when they feel secure."
She said that employees work better "when they feel secure."

Periods are also used with abbreviations, such as *mi.* and *a.m.* However, periods are frequently omitted in common abbreviations that refer to organizations, countries, and well-known people and things, such as JFK, wpm, and USSR. You should also omit periods from shortened forms of some words: *math, 3d,* and *memo,* for instance. A dictionary can tell you when to use periods with abbreviations.

Periods should not be doubled at the end of a sentence that finishes with an abbreviation.

Like periods, question marks also have several uses:

Direct question: Where did you put the new merchandise that arrived yesterday?
Question at end of statement: You've already applied, haven't you?
Question within sentence: The solution—can you believe it?—was within reach all along.
Quoted question within sentence: "What color would you prefer?" the clerk asked.
Expression that stands for complete question: Why not?
Statement subject to uncertainty: On January 14, 1957 (?), the industry was born.

Never use a comma or a period immediately after a question mark:

> "Should I transfer the files?" she asked.
> She asked, "Should I transfer the files?"

Exclamation points are seldom used in business writing—except in advertising copy and sales letters. They are used only to express or generate strong emotion:

> I can't believe he has taken a job with our competition!
> Don't forget!
> Can you believe this price!
> Now!

As with question marks, exclamation points should never be followed immediately by a comma or a period.

In the following exercise, add periods, question marks, and exclamation points wherever they are appropriate. For your convenience, each line of the letter is numbered:

1. Dr Eleanor H Hutton

2. 1358 N Parsons Avenue

3. Tulsa, OK 74104

4. Dear Dr Hutton:

5. Your request for information on TaskMasters, Inc has

6. been passed on to me We truly appreciate your asking

7. TaskMasters has been in existence for three years,

8. and in that time we have experienced a phenomenal growth

9. of 800 percent That qualifies us as a rapidly growing

10. new company, don't you think

11. Our company's president, Daniel Gruber, is a CPA On

12. your behalf, I asked him why he started at TaskMasters His

13. initial response: "Why does Dr Hutton want to know

14. Maybe she plans to become a competitor" (He was

15. joking, of course He knows all about your research

16. Mr Gruber started the company because so many of his

17. regular accounting clients were disorganized Now they

18. can hire us to take care of all their paperwork

19. Is this the sort of information you wanted If you

20. still have questions, you can call me here before 3 pm

21. I have a request for you too Would you possibly mind

22. filling out the enclosed questionnaire We are

23. currently conducting a survey on clients' and potential

24. clients' needs And although you are not yet a client, you

25. may be someday

You can learn more about this subject by looking up the following topics in a grammar book:

exclamation points/marks   periods   question marks

You may also wish to refer to Sections 2.1, "Periods," 2.2, "Question Marks," and 2.3, "Exclamation Points," in Appendix I, "Fundamentals of Grammar and Usage," in *Business Communication Today*, Fourth Edition.

Lesson 13

Punctuation: Commas and Semicolons

Perhaps the most difficult punctuation mark to use correctly is the comma, which indicates a pause—not the full stop indicated by a period. The semicolon, the comma's cousin, indicates a pause greater than a comma but less than a period.

One use for commas is the linking of two independent clauses (sentence parts that contain both a subject and a predicate and can stand alone):

We shipped the ordered items on November 15, and you confirmed receipt on November 20.

The comma is necessary in this sentence because both parts have a subject and a predicate and are equal in importance. Independent clauses like these are joined by the conjunctions *and, but, for, not, or, so,* and *yet.*

Sometimes independent clauses are linked by semicolons instead of commas (no conjunction necessary):

We shipped the ordered items on November 15; you confirmed receipt on November 20.

But do not use semicolons to link sentence elements that are not equal—such as clause to phrase or independent clause to dependent clause. The use of a semicolon in the following sentence is wrong:

We closed down the warehouse yesterday; because we needed to conduct an inventory.

The clause that begins with *because* cannot stand alone and is therefore dependent rather than independent.

Semicolons are also used when a transitional expression such as *however, for example,* or *therefore* is used between independent clauses:

We shipped the ordered items on November 15; however, you confirmed receipt on November 20.

Transitional expressions are followed by a comma when they introduce an independent clause—even when it stands alone as a sentence:

In fact, the first shift is understaffed at present.

Modifying elements (clauses and phrases) that introduce a sentence are also followed by a comma. For example:

Because your application reached us after the deadline, you will be considered for a position at a later time.
Judging from your background, I assume that you will be considered for a position at a later time.
Yes, you will be considered for a position at a later time.

However, commas may be left out if the introductory element is a short prepositional phrase (no subject and predicate) and cannot be misread:

<u>With your help</u> we will soon begin.

Be careful not to confuse readers by omitting necessary commas. Can you tell exactly what the following sentence means without backtracking or reading it twice?

Before leaving Ms. Danforth passed out some assignments.

The meaning becomes much clearer if a comma is added after the prepositional phrase:

Before leaving, Ms. Danforth passed out some assignments.

Within sentences, adjectives are sometimes used in combination to modify a single noun. When the order of the adjectives can be switched without affecting the meaning of the sentence, they are separated by commas (never semicolons):

A <u>stale</u>, <u>metallic</u> taste permeates the water.

But leave out the comma if the order of the two adjectives cannot be switched:

The <u>last promising</u> applicant has been interviewed.

Commas are also used to set off a variety of parenthetical words and phrases within sentences, including state names, dates, abbreviations, quotations, transitional expressions, and contrasted elements. Notice in the following examples that the commas are paired if the parenthetical element falls in the middle of the sentence:

Jerry noticed, before anyone else did, that the numbers don't add up.
They were, in fact, prepared to submit a bid.
Tall buildings, reaching for the sky, soon dominated the cityscape.
The best worker in the department is Ken, who joined the company just a month ago.
Habermacher, Inc., went public in 1986.
Our goal was increased profits, not increased market share.
Service, then, is our main concern.
"The Grant Avenue store," she said yesterday, "is next in line for renovation."
The new factory has been built in Chattanooga, Tennessee, to take advantage of the labor pool there.
Joanne Dubik, M.D., has applied for a loan from First Savings.
I started to work for this company on March 1, 1989, and soon received my first promotion.
Send the letter to Deborah Schneider, 1779 Church Street, Elmhurst, Illinois 60126.

Another common use for commas is to separate three or more items in a series. A comma follows every item except the last:

Send us the main unit, all available peripherals, and an operating manual.
Go to the personnel office, turn in your forms, and return here by 1:15.

Semicolons should be used to separate the items in a series when one or more of the items includes a comma:

The participants were Everett Johnston, Nagle Corporation; DeLynn Buckley, Restaurants Unlimited; and Connie Crichton, Tandem, Inc.

Insert required commas and semicolons in the following exercises, crossing out unnecessary words:

1. Send us four cases of filters two cases of wing nuts and a bale of rags.

2. Can you help teachers and office workers and sales representatives?

3. Mr. Pechman I hope to see you at our next meeting.

4. Your analysis however does not account for returns.

5. As a matter of fact she has seen the figures.

6. Before May 7 1990 they wouldn't have minded either.

7. You can reach me at this address: 717 Darby Place Scottsdale Arizona 85251.

8. Transfer the documents from Fargo North Dakota to Boise Idaho.

9. Sam O'Neill the designated representative is gone today.

10. An outstanding new product has just hit the market.

11. Beginning next week and continuing until January 3 our Austin offices will be closed.

12. She may hire two new representatives or she may postpone filling those territories until the spring.

13. After Martha has gone talk to me about promoting her.

14. Stoneridge Inc. will go public on September 9 1991.

15. We want the new copier not the old model.

16. "Talk to me" Sandra said "before you change a thing."

17. This letter looks good that one doesn't.

18. The Zurich airport has been snowed in therefore I won't be able to meet with you before Thursday January 27.

19. Because of a previous engagement Dr. Stoeve will not be able to attend.

20. Send a copy of the memo to Mary Kennedy Vice President of Marketing Robert Bache Comptroller and Dennis McMurphy Director of Sales.

21. She started attracting attention during the long hard recession of the mid-1970s.

22. We have observed your hard work and because of it we are promoting you to manager of your department.

23. After we see the outcome of the survey we will choose which product to introduce first.

24. Yes we will be able to supply you with all you need.

25. Tolbert & O'Toole is of course a leader in its industry.

To learn more, consult a grammar book on the following topics:

appositives	independent clauses	nonrestrictive modifiers
conjunctions	introductory clauses	parenthetical elements
contrasted elements	introductory phrases	series

You may also wish to consult Sections 1.7.4, "Fused Sentences and Comma Splices," 2.4, "Semicolons," and 2.6, "Commas," in Appendix I, "Fundamentals of Grammar and Usage," in *Business Communication Today*, Fourth Edition.

Lesson 14

Punctuation: Asides and Additions

Some marks of punctuation—colons, parentheses, brackets, and dashes—are used to set off supplementary information from the main part of a sentence.

A colon, for example, calls attention to the words that follow—as if the colon meant "for example" or "that is." Therefore, colons are frequently used to introduce a word, phrase, or sentence of explanation:

Only one word can describe your proposal: fantastic!
This, then, is our goal for 1991: to increase sales 35 percent.
Remember this rule: When in doubt, leave it out.

Colons are also used to introduce lists, although lists that are necessary to complete a thought are not set off by colons. Observe the difference between these two sentences:

Next year we will have to hire a typist, a bookkeeper, and a receptionist.
Next year we will have to hire three people: a typist, a bookkeeper, and a receptionist.

In the first example, the list actually serves as the object of the sentence (*What will we have to hire?*) and cannot be separated from the subject and predicate by a colon. But in the second example, the part before the colon could stand on its own as a sentence. It is a complete thought in itself and must be separated from the list.

Colons also introduce formal quotations:

Chairman Dana Gerster announced: "Aquatec today acquired the assets of Marine Corp."

Finally, colons have several specialized uses. In letters, of course, they are used with closed or mixed punctuation following the salutation (*Dear Ms. Norden:*); they are used with memo headings (*TO:*); and they are used to separate hours from minutes in time designations (*11:30 a.m.*).

Parentheses are also used to set off information from the main part of a sentence. Some sentences use commas to indicate a supplementary idea; parentheses do much the same thing, but they are used when the idea has little importance to the main part of the sentence. Compare these two examples:

She drove her own car, an '85 Chrysler, last week.
She drove her own car (an '85 Chrysler) last week.

The only difference between these two sentences is the degree of emphasis given to the type of car being discussed. Context and judgment should tell you whether to use commas or parentheses in a given situation.

Parentheses themselves are relatively easy to use; what is more difficult is to use other punctuation properly when you're using parentheses. For instance, what kind of punctuation do you use when a complete sentence is embedded in another sentence by means of parentheses? You should never use a period at the end of an embedded sentence, but you can use a question mark or an exclamation point:

When you hear from her (have you already heard?), call me.

240

Notice that the embedded sentence is not capitalized. Notice also that the comma that would normally be used at the end of the introductory clause is still included, although it follows the parenthetical statement. Semicolons and colons are also included after the closing parenthesis if necessary to the main part of the sentence.

If the material between the parentheses is a sentence by itself and is not embedded in another sentence, its punctuation is self-contained:

Our company's profit history is irregular. (See Table 2 for a complete rundown on company profits over the past ten years.)

Brackets, which look similar to parentheses, have a specialized use. In quoted material, they set off the writer's comments from the comments of the person being quoted:

"In the past seven years [during which Cass has dominated the market], we have exceeded our goals," Dr. Blevins noted.
"The closest airport of any size," said Carol Nichols, "is about 25 kilometers [15.5 miles] away."

One other way that you can insert parenthetical material into a sentence is to use dashes (which are typed as two hyphens with no extra spaces between or on either side). Dashes give inserted material more emphasis than either commas or parentheses and should be used sparingly.

Compare these sentences and note the weight given to the parenthetical thought by the three types of punctuation:

Model 7-103, the latest in our line of quality conveyors, will be introduced at the convention in Chicago.
Model 7-103 (the latest in our line of quality conveyors) will be introduced at the convention in Chicago.
Model 7-103—the latest in our line of quality conveyors—will be introduced at the convention in Chicago.

Abrupt interruptions to the main thought are also set off by dashes:

The file on Marian Gephardt—yes, we finally found it—reveals a history of late payments.

Dashes or parentheses, not commas, are used when the parenthetical statement itself contains commas:

Three qualities—speed, accuracy, and reliability—are desirable in any typist employed by our department.

Dashes are also used when a sentence begins with a list and then finishes with a summarizing statement:

Speed, accuracy, and reliability—these are the qualities we look for in any typist employed by our department.

In the following exercises, insert colons, parentheses, brackets, and dashes wherever necessary:

1. Only one thing increased productivity will save us.

2. Stealth, secrecy, and surprise those are the elements that will give us a competitive edge.

3. The clients were most interested in income statements, balance sheets and payroll statements.

4. Her response see the attached memo is disturbing.

5. His motivation was obvious to get Meg fired.

6. Only two firms have responded to our survey J. J. Perkins and Tucker & Tucker.

7. Only two sites maybe three offer the things we need.

8. Sarah O'Roarke an appraiser will be here on Thursday.

9. The typist the one who just had a baby will have the document ready later today.

10. Kevin Langhans our top sales representative last year is at the bottom of the pile so far this year.

11. Your training kit consisting of a manual, supplementary reading, and product samples has already been shipped.

12. Please be sure to interview these employees next week Henry Golden, Doris Hatch, and George Iosupovich.

13. The new offices will be spacious, well-lit, and inviting.

14. The convention kit includes the following response cards, giveaways, brochures, and a display rack with samples.

15. Glenda she's the union representative has been helpful.

16. Professor Pettit had this to say: "We cannot assume a larger market, even with an increase in population. Demographic patterns have changed radically."

17. Send the memo to all the sales reps, the sales managers, and the director of marketing.

18. Ron Franklin do you remember him? will be in town Monday.

19. I want to make one thing perfectly clear: neither of you will be promoted if the sales figures do not improve.

20. Four items ladders, workbench kits, fluorescent light fixtures, and pegboard supplies will go on sale March 1.

21. Service and value those are Krasner's watchwords.

22. We will operate with a skeleton staff during the holiday break December 21 through January 2.

23. Refinements in robotics may prove profitable. More information about this technology appears in Appendix A.

24. Please return it before the deadline January 31, so we may send all the documents to you by the end of February.

25. Lucy has a math background an enormous advantage.

To learn more about these types of punctuation, consult a grammar book on the following topics:

brackets	dashes	parentheses
colons	embedded sentences	parenthetical elements

You may also wish to refer to Sections 2.5, "Colons," 2.7, "Dashes," and 2.11, "Parentheses," in Appendix I, "Fundamentals of Grammar and Usage," in *Business Communication Today*, Fourth Edition.

Lesson 15

Punctuation: Quotations

You may often want to use someone else's words in your business writing, especially in reports and persuasive sales letters. Quotation marks are indispensable for reporting what someone else has said:

> Dan Hurtig said, "Only five companies will remain after the coming shakeout in our industry."
> According to Inez Castro, the hospital supply department is "coping heroically under difficult circumstances."
> "Where there's a will, there's a way," she remarked.

Notice that the first word of a quotation is capitalized only when the quotation begins a sentence (as in the third example) or is itself a sentence and is preceded by a word like *said* (as in the first example). When the quotation is only part of a sentence and serves as the object of the sentence, the first word is not capitalized (as in the second example).

Direct quotations, whether spoken or written, should always be put between quotation marks and attributed to the person who originated them. Indirect quotations, however—paraphrased statements—do not require quotation marks. In the following sentence, the introductory word *that* is a clue that the quotation is indirect:

> Alice Montero said that few of the new employees have opted for day-care benefits.

Quotation marks are also used to set off words and phrases that are being treated with irony or are being used in a special context.

> The "benefits" of working for him include frequent criticism and scant praise.
> A "request for proposal" is a government notice that proposals will be accepted.

When you are defining a word, put the definition in quotation marks:

> The word *etc.* means "and so forth."

Quotation marks are also used in reference notes to set off the titles of articles, book chapters, and other small works or parts of larger works:

> Did he find "Seeking Profits in the Nineties" in *Business Today?*

Periods and commas always fall within the last set of quotation marks, but semicolons, colons, and dashes always fall after the last set:

> "Given their recent performance," she said, "we probably should not risk a large investment."
> They note "a marked lack of respect"; however, Drake was not working directly for them at that point.
> Two things affect "demand curves": price and quantity.
> Harry DeLuca—our plant's "labor analyst"—should undertake that project.

In using quotation marks with question marks and exclamation points, however, you must use your judgment. If the quoted passage is itself a question or an exclamation, the punctuation should be placed inside the last set of quotation marks:

> "Can you find the source of the problem?" she asked.
> He spoke in frustration: "These developers! I wish they would just accept the zoning plan!"

Notice in the first example that no comma is used to set the quoted passage apart from the rest of the sentence. Do not use a comma in combination with a question mark or an exclamation point.

Question marks and exclamation points are set outside the quotation marks when the quoted material is merely part of a sentence that is itself a question or an exclamation:

> They themselves drew our attention to these "irregularities"!
> Do you know who asked for "bilateral decisions"?

When quoting a long passage (more than three lines), you should set off the material by indenting it on both sides and single-spacing. This treatment makes quotation marks unnecessary.

Sometimes you will find that material you want to quote contains more than you need. In that case, use points of ellipsis to indicate that you have left out words:

> "It is in our nature . . . to look for advantage."

Ellipses (omissions) are always indicated with only three dots, although a fourth dot—a period—is included when necessary:

> "It is in our nature to look for advantage. . . ."

Underlining and italics are often used in connection with quotations, for citing a printed source. If possible, use italics for the titles of books, magazines, newspapers, movies, and other inclusive reference materials; otherwise, underline the titles:

> Our ad will appear in *The Wall Street Journal*.
> The Wealth of Nations proposed an early version of this notion.

Underlining and italics are also used to mark words used as words and to emphasize (sparingly) words and phrases:

> The word *profit* has a variety of meanings.
> The result of this campaign did not justify the expense.

In the following exercises, insert all necessary punctuation in the right places:

1. Be sure to read How to Sell by Listening in this month's issue of Fortune.

2. Contact is an overused word.

3. I don't care why you didn't fill my order; I want to know when you'll fill it.

4. We all make mistakes sometimes, the letter said.

5. Where did you put the Hartnet files? he asked.

6. Do you remember who said And away we go?

7. I can't believe that she doesn't know how to find, as Dr. Frankel puts it, sufficient resources.

8. Whom do you think Time magazine will select as its Man of the Year?

9. Bah! Humbug! said Scrooge.

10. The term up in the air means undecided.

11. As the report that I read concluded, Crown Products' best avenue for growth is the consumer market; I believe we should follow up on this analysis.

12. Susan said that she could not find the source of the error.

13. A computer nerd would have no trouble with it.

14. Professional bookkeepers use the double-entry method.

15. Business is the lifeblood of our country! she exclaimed.

16. Can you see the difference between debits and credits?

17. Only two were listed in the manager's little black book: Cathy Navasitis and Jeff Stamper.

18. Stephen Roussin made this point: The element of surprise would be of little use to us in this case; therefore, we should seek information wherever we can find it.

19. Then she asked, Do you have any disabilities that would prevent you from taking this job?

20. Can you believe that he would say something like We're only here to serve larger corporations?

21. Do you know anything about read-only memory?

22. The SBP's next conference, the bulletin noted, will be held in Minneapolis.

23. Patrick Henry is supposed to have challenged them with Give me liberty, or give me death!

24. Let's subscribe to Advertising Age.

25. What about taxes? we asked.

If you want to learn more about quotations, consult a grammar book on these topics:

direct quotations	indirect quotations	quotation marks	underscoring
ellipses	italics	reference notes	

You may also wish to consult Sections 2.10, "Quotation Marks," 2.12, "Ellipses," and 2.13 "Underscores and Italics," in Appendix I, "Fundamentals of Grammar and Usage," in *Business Communication Today*, Fourth Edition.

Lesson 16

Punctuation: Within Words

The main marks of punctuation used within words are apostrophes and hyphens. Apostrophes are used to indicate left-out letters; hyphens are used to link words or parts of a word into one.

One use for apostrophes is within contractions like the following:

don't	do not	it's	it is
we'll	we will	'90	1990

In the most formal writing, contractions should be avoided. They are acceptable, however, in speech and in informal writing.

Be careful that you do not confuse contractions with possessive pronouns. *It's* and *its* are often confused, as are *there's* and *theirs* and *they're* and *their*. If you have trouble deciding which one to use, take a moment to remember what words the contraction stands for. If the sentence still makes sense when you substitute those words, you can use the contraction. Otherwise, use the possessive pronoun.

What makes the distinction between contractions and possessive pronouns so confusing to some people is the fact that apostrophes are also used to make words possessive:

Robert's pen report's cover employees' wages

Be careful to use the possessive form only when "ownership" is indicated; change the words around and add *of* as a test:

Robert's pen	pen of Robert
report's cover	cover of the report
employees' wages	wages of the employees

It is sometimes hard to figure out where to put the apostrophe when showing ownership. As a rule, you simply add *'s* to the end of any word that does not already end in *s*, whether the word is singular or plural:

Sarah Boswell's letter	children's books
Grady Inc.'s main office	people's needs

If the word is plural and ends in *s* and an *s* sound, you usually add just an apostrophe at the end:

consultants' recommendations	twenty dollars' worth
Morrises' home	companies' plans

You add *'s* to singular words that end in one *s* or *s* sound, an apostrophe alone when the word ends in two *s* sounds:

boss's chair	analysis' limitations
Mr. Sanchez's office	Ms. Tarses' job

248

With compound nouns, add the apostrophe to the last word:

mother-in-law's idea   attorney general's opinion

When two or more individuals each own something separately, you should use the apostrophe with both names. But when they own something together, use the apostrophe with only the second name:

Paul's and Sam's offices   Paul and Sam's office

The use of apostrophes in business can become complicated. For example, some organizations use the apostrophe and some don't:

Harrison's Hardware, Inc.   United States Post Office

There is no hard and fast rule for using apostrophes with the names of organizations. Check the organization's letterhead or a directory.

Nor is there a rule you can consult to decide whether to use an apostrophe in phrases like these:

employee handbook   employees' handbook   employee's handbook

Consult other company documents for guidance in these cases—or use your judgment to figure out the real meaning behind the words you are using.

With most abbreviations, the apostrophe is used to form possessives just as it would be with any other word—although you must be careful to put the apostrophe after the period, if there is one:

CBS's report   R.N.'s schedule

You should not use an apostrophe to indicate plural numbers (for example, 1990s is correct), but you should use apostrophes with letters used as letters (A's and B's).

Test your ability to use apostrophes properly by adding them wherever necessary in the following exercises:

1. Collect every employees timecard on Friday.

2. Is that Tracys or Nicks?

3. The outcome of the test is anyones guess.

4. All the attorneys offices are cleaned every night.

5. Well discuss the mens coat department tomorrow.

6. Mr. Dunne completed the course in the 1960s with all As.

7. Its hard to see how their situation could improve.

8. We might buy a thousand dollars worth.

9. Where did you get IBMs annual report?

10. The electronics industry gives its best wages to Ph.D.s.

The other type of punctuation mark commonly used within words is the hyphen. Hyphens are always used to separate the main part of a word from the prefixes *all, ex,* and *self;* the main part from the suffix *elect;* a prefix from a capitalized word; and a prefix or suffix from numbers or letters:

all-inclusive	ex-athlete	self-controlled
chairperson-elect	non-European	mid-1990s

Other words that combine parts may or may not use a hyphen. In fact, they may or may not be two separate words:

half hour	half-baked	halfway

The best way to find out whether to use a hyphen in words like these is to look them up in a dictionary. (However, remember that dictionaries take different approaches to hyphenating words.) If the combined word does not appear in the dictionary, it should be written as two separate words.

Hyphens are used to combine whole words too. For example, the following nouns use a hyphen:

programmer-analyst	sister-in-law

Hyphens are more often used in adjectives that combine two or more words—but only when they come before a noun:

often-used formula	formula that is used often
high-level manager	manager at a high level
fact-finding mission	mission for finding facts
how-to manual	manual describing how to . . .
all-inclusive set	set that includes all
well-organized report	report that is well organized
up-to-date styles	styles that are up to date
blue-green paint	paint combining blue and green

But do not hyphenate combinations of an adjective and a modifier ending in *ly*—because a modifier that ends in *ly* is actually an adverb: *poorly marketed product, newly hired employee.*

When a sentence contains a series of hyphenated words that are similar, you may shorten it by dropping the repeated word:

We need to order some three- and four-compartment servers.

Hyphens may also be used to prevent misreading. Notice how the meaning of the first sentence changes with the addition of a hyphen:

We plan to start a <u>small business</u> publication. (a business publication that is small)
We plan to start a <u>small-business</u> publication. (a publication for small businesses)

Here is another example:

Ask the intern to prepare a <u>short term</u> paper. (a term paper that is short)
Ask the intern to prepare a <u>short-term</u> paper. (a paper dealing with the short term)

Insert hyphens only where necessary in the following exercises:

11. A highly placed source explained the negotiations.

12. They're selling a well designed machine.

13. A bottle green sports jacket is hard to find.

14. How many owner operators are in the industry?

15. Your ever faithful dog deserves Meaty Max.

16. The table is well placed in the text.

17. Myrna Talefiero is the organization's president elect.

18. I need a small business loan of $10,000 so I can expand my boutique.

19. How can we possibly please all the higher ups?

20. Try to eliminate your self consciousness.

21. We must carefully limit aid to truly needy residents.

22. High living bureaucrats receive extra scrutiny.

23. Your devil may care attitude affects us all.

24. His new office is well decorated.

25. What decision making processes will the group use?

To learn more about punctuation within words, you may wish to consult a grammar book on the following topics:

apostrophes	hyphens	suffixes
compound words	prefixes	

You may also wish to consult Sections 1.1.3, "Possessive Nouns," 2.8, "Hyphens," and 2.9, "Apostrophes," in Appendix I, "Fundamentals of Grammar and Usage," in *Business Communication Today*, Fourth Edition.

Lesson 17

Mechanics: Numbers

In general, numbers from one to ten are spelled out, and numbers over ten are written in figures. (If your organization has adopted its own style for dealing with numbers, use it.) But when a number begins a sentence, it should always be spelled. You can avoid writing an awkwardly large number (more than two words) at the beginning of a sentence by rewriting the sentence. For example:

Awkward:	Five hundred thirty-seven people have signed up.
Better:	Sign-ups number 537.
Better:	About 540 people have signed up.

Approximate numbers that can be expressed in one or two words are also spelled out (notice the use of hyphens with some numbers):

> About twenty-five people have applied for the job.
> Over one hundred software titles are in stock.
> We're looking for something in the seventy-five-dollar range.

In dealing with numbers over 999, remember to use a comma to separate thousands from hundreds: 2,384. Numbers in the millions and billions combine words and figures: *7.3 million, 2 billion.*

Usually, however, words and figures should not be combined. In a series of related numbers, spell all (if all are ten or under) or write all in figures:

> Please send 12 copies of <u>Bridge for Beginners</u>, 6 copies of <u>Bridge Strategies</u>, and 3 copies of <u>Secrets of the Life Masters</u>.

The general rule about using words and figures may also be ignored when two numbers fall next to each other in a sentence. Regardless of the size of the numbers, use figures for the number that is largest, most difficult to spell, or part of a physical measurement; use words for the other:

> I have learned to manage a classroom of 30 twelve-year-olds.
> She's won a bonus for selling 24 thirty-volume sets.
> You'll need twenty 3-inch bolts.

In money expressions, approximate dollar amounts may be expressed in words: *five dollars.* But specific dollar amounts are written in figures with a dollar sign: *$5.95, $27, $3 million.*

For amounts less than one dollar, use figures and the word *cents*: *5 cents.* But if you are writing a series of money expressions and at least one has a dollar sign, all the rest should too. Remember also to include cents with all the numbers if one of them is not an even dollar amount:

> The skins retail for $12.00 each; the hole punches, $3.59 each; and the grommets, $0.19 each.

In dates, the month is always spelled out, and the date and year are written in figures: *August 29, 1991*. In foreign, military, and some government correspondence, however, the order of the date and month is reversed: *29 August 1991*. Observe how dates are written when the year is not specified:

29th of August   August 29   the 29th

References to centuries or decades may be in words or in figures:

twentieth century   20th century
sixties   1960s

Time expressions that use *a.m.* or *p.m.* should be written in figures, but time expressions that use *o'clock* should be written in words. Compare:

The meeting starts at 9:30 a.m.
The meeting starts at eleven o'clock.

Most other time expressions are spelled out for the numbers ten and under and written in figures for the numbers over ten. The only exception is that figures are sometimes used for emphasis in detailing the terms of doing business:

Your account will be credited within 5 working days.

In addresses, all street numbers except *One* are in figures. So are suite and room numbers and ZIP codes. But what about street names that are numbered? Because practice varies so widely, you should use the form specified on an organization's letterhead or in a reliable directory. All the following are correct:

One Fifth Avenue   297 Ninth Street
1839 44th Street   11026 West 78 Place

Telephone numbers are always expressed in figures. Usually, parentheses separate the area code from the rest of the number, but a slash or dash may be used instead if the entire phone number is enclosed in parentheses:

(602) 382-8329   (602/382-8329)   (602-382-8329)

Figures are also used for extension numbers: *(602) 382-8329, extension 71.*

Percentages are another type of number that is always expressed in figures. The word *percent* is used in most situations (for example, *27 percent*), but % may be used in tables, forms, and statistical writing.

Physical measurements—distance, weight, and volume—are also often expressed in figures (*9 kilometers*). Notice that no comma is used in expressions like the following: *5 feet 3 inches, 7 pounds 10 ounces.*

Ages are usually expressed in words—except when a parenthetical reference to age follows someone's name:

Mrs. Margaret Sanderson is seventy-two.
Mrs. Margaret Sanderson, 72, swims daily.

And ages expressed in years and months are treated like physical measurements that combine two units of measure: *5 years 6 months.*

Figures are used to designate a great many other things as well, such as parts, forms, pages, and accounts. Even if these numbers have four or more digits, they do not use commas:

Section 7   Serial No. 38293   page 84

When you need to indicate numbered order, spell out ordinals from first to tenth and use the abbreviations *st, d,* and *th* with ordinals over 11th:

fifth grade   first floor
23d day   20th century

Use figures and ordinal abbreviations for editions of books in bibliographies:

2d ed.   4th ed.

Decimal numbers are always written in figures. In most cases, add a zero to the left of the decimal point if the number is less than one and does not already start with a zero:

1.38   .07   0.2

In a series of related decimal numbers with at least one number greater than one, make sure that all numbers smaller than one have a zero to the left of the decimal point: *1.20, 0.21, 0.09*. And express all decimal numbers in a series to the same number of places by adding zeroes at the end:

The responses were Yes, 37.2 percent; No, 51.0; Not Sure, 11.8.

Simple fractions are written in words, but more complicated fractions are expressed in figures or, if easier to read, in figures and words:

two-thirds   9/32   2 hundredths

A combination of a whole number and a fraction should always be written in figures. Note that a hyphen is used to separate the fraction from the whole number when a slash is used for the fraction: 2-11/16.

In the following exercises, correct numbers wherever necessary:

1. Let's invite about 20 outstanding college students.

2. Fifty-two typewriters were purchased.

3. We need to hire one office manager, four bookkeepers, and twelve clerk-typists.

4. They want to spend about $300.

5. The population of Guatemala is almost six million.

6. The agency's report totaled 1835 pages.

7. The 1st person who makes a purchase wins a prize.

8. Our offices are open between 9 o'clock and 5 o'clock.

9. Can you make it on the 7th?

10. We have enclosed checks for $45 and $37.50.

11. Deliver the couch to 1 South Thirty-eighth Avenue.

12. 95 percent of our customers are men.

13. Your measurement appears to be off by .7 centimeter.

14. Over 1\2 the U.S. population is female.

15. Our building is three miles past the intersection.

16. Hanna Hilgersen just turned thirty.

17. You'll find a definition of coverages on page five.

18. Of the fifteen applicants, seven are qualified.

19. Last year I wrote twenty one fifteen-page reports.

20. Set up enough chairs for an audience of at least 100.

21. 50,000,000 Americans can't be wrong.

22. This is the thirty-fifth request for confirmation.

23. Plan to be here for interviews from 1:00 to 4:30 p.m.

24. We need a set of shelves ten feet, eight inches long.

25. Check the following specifications: A, 2.39; B, .5; C, .09.

To learn more about this subject, consult a grammar book on the following topics:

decimals   hyphenated numbers
fractions   ordinals

You may also wish to consult Section 3.3, "Numbers," in Appendix I, "Fundamentals of Grammar and Usage," in *Business Communication Today*, Fourth Edition.

Lesson 18

Mechanics: Abbreviations and Symbols

Abbreviations and symbols provide a short, convenient way to express yourself, but some readers may not know what they stand for. Even if you think that readers will recognize them, you should generally limit their use to tables, graphs, lists, forms, technical documents, and informal memos. In any case, approach the abbreviation decision with this rule in mind: When in doubt, spell it out.

One way to handle an abbreviation that you want to use throughout a document is to spell it out the first time you use it, follow it with the abbreviation in parentheses, and then use the abbreviation in the remainder of the document.

The commonly used abbreviations for most organizations are capitalized and lack periods:

AT&T   UNICEF   NFL   WETA-TV

Some abbreviations of organizations' names are more than just initials; instead, they are shortened versions of the full name:

Bell Labs   Georgia Tech   the States

You may use these shortened names only in informal writing.

Abbreviations are also commonly used in addresses. Company names, for instance, often end with Inc., Ltd., Co., or Corp. If the company uses any of these abbreviations in its letterhead or in references to itself, you should use them too. For repeated reference to the same company, however, you may drop such abbreviations and use only the main part of the name.

Compass points (north, south, east, west) are usually not abbreviated when they come before a street name; however, the compass points that sometimes follow a street name (NW, NE, SW, SE) are usually abbreviated. Do not abbreviate other parts of the street name (such as *Street* and *Avenue*) unless you have very little space.

Most place names are not abbreviated: Fort Lauderdale, Port Arthur, Mount Pleasant, South Milwaukee. The exception is place names that include the word *Saint*: St. Louis.

Within addresses, use the two-letter postal abbreviations for state names, such as *KY* and *CO*. If you must abbreviate state names elsewhere but are not using ZIP codes, you may use such abbreviations as *Ky.* and *Colo.*

The names of countries are usually spelled out, both in addresses and in the body of letters, memos, and reports. The two most common exceptions are *USSR* and *U.S.*

What about the names of people? Do not abbreviate unless a person wants to be known by first and middle initials or by an abbreviated first name (B. J. Brooks, Geo. F. Carlisle). Notice that the initials are separated by a space.

Titles are another matter. The abbreviations *Mr.*, *Ms.*, *Mrs.*, and *Dr.* should always be used when they appear before a person's name. (Do not use *Mr.*, *Ms.*, *Mrs.*, *Dr.*, or *Esq.* [Esquire] with any other title.) Other titles that come before a person's name may or may not be abbreviated if they are used with the person's full name but should never be abbreviated if they are used with the last name alone:

Sen. Elizabeth Clarke   Senator Clarke
Capt. Robert Leinert   Captain Leinert
Prof. Patricia Stone   Professor Stone

256

Another sort of abbreviation comes after a person's full name:

Nathaniel Grob, Jr.   Artis Remer, M.B.A. (or MBA)
Richard Taylor, Esq.   Peggy Klein, D.V.M. (or DVM)

In statistical or technical writing and in tables and charts, you may use abbreviations for units of measurement. For example:

gal.   ft.   mpg   m   wpm   kg   cu. yd.

Notice that metric measures (m, kg) have no period; nor do the abbreviations for miles per gallon and words per minute.

Some references to time are typically abbreviated:

a.m.   A.D.   CST (Central Standard Time)

The following list shows one way of using periods and capital letters in abbreviations of some business terms; your source may recommend another:

acct.	account	LIFO	last in, first out
A/P	accounts payable	mdse.	merchandise
ASAP	as soon as possible	mfg.	manufacturing
bal.	balance	mgr.	manager
b/l	bill of lading	MIS	management information system
cc	carbon copy	mtg.	meeting
CEO	chief executive officer	N/30	net due in 30 days
c/o	care of	no.	number
C.O.D.	cash on delivery	p., pp.	page, pages
CPS	Certified Professional Secretary	pd.	paid
cr.	credit	PR	public relations
CRT	cathode ray tube	P.S.	postscript
cwt	hundredweight	R&D	research and development
dept.	department	rm.	room
div.	division	R.R.	railroad, rural route
doz.	dozen	RSVP	please respond (from French)
DP	data processing	std.	standard
ea.	each	ste.	suite
e.g.	for example	VIP	very important person
e.o.m.	end of month	WP	word processing
et al.	and others	/	per
etc.	and so forth	#	number
ext.	extension	%	percent
FIFO	first in, first out	@	at
fig.	figure	$	U.S. dollar
F.O.B.	free on board	Can$	Canadian dollar
FYI	for your information	™	trademark
GDP	gross domestic product	¶	paragraph
GNP	gross national product	®	registered
i.e.	that is	©	copyright

For the following exercises, assume that the reader is an "insider," and substitute abbreviations wherever possible:

1. Paul Hansen, Registered Nurse, is joining our staff.

2. The Young Men's Christian Association has a center here.

3. Send it to Mister H. K. Danforth, Rural Route 1, Warrensburg, New York 12885.

4. She is a candidate for the master of business administration degree at the University of Michigan.

5. Call me at 8 in the morning, Pacific Standard Time.

6. The data processing department will work on it as soon as possible.

7. The core sample weighs 1.7 kilograms.

8. The Securities and Exchange Commission sent notice to them.

9. General George Armstrong Custer fought in the West.

10. We are sending it cash on delivery, net due in 15 days.

For the remaining exercises, assume that the reader is an "outsider," and spell out abbreviated words wherever possible:

11. The FBI is based near Washington, D.C.

12. Nashville, Tenn., is their headquarters.

13. Mr. Geoffrey Finley is the CEO of TrendWell, Inc.

14. Call me at 818-3948, ext. 72, between 10 a.m. and 3 p.m.

15. Send the package to Mr. C. W. Crane, 9382 W. Florida Ave., Ft. Bragg, Calif. 95437.

16. FYI, the Bilbray accts. are past due.

17. I have an M.S. degree for MIT.

18. It's 3 km from our office to the nearest restaurant.

19. Over 50% of our engineering staff have Ph.D.s.

20. Christine Jarvis, CPS, is joining the mfg. div.

21. The UN is headquartered in NYC.

22. The Hon. Donna Stroeb-Atkins will speak at our meeting.

23. Send your std. #10 envelopes, @ $9.95/box.

24. RSVP ASAP.

25. Capt. Macek et al. participated in the setting up of the MIS.

If you would like to study more about this subject, consult a grammar book under the following headings:

acronyms	names
addresses	periods
capitalization	scientific/technical terms
dates	titles and degrees
measurements	trade names

You may also wish to consult Section 3.2, "Abbreviations," in Appendix I, "Fundamentals of Grammar and Usage," in *Business Communication Today*, Fourth Edition.

Lesson 19

Mechanics: Capitals

Capital letters are used, of course, at the beginning of sentences. But they are also used at the beginning of other word groups:

Formal statement following colon: She has a favorite motto: Where there's a will, there's a way.
Phrase used as sentence: Absolutely not!
Quoted sentence embedded in another sentence: Scott said, "Nobody was here during the lunch hour except me."
Set-off list of items: Three preliminary steps are involved:
  1. Design review
  2. Budgeting
  3. Scheduling

Capital letters are also used with proper nouns and proper adjectives, such as the following:

Darrell Greene   Victorian mansion

A proper noun is separated from a prefix with a hyphen:

ex-President   anti-American

People's titles are capitalized when they are used in addressing a person, especially in a formal context. They are not usually capitalized, however, when they are used merely to identify the person. Observe the difference here:

Address the letter to <u>Chairperson</u> Anna Palmer.
I wish to thank <u>Chairperson</u> Anna Palmer for her assistance.
Please deliver these documents to board chairperson Anna Palmer.
Anna Palmer, chairperson of the board, took the podium.

Titles should also be capitalized if they are used by themselves in addressing a person:

Thank you, <u>Doctor</u>, for your donation.

Titles used to identify a person of very high rank are capitalized regardless of where they fall or how much of the name is included:

the <u>President</u> of the United States
the <u>Prime Minister</u> of Canada
the Pope

In addresses, salutations, signature blocks, and some formal writing (such as acknowledgments), all titles are capitalized whether they come before or after the name.

260

The names of organizations are capitalized, of course; so are the official names of their departments and divisions:

> Route this memo to <u>Personnel</u>.
> Larry Tien was transferred to the <u>Microchip Division</u>.
> Will you be enrolled in the <u>Psychology Department</u>?

However, when referring in general terms to a department or division, especially one in another organization, do not capitalize:

> Someone from the <u>engineering department</u> at EnerTech stopped by the booth.
> Our <u>production department</u> has reorganized for efficiency.
> Send a copy to their <u>school of business administration</u>.

Capitalization is also unnecessary when using a word like *company, corporation,* or *university* alone:

> The <u>corporation</u> plans to issue 50,000 shares of common stock.

The names of specific products should be capitalized, although the names of general product types should not be:

> Praxis typewriter   Tide laundry detergent

Many writers have trouble with the capitalization of compass directions. For instance, should you use *south Florida* or *South Florida, north county* or *North County*? Capitalize when the compass direction is part of a place's name, whether in official or in common use; do not capitalize when referring to a direction or general location. Here are some examples:

> the West   the western half of Canada
> the South   southern Minnesota
> the Northeast   northeasterners

Another problem that often arises in writing about places is the treatment of two or more proper nouns of the same type. When the common word comes before the specific names, it is capitalized; when it comes after the specific names, it is not. Observe the capitalization here:

> Lakes Ontario and Huron
> Allegheny and Monongahela rivers

The names of languages, races, and ethnic groups are also capitalized: *Japanese, Caucasian, Hispanic.* But racial terms that denote only skin color are not capitalized: *black, white.*

In referring to the titles of books, articles, magazines, newspapers, reports, movies, and so on, you should capitalize the first and last words and all nouns, pronouns, adjectives, verbs, adverbs, and prepositions and conjunctions with five letters or more. Except for the first and last words, do not capitalize articles, and do not capitalize conjunctions and prepositions with fewer than five letters. For example:

> *Economics During the Great War*
> "An investigation into the Market for Long-Distance Services"
> "What Successes Are Made Of"

When *the* is part of the official name of a newspaper or magazine, it should be treated this way too: *The Wall Street Journal.*

References to specific pages, paragraphs, lines, and the like are not capitalized: *page 72, line 3.* However, in most other numbered or lettered references, the identifying term is capitalized:

Chapter 4   Serial No. 382-2203   Item B-11

Words for specific markings or instructions on documents are also capitalized:

Stamp this letter "Confidential" before it goes out.

Finally, the names of academic degrees are capitalized when they follow a person's name but are not capitalized when used in a general sense:

I received a <u>bachelor of science</u> degree.
Thomas Whitelaw, <u>Doctor of Philosophy</u>, will attend.

Similarly, general courses of study are not capitalized, but the names of specific classes are:

She studied <u>accounting</u> as an undergraduate.
She is enrolled in <u>Accounting 201</u>.

Remember that the principles described here are well accepted but that your organization may have its own rules for capitalization.
In the following exercises, capitalize wherever appropriate:

1. Yates & co. is in suite 303 of park towers.

2. The luxury of chinese silk is yours.

3. Pat swink said, "my research shows something else."

4. The president of the company has adopted this motto: look before you leap.

5. I'm taking two psychology courses.

6. Let's invite dr. lynne jamison, the director of personnel.

7. See page 143 in chapter 5.

8. We plan to establish a sales office on the west coast.

9. The personnel department has submitted its budget.

10. Do you know how to fix the xerox machine?

11. Check in the *dictionary of occupational titles.*

12. We're at the corner of madison and center streets.

13. Did you see the file labeled "overdue accounts"?

14. The staff at university hospital deserves praise.

15. Address it to art bowers, chief of production.

16. Our new tractor, the sodbuster, has been developed to solve the special problems of midwestern grain farmers.

17. See if you can find "in search of a stable economy."

18. We're forming a partnership with a south american corporation.

19. You could reserve the regency and embassy rooms.

20. New caressa skin cream smooths wrinkles.

21. I have a graduate degree in business administration.

22. She characterized the movie as "an orwellian fantasy."

23. Tell me, professor, do you plan to come?

24. The company is forming a new policies group.

25. Maybe we should consider a location in the deep south.

To learn more about this subject, consult a grammar book on the following topics:

abbreviations   proper nouns
addresses   quotations
bibliographies   titles and degrees
personification   trademarks
place names

You may also wish to consult Section 3.1, "Capitals," in Appendix I, "Fundamentals of Grammar and Usage," in *Business Communication Today*, Fourth Edition.

Lesson 20

Words

One of the greatest sources of trouble for business writers is groups of words that look alike, sound alike, or have special connotations. Note carefully the differences in meaning among the following:

accept	to take, to agree	assistance	help
except	excluding	assistants	helpers
access	entry, means of approaching	assure	to personally promise
excess	too much	ensure	to guarantee
		insure	to issue an insurance policy
adapt	to adjust		
adept	skilled	beside	next to
adopt	to take on	besides	other than
adverse	unfavorable	biannual	twice a year
averse	strongly disinclined	biennial	once every two years
advice	recommendation	bloc	group of people
advise	to counsel, to recommend	block	solid mass, to put up an obstacle
affect	to change, to have an impact	born	brought forth by birth
effect	result of action	borne	carried
aggravate	to make a problem worse	breath	air inhaled and exhaled
annoy	to bother	breathe	to inhale and exhale
irritate	to cause anger or impatience		
		capital	money, seat of government
allusion	reference to	capitol	building occupied by a legislature
illusion	appearance of		
		casual	informal
among	referring to three or more	causal	related to a cause
between	referring to two		
		cite	to refer to
anxious	nervously anticipating	sight	vision, to see
eager	enthusiastically anticipating	site	location
appraise	to estimate a value	clothes	garments
apprise	to inform	cloths	fabrics
apt	naturally inclined or able	coarse	rough
likely	probable, appropriate	course	direction, route

264

command	order, to order	eminent	notable
commend	to praise	imminent	impending
complement	something that completes or makes perfect, to make whole	envelop	to surround
		envelope	paper covering for a letter
compliment	expression of praise, to praise, to congratulate	explicit	clearly stated
		implicit	unstated, hidden
compose	to formulate		
comprise	to include, to contain	farther	more distant
		further	more, additional, to advance
confidant	person who hears secrets		
confident	self-assured	feasible	desirable and possible
		possible	able to likely to happen
conscience	sense of right and wrong	practicable	possible given existing conditions
conscious	aware		
		formally	in a formal manner
constant	recurring in the same way	formerly	previously
continual	recurring at frequent intervals		
continuous	ongoing	human	relating to people
		humane	compassionate
core	center		
corps	group	imitate	to copy
		intimate	personal
council	committee		
counsel	adviser, to advise	imply	to hint
		infer	to interpret
deference	submission		
difference	dissimilarity	incidence	rate of occurrence
		incidents	occurrences
dependence	reliance		
dependents	those who rely on someone	ingenious	clever
		ingenuous	naive and innocent
deprecate	to protest, to belittle		
depreciate	to lessen value	instance	case
		instants	moments
detract	to take away from		
distract	to divert	intense	heightened
		intents	purposes
device	mechanism		
devise	to construct	interstate	between states
		intrastate	within a state
disapprove	to condemn		
disprove	to prove wrong	its	of it
		it's	it is
disburse	to pay out		
dispense	to distribute	later	more advanced in time
disperse	to scatter	latter	item closest to the end
discreet	prudent	lead	metal; to show the way
discrete	separate	led	showed the way
elicit	to draw out	lend	to give the use of
illicit	unlawful	loan	something lent

266 English Essentials

liable	legally responsible	presence	attendance
libel	written defamation	presents	gifts
local	of the surrounding area	principal	main, head, capital (money)
locale	place	principle	rule
loose	unrestrained	raise	to lift
lose	to misplace, to fail to win	rise	to get up, to go up
moral	honest, lesson	role	part
morale	mental condition	roll	bread, to throw, to turn over
passed	went by	set	to put down
past	bygone	sit	to take a seat
pedal	foot lever, to move with the feet	stationary	in one place
peddle	to sell	stationery	paper
perquisite	benefit	straight	not curved
prerequisite	qualification	strait	narrow waterway, difficult position
persecute	to harass	than	compared with
prosecute	to start legal proceedings	then	time past
personal	of the person	their	of them
personnel	staff, employees	there	in that place
		they're	they are
perspective	view		
prospective	potential, forthcoming	to	opposite of from
		too	overly, also
populace	inhabitants	two	2
populous	having many people		
		vice	immorality
practicable	able to be done	vise	instrument for gripping
practical	workable (things), sensible (people)		
pragmatic	hard-headed, realistic	waiver	abandonment of a right
		waver	to flicker, to hesitate
precede	to go before		
proceed	to continue	who's	who is
		whose	of whom
preposition	a part of speech		
proposition	scheme	your	of you
		you're	you are

Underline the correct word in each of the following exercises:

1. Everyone accept/except Barbara King has registered.

2. The whole debt was born/borne by his parents.

3. We need to find a new security device/devise.

4. They decided to sue for liable/libel.

5. The passed/past few days have been hectic.

6. How much farther/further is the convention center?

7. Just set/sit it on the credenza.

8. Enter the number of dependence/dependents in this box.

9. Were you able to determine their intense/intents?

10. You will be asked to sign a waiver/waver.

11. I assure/ensure/insure you that all will be ready.

12. From my perspective/prospective, this is a bad move.

13. The moral/morale is this: Expect the worst.

14. Your experience is a good complement/compliment to my enthusiasm.

15. I'd like a later/latter appointment.

16. Scientists have established a direct casual/causal relationship between sunburn and skin disorders.

17. He didn't mention it outright, but his need for a decision was explicit/implicit.

18. This month's balance is greater than/then last month's.

19. Can you appraise/apprise us of her qualifications?

20. Look up their/there/they're address.

21. We can't let outside events detract/distract us now.

22. The study group will compose/comprise all the analysts.

23. I'd like to precede/proceed my remarks with a question.

24. An ambitious person will raise/rise above challenges.

25. Dr. Khoury is an eminent/imminent chemist.

If you need help in using words correctly, you may wish to consult a grammar book on the following topics:

diction   usage
homonyms   vocabulary
idioms

You may also wish to consult Sections 4.1, "Frequently Confused Words," 4.2, "Frequently Misused Words," and 4.3, "Frequently Misspelled Words," in Appendix I, "Fundamentals of Grammar and Usage," in *Business Communication Today*, Fourth Edition.

SOURCE NOTES

Chapter 1 (Where the Jobs Are), p. 5.

Adapted from *Jobs and Opportunities for Writers*, by the editors of *Writer's Digest* (Cincinnati, Ohio: Writer's Digest Books, 1972), 1–16. Copyright © 1972 by *Writer's Digest*. Reprinted by permission of *Writer's Digest Books*, a division of F & W Publications, Inc., Cincinnati, Ohio 45242.

Chapter 2 (Reading the Nonverbal Communication of Office Settings), p. 15.

Adapted from Patricia A. Thompson and Brian H. Kleiner, "How to Read Nonverbal Communication," *The Bulletin of the Association for Business Communication* LV, no. 3 (September 1992): 81–83.

Chapter 4 (When Your Office Isn't at the Office Anymore), p. 30.

Adapted from Geoff Lewis, Jeffrey Rothfeder, Resa W. King, Mark Maremont, and Thane Peterson, "The Portable Executive: From Faxes to Laptops, Technology Is Changing Our Work Lives," *Business Week*, 10 October 1988, 102–112; John Schwartz and Dody Tsiantar, with Karen Springen, "Escape from the Office," *Newsweek*, 24 April 1989, 58–60; Donna Whittingham-Barnes, "Making Your Office User Friendly," *Black Enterprise*, April 1990, 60; "When Going to Work Means Staying Home," *Modern Office Technology*, June 1987, 30; Cynthia Crossen, "Where We'll Be," *Wall Street Journal Reports*, 4 June 1990, 6–10.

Chapter 5 (Winning Friends and Influencing People), p. 37.

Adapted from Dale Carnegie, *How to Win Friends and Influence People* (New York: Simon & Schuster/Pocket Books, 1972), 111–185.

Chapter 6 (How to Tap Your Creativity), p. 45.

Adapted from Rudolf Flesch, *The Art of Clear Thinking* (New York: Harper & Row, 1951), 138–148; Vincent W. Kafka, "Lncourage the Use of Creative Energy," *Supervisory Management*, October 1975, 32–35; Rudolf F. Sirny, "How's Your Management Momentum?" *Supervisory Management*, March 1976, 18–26.

Chapter 7 (Readability = Ease + Interest), p. 54.

Adapted from Rudolf Flesch, *The Art of Readable Writing* (New York: Harper & Row, 1949), 20–21, 151, 213–216. Copyright © 1949 by Rudolf Flesch. Reprinted by permission of Harper & Row, Publishers, Inc.

Chapter 8 (The Meek Person's Guide to Asking for Help), p. 63.

Adapted from Merna Dee Galassi and John P. Galassi, *Assert Yourself* (New York: Human Sciences Press, 1977), 97–98. Copyright © 1977 by Merna Dee Galassi and John P. Galassi. Reprinted by permission of Human Sciences Press.

Chapter 9 (A "Magic" Formula for Business Success), p. 71.

Adapted from Thomas J. Peters and Robert H. Waterman, Jr., *In Search of Excellence* (New York: Harper & Row, 1982), 157–159.

Chapter 11 (How to Increase Your Credibility), p. 87.
   Adapted, by permission of the publishers, from Judi Brownell, "Increasing Your Credibility," *Supervisory Management*, December 1982, 32, 34. Copyright © 1982 AMACOM Periodicals Division, American Management Association, New York. All rights reserved.

Chapter 13 (The Assertive Interviewee), p. 104.
   Adapted from Richard A. Lynch, "Ten Questions to Ask Before Accepting a Job," *Money*, February 1985, 109–114.

Chapter 15 (Techniques for Picking an Expert's Brain), p. 121.
   Adapted from personal interview with Angela Fox Dunn, 1983, and from "How to Pick an Expert's Brains," *Nation's Business*, February 1982, 56.

Chapter 16 (Pictures That Tell the Wrong Story), p. 129.
   Adapted from Darrell Huff, "How to Lie with Statistics," in Kevin J. Harty, ed., *Strategies for Business and Technical Writing* (New York: Harcourt Brace Jovanovich, 1980), 241–248; Rudolf Flesch, *The Art of Clear Thinking* (New York: Harper & Row, 1951), 157–159; Robert Lefferts, *How to Prepare Charts and Graphs for Effective Reports* (New York: Barnes & Noble Books, 1981); J. C. Mathes and Dwight W. Stevenson, *Designing Technical Reports: Writing for Audiences in Organizations* (Indianapolis, Ind.: Bobbs-Merrill), 1976, 185–189.

Chapter 17 (You Be the Editor), p. 137.
   Data for "The Market for Home Health Care" taken from "Home Health Care Revenues to Top $24 Billion by 1995," *Predictions from Predicasts* (Cleveland, Ohio: Predicasts Research Division, October 1984), 1.

Chapter 17 (A Look at Annual Reports), p. 138.
   Adapted from Carol McFarland Baxter, *Business Report Writing: A Practical Approach* (Boston, Mass.: Kent Publishing, 1983), 276–287; John A. Byrne, "This Year's Annual Reports: Show Business as Usual," *Business Week*, 13 April 1987, 42; "Leaner Reports Still Rare," *USA Today*, April 6, 1987, 6B.

Chapter 18 (In Brief), p. 145.
   Adapted from Christian K. Arnold, "The Writing of Abstracts," in Kevin J. Harty, ed., *Strategies for Business and Technical Writing* (New York: Harcourt Brace Jovanovich, 1980), 213–217.

Chapter 19 (How to Negotiate Like a Pro), p. 153.
   Adapted from David D. Seltz and Alfred J. Modica, *Negotiate Your Way to Success* (New York: New American Library, 1980), 183–200; Kay Cassill, *The Complete Handbook for Freelance Writers* (Cincinnati, OHIO: *Writer's Digest* Books, 1981), 220–221; Herb Cohen, *You Can Negotiate Anything* (Secaucus, N.J.: Lyle Stuart, 1980).

Chapter 20 (A Master's Voice), p. 161.
   Adapted from Milton Dickens, *Speech: Dynamic Communication*, 3d ed. (New York: Harcourt Brace Jovanovic, 1974), 172–187; John A. Grasham and Glenn G. Gooder, *Improving Your Speech* (New York: Harcourt Brace Jovanovich, 1960), 303–310; Louise M. Scrivner and Dan Robinette, *A Guide to Oral Interpretation: Solo and Group Performance*, 2d ed. (Indianapolis, Ind.: Bobbs-Merrill, 1980), 76–87.

Component Chapter B (How to Take Better Notes Faster), p. 178.
   Adapted from Rudolf Flesch, *The Art of Clear Thinking* (New York: Harper & Row, 1951), 154; Joe M. Pullis, *Principles of Speedwriting Shorthand*, Regency Edition (Indianapolis, Inc.: Bobbs-Merrill, 1984), 433–436, 447–450, 455–459.